D1607804

# Mitteleuropa

*Studies in European Unity*

SERIES EDITORS
Michael L. Smith, Peter M. R. Stirk and David Weigall

# Mitteleuropa

## History and Prospects

*Edited by Peter Stirk*

EDINBURGH UNIVERSITY PRESS

© Edinburgh University Press, 1994

Edinburgh University Press Ltd
22 George Square, Edinburgh

Typeset in Linotron Bembo
by Koinonia Ltd, Bury, and
printed and bound in Great Britain by
Redwood Books, Trowbridge

A CIP record for this book is available from
the British Library

ISBN 0 7486 0449 9

# Contents

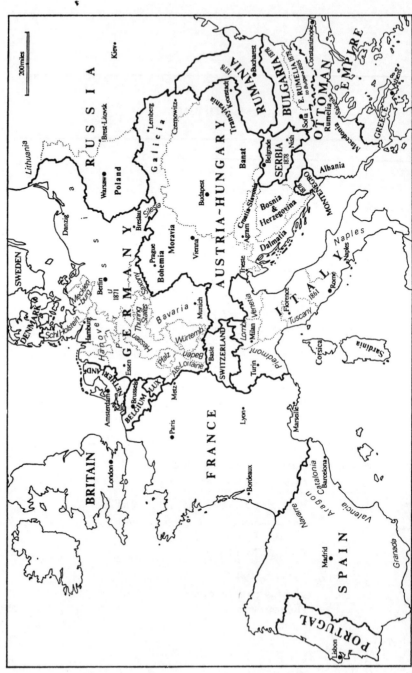

MAP 1: Europe in 1878.
Source: James Joll, *Europe since 1870* (Weidenfeld and Nicolson, 1973), p. 17.

# Acknowledgements

The increased, and often irrational, demands of contemporary academic life have made collaborative enterprises even more difficult. I am grateful to the contributors to this volume for overcoming them. At Edinburgh University Press I am indebted to Maureen Prior and Penny Clarke, both for their efficiency and for their sense of humour. I am grateful to Jonathon Price for his commitment to this series and for his clear sense of direction in developing it. Members of the Research Seminar in the Department of Politics at Durham University pointed to some ambiguities in a draft of the Introduction. Dr J. Dresch kindly translated Dietmar Stübler's contribution from the original German text.

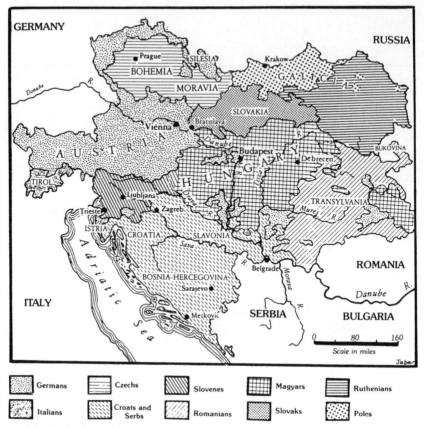

MAP 2: Nationality Map of Austria–Hungary.
Source: Barbara Jelavich, *Modern Austria* (Cambridge University Press, 1987), p. 90.

MAP 3: Eastern Europe under the Treaty of Brest-Litovsky, March to November 1918.
Source: J. M. Roberts, *Europe 1880–1945* (Longman, 1970), p. 281.

MAP 4: Versailles Eastern Europe 1919–38.
Source: Martin Gilbert, *Recent History Atlas* (Weidenfeld and Nicolson, 1966), p. 43.

# Preface

The theme of Mitteleuropa presents a variety of challenges. The first of these is the choice of terminology. Not only is Mitteleuropa a German word, but it is also one which has carried with it distinct political and cultural implications, suggesting both a political programme for German hegemony in the heart of Europe, and a transnational culture embracing Germans but not being reducible to Germanic culture. There are alternatives to the term. Central Europe – also expressible in German (*Zentraleuropa*) and often used as a synonym for Mitteleuropa – East Central Europe and Eastern Europe have all been used to cover all or part of the region and the trends discussed in this volume.[1] All these will be found in the various contributions. Precisely because of the implicit or explicit connotations, which vary with time, place and standpoint, no attempt has been made in this volume to insist upon uniform usage across the different chapters. To have insisted upon consistency would have meant sacrificing the nuances, and even the systematic ambiguity, which characterize the history and prospects of the region, to uniformity. More would have been lost than gained in the process. For the same reason a flexible approach has been adopted to usage within individual chapters.

It might well then be asked: why choose Mitteleuropa as a title? Although all the chapters refer to non-Germanic perspectives, some more strongly than others, the role of Germans and German perspectives looms large in most of the contributions. As several chapters make clear, Germans played a disproportionate part compared with other peoples. This is, of course, not the only perspective which can guide a volume on Mitteleuropa but it does provide a unifying theme to this one.

Nevertheless, there is a second problem associated with the choice of title and theme. To write of Mitteleuropa – or Central Europe, East Central Europe, Eastern Europe – is at least to raise the presumption that there is some kind of regional identity which can be distinguished by this term. However, the traditional choice of national units as a historiographical theme has come under increasing criticism. To that extent Mitteleuropa has the advantage of stepping outside the orthodox framework of national histories: histories which carry their own connotations and distortions.[2] Especially in a part of the world in which the nation state arrived comparatively late on the scene and has not enjoyed undisputed support, there are attractions to avoiding the constrictions of national histories. Yet the identity and integrity of Mitteleuropa is no sure basis either. The presumption of unity, as the individual chapters demonstrate, has become questionable and in some respects always was.

The approach adopted here is to explore aspects of Mitteleuropa without ceding too much ground in advance to the case for or against it. Within this framework, the Introduction provides an overview of the career of the idea of Mitteleuropa, seeking to relate this to the underlying political, social and economic realities. The succeeding chapters focus on different facets. In Chapter 1 Walter Weitzmann presents the ideas of the nineteenth-century visionary and opponent of Bismarck, Constantin Frantz, as a prism through which the obstacles to integration can be displayed. He also points out the vicissitudes of the advocacy of unity, the way in which Frantz's ambiguous legacy could be bent into a new, and less benign, vision by Pan-Germanists and ultimately by the Nazis. In Chapter 2 Steven Beller also points to the systematic dilemma of integration in Mitteleuropa: how to achieve unity without embarking upon an imperialist course. Failure to resolve this dilemma, as this chapter demonstrates, was to have baneful consequences for Mitteleuropa's two transnational élites: Jews and Germans. In Chapter 3 Peter Stirk considers attempts to recapture some semblance of unity in the interwar period, when the nation state seemed triumphant and integration in Mitteleuropa, and elsewhere gave way to economic nationalism. But as with Chapter 2, the conclusion is that Mitteleuropa's dilemmas are soluble only within a broader European pattern of integration.

This point is also evident in Chapter 4, by Alan Foster, which looks at the region from an internal (British) perspective, focusing again on the interwar period. It demonstrates that there were severe limits to the commitment which the Western Europeans were willing to extend to the peoples of Mitteleuropa. In Chapter 5 Anthony McElligott assesses a vital consequence of that limited commitment, the economic fate of the region under wartime German hegemony. He challenges assumptions that Germanocentric integration could have been viable, if shorn of the brutalities of the Nazi political programme. By extension this chapter also questions the viability of a Germanocentric model in the region's future, illustrating the chaos bequeathed by this last attempt of Mitteleuropa to resolve its problems on its own. In the wake of the Second World War much of what had been mitteleuropäisch was suppressed beneath another political and economic regime. Chapter 6, by Dietmar Stübler, compares the two ends of the period covered in this volume, the Revolutions of 1848–1849 and 1989. It suggests that the recent events in Mitteleuropa should be seen as part of a wider European process stretching over two centuries, and outlines the possibility of precisely that pan-European integration, for want of which Mitteleuropa had torn itself apart.

## NOTES

1. For a discussion of the diverse categories, see Robin Okey, 'Central Europe/Eastern Europe: Behind the Definitions', *Past and Present*, No. 137 (1992), pp. 102–33.
2. See, for example, James J. Sheehan, 'What is German History? Reflections on the Role of the *Nation* in German History and Historiography', *Journal of Modern History*, Vol. 53 (1981), pp. 1–23.

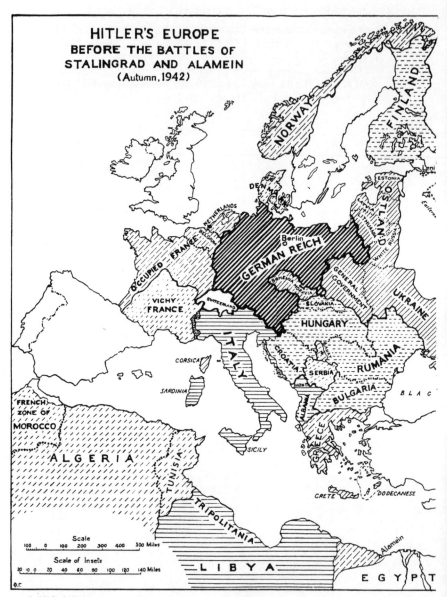

MAP 5: Hitler's Europe.
Source: Royal Institute of International Affairs, *Survey of International Affairs 1939–1946. Hitler's Europe* (Oxford University Press for the Royal Institute of International Affairs, London, 1954 © RIIA).

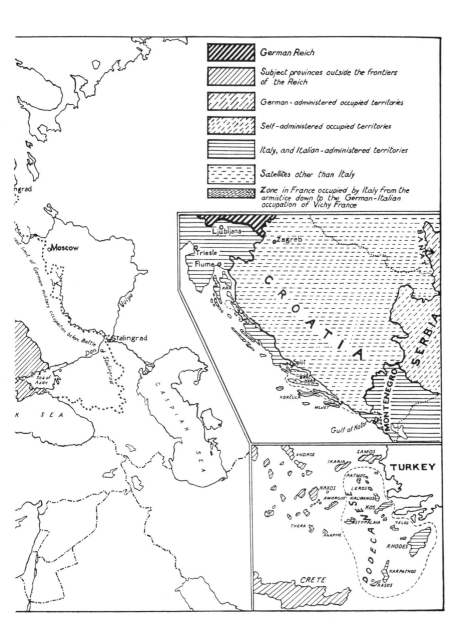

German Reich

Subject provinces outside the frontiers of the Reich

German-administered occupied territories

Self-administered occupied territories

Italy, and Italian-administered territories

Satellites other than Italy

Zone in France occupied by Italy from the armistice down to the German-Italian occupation of Vichy France

Ljubljana

Zagreb

Trieste

Flume

BANAT

C-R-O-A-T-I-A

SERBIA

Split

KRK

KORČULA

MLJET

Gulf of Kotor

MONTENEGRO

ingrad

Moscow

west limit of German military occupation before Battle

Stalingrad

Volga

Don

Stalingrad

Sea of Azov

K SEA

CASPIAN SEA

ANDROS

IKARIA

SAMOS

TURKEY

PATMOS

NAXOS

LEROS

AMORGOS

KALYMNOS

KOS

THERA

ASTYPALAIA

TELOS

ANAPHE

RHODES

DODECANESE

KARPATHOS

KASOS

CRETE

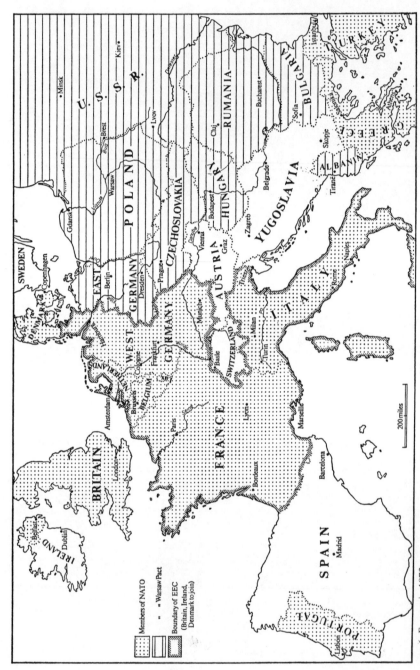

MAP 6: Europe in 1972.

Source: James Joll, *Europe since 1870* (Weidenfeld and Nicolson, 1973), p. 424.

Introduction

# The Idea of Mitteleuropa

## *Peter M. R. Stirk*

The term Mitteleuropa has had an effervescent and contentious career. It con-
jures up a sense of unity which was associated with the Habsburg Empire but
also carries with it a sense of the conflicts which led to the demise of that multinational state at the end of the First World War. Whenever it has flourished on
the political landscape it has been stretched between those two characteristics:
the implication of unity, the idea that there is a region which might be desig-
nated Mitteleuropa, and resistance to integration, the desires of the peoples of
the hypothetical region for autonomy. The tension between these two characteristics points to a third: the vulnerability of political arrangements within the
area. Among the many attempts to define the region images of transience
abound. It has been suggested that just as Britain's character was stamped by its
island nature so too Mitteleuropa has been stamped by the openness of its borders.[1] For Mitteleuropa at least the point is persuasive. Geographical boundaries
are lacking and the most prominent geographical features – the Danube, the
Vistula and the Carpathian mountains – cut across the region rather than demar-
cating it. Empires and states have risen, fallen, or more frequently been de-
voured, and sometimes, resurrected. These lands have been described, as 'organ-
isms with vertebrae and arteries but no external shell'.[2]

The most obvious features of the region confirm this image of vulnerability.
Although Western Europe is far from enjoying the full coincidence of nation
and state upheld as an ideal by the doctrine of nationalism, Mitteleuropa has
exhibited an ethnic diversity and intermingling which goes far beyond anything
found in the West. In the wake of the Congress of Vienna this diversity was
masked by the domination of the region by the four major empires of Prussia,
Russia, the Ottomans and the Habsburgs (see Map 1). It was, politically, also
latent, in so far as the age of nationalism was only beginning to penetrate the
region. As the different ethnic groups discovered or constructed their collective
national identities, the question of the unity or disunity of the region became
increasingly important. The peoples were implicitly faced with three possible
futures. They could continue to live within multinational empires or states and
find a way to reform these in a federalist direction which could better accommodate their national autonomy. In practice this option was associated with

proposals for the reform of the Habsburg Empire. It should not be forgotten, though, that both Prussia and the subsequent German *Reich* and Russia as well as most of the states established at the end of the First World War were multinational. Interwar Poland, for example, was no more than 70 per cent Polish. The relevance of a federal solution, or, to put it differently, the inappropriateness of the idealized nation state, stands out indeed as one of the major defining features of the region. Alternatively, the stronger of the peoples could resolve the problem by the assertion of imperialist hegemony. For the advocates of national identity this was in fact precisely what had already happened. The multinational empires were, it was argued, built upon the oppression of nations by dominant groups, Germans in Prussia and the Habsburg Empire, Russians in the Tsarist Empire. From the same perspective the third future involved the break up of the empires and the liberation of the oppressed peoples. But what would succeed the empires, as the interwar period demonstrated, was not a region of nation states, but, with few exceptions, a region of multinational states. The third future also contained a hidden agenda. It pointed in the direction of refashioning the ethnic as well as the political map. It pointed to the purgation of nations and states. Nation states could be constructed if alien peoples were either driven out or converted.

Bound up with these possible futures was the disequilibrium of the region. Germans were more numerous than the other peoples and they were in command of two of the multinational empires. As German nationalism grew and as the traditional fragmentation of political power to the north of the Habsburg Empire gave way to the concentration of power under Prussian leadership the disequilibrium became acute. It is in this context that it is as well to admit that the term Mitteleuropa entails unwelcome connotations for some. Its German provenance points to the reason for the concern. According to Felix Gilbert, writing at the end of the Second World War:

> The adherents of Mitteleuropa assign to Germany the role of organizing the central area of Europe under German leadership. In other words, the Mitteleuropa idea expresses a political aim. It is a political idea rather than a descriptive or geographical one.[3]

Gilbert was right to point to the imperialist use to which Mitteleuropa had been put, but he was wrong to claim that it was not also a descriptive term. The Germans were a physical presence throughout the region, the German language served as a lingua franca and German economic and military power, the inherent disequilibrium of Mitteleuropa, was a distinctive feature of the region.

The looming presence of Russia was the other major source of disequilibrium. It was a reality long before the Soviet Red Army liberated Eastern Europe, helped to divide Germany and excluded German influence for four decades. It was, after all, Polish attempts to reform their weakened state and escape from subordination to the Tsars in the eighteenth century which led to the successive partitions of Poland and the disappearance of Poland from the

European map for over a hundred years.[4] Yet the Russian presence was different from the German one. The Russians were not part of Mitteleuropa in the same way as the Germans. It is not necessary here to agree with those who argue that Russia was, and is, politically and culturally distinct from the Europe in order to accept this point.[5] Russians were simply not physically present in the way in which Germans were. There were no Russian communities scattered through-out the region. Until the middle of this century German economic and military strength outpaced Russian strength and influence.

Alongside its ethnic complexity and the disequilibrium of power, the region was vulnerable in a third sense. Within the wider context of socioeconomic development much of the region, East of the Elbe, developed more slowly than Western Europe and North America. The difference, according to Jeno Szucs, was sufficient to define East Central Europe[6] as a third region between Western Europe and Russia. The main distinguishing feature is traced back by Szucs to the emergence of the modern period. East Central Europe had followed the West in developing an independent nobility and many of the contractual rela-tionships which were to form the basis of Western freedoms. The difference was that in the West economic development became dependent upon an urban economy at a very early stage. Szucs dates this change to around 1300. But in East Central Europe the nobility:

> succeeded after 1500 in doing what the nobility of the West had failed to do after 1300 ... shifting the burden of the crisis onto the peasantry. The unmistakeable legislative omens of the 'second serfdom' appeared with awesome synchroneity in Brandenburg (1494), Poland (1496), Bohemia (1497), Hungary (1492 and 1498).[7]

For Szucs this assertion of the power of the nobility went along with the stifling of urban development and consequently the failure to follow the Western lead in economic growth. It is important here to note that there are two aspects to this experience: the economic, which gains its full significance only in terms of the comparison with the West, and the social structure of the region. Strictly speaking Szucs' model fits the Polish and Hungarian cases the best. It was only here that an indigenous nobility developed which was strong enough to domi-nate political affairs and to consistently retard economic progress.[8] The indig-enous Czech nobility was decimated at the battle of the White Mountain in 1620, its lands distributed to foreigners and its remnants Germanized. The de-velopment of the nobility in South Eastern Europe was severely hampered by the long Ottoman occupation. This can be seen most clearly in the case of the Romanian provinces of Wallachia and Moldavia, where in the eighteenth and early nineteenth centuries the Ottoman Empire imposed its own agents, mainly Greeks, for the better exploitation of the peasantry.

Despite this contrast between the experience of the historic nations, the Poles and Hungarians, and the peoples of South Eastern Europe, there is also an im-portant similarity. In East Central Europe distinctions of class were often also ethnic distinctions. Thus, Lithuanian and Ukrainian peasants were exploited by Polish or Polonized nobles, Slovak peasants by Magyar or Magyarized nobles. Urban populations, especially the emergent, small middle class often exhibited similar ethnic divergence from the population of the countryside, with Germans and Jews forming significant elements. In Hungary, at least until the middle of the nineteenth century, Greeks, Serbs and Armenians dominated the commercial class, although they were in the process of being assimilated into the Magyar nation.[9] The ethnic complexity of the region was, then, more than just the intermingling or juxtaposition of peoples across the region. On top of that there was also a functional side to the complexity. In terms of the economies of the region, ethnic diversity was part of a symbiotic pattern; though that in no way meant it was a harmonious pattern.

During the nineteenth century the persistence of a large peasant class and the weakness of urban and industrial development became ever more problematic. Even in the interwar period the percentage of the labour force employed in agriculture was high, ranging from 51 per cent in Hungary, through 60 per cent in Poland to 80 per cent in Albania. The percentage employed in the industrial sector was correspondingly low. Of the male labour force only 9 per cent were employed in industry in Lithuania, 22 per cent in Poland and 26 per cent in Hungary.[10] Within the agricultural economy, population growth from the nineteenth century onwards contributed to massive rural underemployment. It was this that drove the waves of emigrants to the Americas in the nineteenth century. But neither emigration, nor the land reform which followed the First World War, solved the problems of 'the politics of population pressure'. It was not to be until after the Second World War, under the strategy of an imposed industrialization, that a fundamental break with this social structure was to occur.[11]

The idea of Mitteleuropa represents an attempt to come to terms with and find solutions for these features of the region, its ethnic complexity, its inherent disequilibrium and its socioeconomic plight. The term itself along with associated phrases like 'middle powers' go back to the early nineteenth century. It was taken up in the 1830s and 1840s by economists and political publicists.[12] The concern here however is with the idea rather than the term. To be more precise the concern is with programmes for solving those underlying problems which mark out the region: the ethnic complexity, the inherent disequilibrium and the socioeconomic problems. From this perspective, terminology is not too important. Nor for that matter is the precise delimitation of the region, for the territorial extent implied by the idea would depend upon the nature of the solution to those underlying problems.

A striking example of this comes from Count Valerian Krasinski, a Polish *émigré* from Russia writing amidst the intense debates on the reform of Mitteleuropa in 1848–9. Krasinski was primarily concerned with the inherent disequilibrium of the region and its wider European ramifications. His main fear was of Russian-dominated pan-Slavism and, to a slightly lesser extent with the

German threat from the West. His solution was quite simple, if not very practical:

> The only effective means which Europe possesses to counteract the es-
> tablishment of a Russo-Panslavic empire is … the transformation of Aus-
> tria into a Slavonic state, which would comprehend Poland, Bohemia,
> Hungary and all the Austrian provinces where the Slavonic element pre-
> vails … Should … the politicians of Germany persevere in their preten-
> sions to make the western Slavonians the subjects and not the allies of
> their country the latter must sooner or later be thrown into Russian
> Panslavism.[13]

Krasinski's solution deals with two of the major problems, the disequilibrium
and the ethnic complexity, albeit at the expense of simplifying the latter, to the
benefit of the Poles who would be the dominant group in the proposed
Slavonian Habsburg empire. All the supposed answers to the region's problems
involved some element of exclusion as well as integration. According to the
prime focus of the solution, the institutional starting point, if any, and the loyalties and ambitions of their authors, Mitteleuropa could be stretched as far West
as the mouth of the Rhine or as far East as Kiev, and possibly even beyond. It
could be constituted by a divison between Slavs and Germans or presume their
common membership of the region. The region, and here both Gilbert and
Meyer are right, was always a political project as well as an ethnic cockpit or a
socioeconomic pattern.

When Krasinski wrote his appeal for a Slavonic empire located between the
Germans and Russia he was responding to the beginnings of a cultural division
which would later have fateful consequences for Mitteleuropa. Amidst the revolutions of 1848, sparked off by events in Paris, German liberals had established a
Parliament at the Paulskirche in Frankfurt to work, among other things, on a
new constitution for the German nation. They had invited representatives from
Bohemia, which formed part of the German Confederation, to attend, only to
receive a reply from the leading Czech nationalist Palacký affirming his identity
as a 'Czech of Slav race'. In response to the Frankfurt Assembly Palacký called
the first Pan-Slav Congress which met in Prague in 1848.[14] Pan-Germanism and
Pan-Slavism were beginning, but only beginning, to emerge as two conflicting
loyalties which would ultimately be used to justify the conflict of the First
World War. How far removed 1848 was from this manichean stance can be seen
from Palacký's support for the continued existence of the Habsburg Empire – as
a federation between equal peoples. In Palacký's famous assertion, 'Truly, if the
Austrian Empire had not already existed for a long time, the interests of Europe
and the interests of humanity would demand its speedy creation.' [15] The driving
force behind these incipient divisions was, however, in a sense intra-German
relations.[16] The Germans, fragmented into numerous states with two – Prussia
and the multinational Empire – standing out, were being called upon to unite.
The Empire could not in fact accept the idea of a German nation state without committing suicide as a political entity, for so much of its territories was

occupied by non-Germans. At the end of its deliberations the Frankfurt Assembly opted for a *kleindeutsch* solution: that is, unification of Germany without Austria, as opposed to a *grossdeutsch* solution.

This decision, embodied in the draft constitution of March 1849, was not yet to be implemented. The dynastic houses, temporarily disoriented by the revolutions of 1848, recovered their nerve and power and suppressed the Parliament. When the decision was effectively taken by the 1866 victory of Prussian-led armies over the Habsburg Empire and its allies, it was motivated by Otto von Bismarck's pursuit of the dynastic interests of Prussia, not in pursuit of the national idea *per se*. That decision was unsatisfactory in several respects. The achievements of Prussian armies did force the Empire out of German affairs to the north of its borders but it left the German nation divided. It signified the fragmentation as much as the unity of the German nation. Perhaps more importantly it forced the Habsburgs to make concessions to the Magyar aristocracy, through the *Ausgleich* of 1867, and hence strengthened the hand of the Magyar ruling class against the non-Magyar peoples within the boundaries of the Hungarian part of the Empire. The outcome was that the prospects for realizing a less antagonistic, and more all-embracing, solution to the problems of Mitteleuropa were seriously, and perhaps irrevocably, weakened. A partial German integration was outpacing attempts to find a broader solution. Considerations of power, primarily dynastic power, were riding rough shod over the prospects of integration on the basis of economic interests.

The idea that there should be a reorganization of Mitteleuropa on the basis of commercial interests had been widely espoused during the 1830s and 1840s. Friedrich List was the most famous political economist to advocate a customs union embracing the German states and the Habsburg Empire. He argued that not only would this provide an enlarged market for German products but also that it would provide, by means of its external tariff, the protection necessary for the infant industries of these states. [17] List is the most well-known but he was accompanied by a host of others including Freiherr von Andrian-Werburg, the Rhineland industrialist Gustav von Mevissen, the Minister of the Interior for Baden, C. F. Nebenius and Gustav Höfken. List and Höfken shared an interesting common assumption. List believed that Belgium, Holland, Denmark and Switzerland would soon join his proposed customs union. Höfken also wanted to include the Scandinavian states along with Belgium and Holland.[18] This made a great deal of sense. Much of Prussia's burgeoning industry was oriented towards Belgium, Holland and beyond. The more developed markets of North West Europe offered better prospects than the uncertain and limited ones of the Empire and the Balkans. The point was made frequently by North German industrialists when they were consulted on the various propsals for a Prussian-Austrian or North German-Austrian customs union. This North Western expansion of the Mitteleuropa idea, which was to recur later, would however have posed an unacceptable threat to the neighbours of the union, namely France and Britain. Mitteleuropa would signify not just a solution to the indigenous problems of Mitteleuropa but would represent such a concentration of power that it could only be achieved by means of military victory over those whom it potentially threatened. As yet Prussia was not even interested in a customs union with the Empire. Prussia had successfully built up its own customs union, initially with North German states but extending successfully southwards. Contra List's protectionist arguments, Prussia was committed to a moderate tariff policy. There were Prussians who were more sympathetic to protectionism, including the head of the Board of Trade, von Rönne, who later chaired the economic committee of the Frankfurt Parliament. They made little headway against the free traders and the government advocates of a continuation of the moderate tariff policy.

It was to be the vice-chairman of the Frankfurt committee, Karl Ludwig Freiherr von Bruck, who made a more forceful move towards a customs union of Mitteleuropa. Bruck had become Austrian Minister of Commerce in November 1848. He was a founder of the Trieste-based shipping company, Austrian Lloyd, a fact which was to give a distinct focus to his conception of Mitteleuropa. Bruck hoped to build up Trieste and control of Mediterranean shipping, channelling trade between the German lands and the Levant, and trade between England and India through Trieste. In *Die Aufgaben Österreichs*, written in 1859 shortly before his tragic suicide, he advocated an Italian federation alongside the Swiss and German federations. Together they would be able to exclude 'illegitimate foreign influence'. By the latter he meant French, English and Russian influence.[19] Bruck launched his proposal for a customs union of Mitteleuropa in October 1849. He clearly recognized that this had to be linked with internal reforms within the Empire and was soon able to make progress on that front. A major achievement, the abolition of the customs barrier between the Austrian and Hungarian parts of the Empire in June 1850, was made possible by the military defeat of the Hungarian revolt which formed part of the wave of revolutions set off in 1848.

Prussia was different. She could not be compelled to accept a customs union. She had to be persuaded. The leader of the Prussian negotiators, Rudolf von Delbrück, had no intention of accepting Bruck's proposal. His opposition was not merely due to Bruck's attempt to retain protective tariffs for the union. It was also the respective power of the two German states that was at stake. This was true for both sides. Though Bruck genuinely believed in the advantages and virtues of his proposals – proposals whose vision extended beyond the European heartland – the Austrian Prime Minster, Schwarzenberg, saw them primarily as a means of weakening Prussian power by dissolving it within a larger framework.[20] Whatever the virtues of the respective economic arguments, the economic unification of Mitteleuropa would remain caught up in the struggle for political power between Berlin and Vienna even after the Habsburg Empire had ceased to exist. Herein lay a substantial part of the difficulty. The problems of Mitteleuropa were interlinked. Even supposing economic interests did point in the same direction, considerations of the distribution of power between states, the relationship between ethnic groups and even considerations of social structure all had to be taken into account. Occasionally, one of them could be ignored, as when military defeat of the Magyar revolt opened up the way to the abolition of the customs barrier between Austria and Hungary. More usually what made sense in one dimension had unwelcome, for some, implications in another. Links which pointed in the same direction were difficult to establish.

The problem was apparent in the repeated and unsuccessful attempts to reform the Empire. At the end of the day three problems stood out: the sheer ethnic complexity of the Empire, the relative strength of the two dominant but mutually distrustful peoples, the Germans and the Magyars, and divergent conceptions of the root cause of the Empire's internal tensions. For German liberals, and for the majority of German socialists, the root of the evil was political oppression which in turn engendered a growth of nationalism. The persistence of this view for over half a century, from the 1848 Revolution through to the eve of the First World War, is remarkable. As the Constitutional Committee of the Austrian parliament, which had been exiled to Kremsier, sought to complete its work, it drew heavily upon a draft by a German Moravian Cajetan Meyer. In Meyer's eyes political oppression, not national oppression, was the main problem. Hence Meyer and many of the German liberal representatives favoured the maintenance of a centralized Empire, with a system of representative bodies stretching up from the municipalities and ethnically homogenous districts (*Kreise*). In true liberal fashion, they offered Austria's peoples self-government and representative government. The Slav delegates sought instead to preserve and enlarge the powers of the Crownlands, the historic constituent units of the Empire. The reason for their preference was simple. They saw these historic units as the basis for *national* autonomy.[21]

Yet German liberals would continue to suggest programmes of decentralization, sometimes with federalist modifications to take account of the intractable nationalities' problem. The best representative of this approach was Adolf Fischhof who argued for thorough-going decentralization along with a bicameral central parliament in which the second chamber would be indirectly elected in accordance with the strength of the different nationalities. He also wanted a central Court of Arbitration in which conflicting nationalities would be equally represented but in which the chairman would be elected by the nationalities, not party to the particular dispute.[22] Fischhof himself recognized the obstacles posed by the the dualist structure established in 1867 and the likely hostility of the Empire's centralized bureaucracy. Equally significant, Fischhof could not free himself from assumptions about the role of German culture which non-Germans saw as cultural arrogance.[23]

Towards the end of the century Austria's socialists were still convinced that the problem was one of political oppression. As socialists they also believed that opponents of democratic reform were deliberately manipulating and fuelling ethnic tensions to head off reform and, of course, to divide the working class of the Empire. They did not, however, pretend that the ethnic problem was purely artificial. On the contrary: the most interesting proposals for reform which would meet the claims of the Empire's peoples came from her socialists. But the German socialists still clung to what was essentially a liberal conception of the national problem. They saw nationalities as cultural and linguistic entities. This profoundly affected the kinds of concessions they were ready to make. The general assumptions they made were embodied in the resolution on the nationalities problem which was passed at their Party Conference at Brunn in 1898. It began:

> Since the national troubles in Austria cripple any political progress and any cultural development of the peoples, since these troubles can be traced back, in the first instance, to the political backwardness of our public institutions and, especially, since the continuation of the nationalities conflict is one of those means by which the ruling classes secure their domination and block any forceful expression of the real interests of the people ...[24]

The most imaginative approach to the ethnic conflict was advanced by Karl Renner. Renner, though still clinging to the assumption that national identity was cultural and linguistic, favoured a solution which would take account of the ethnic complexity of the Empire, of the impossibility of drawing new territorial borders which would separate out the different nationalities. His solution was to organize the state on differing bases for different purposes. Thus economic and political affairs were to be dealt with through a federal system based on territoral units. In addition to this, matters affecting national identity were to be dealt with by a separate system according to which members of a national group were to be represented by their co-nationals, regardless of their place of residence.[25] Leaving aside the uncomfortable fact that Renner was putting forward a solution which would have required considerable tolerance and sophistication at a time when the tensions between the nationalities were becoming increasingly crude, his scheme was flawed by its fundamental assumptions. Whereas the German socialist Renner still thought that the problem was one of cultural and linguistic differences, the Czech socialist Modracek bluntly asserted that: 'The conflict of nationalities has its roots in the unequal economic development of the peoples ...'.[26] Renner, like so many other advocates of reform in the Empire, believed that economic development and economic self-interest would cut across ethnic identities, in the long run at least. As a Marxist Renner had quite evident reasons for believing this. Reformers of a distinctly different political persuasion could also make the same assumption. Amidst the decay of the Empire towards the end of the First World War, Count Polzer-Hoditz, chief of the Emperor's cabinet until 1917, suggested dividing the parliament into two: a political assembly and an economic assembly. The latter, in which representation was to be organized on a corporate basis, was supposed to help to diffuse the division of people on the basis of national identity.[27]

Renner was probably right in arguing that economic interests cut across ethnic barriers, though not always so; he was right that ethnic tensions were consciously inflamed by conservative and radical-nationalist forces; he was certainly right in pointing out that the smaller nationalities had much to gain from a supranational state in which some kind of rule of law prevailed than in the jungle of independent states.[28] But he was wrong in judging that enlightened economic self-interest would prevail and wrong in believing that the national issue could be solved largely in terms of cultural and linguistic autonomy.

By the time Renner formulated his proposals, the wider context of the Mitteleuropa debate had changed significantly from Bruck's day. By the end of the 1850s a new dimension was being added to the debate. The term Mitteleuropa indicates a central position. But central to what? Russian, or in some versions Pan-Slav, pressure provided one pole. Initially French ambitions and English competition provided the other. In the middle of the century the Western threat was being enlarged. List and others had already pointed to the eventual hegemony of the United States of America over England. In the 1850s these two threats were being brought together to form the idea of the looming threat of two continental powers, different in extent, resources and culture from the Old World and against which Mitteleuropa had to unite if it wanted to survive in the long run. In the middle of the century these fears were being expressed by publicists like Joseph Edmund Jorg, editor of the influential catholic *Historisch-politischen Blätter*. He was warning, from 1853 at the latest, of the coming hegemony of the United States and Russia. The European balance of power, he said, was now, obsolete. His conclusion was that Prussia and Austria should unite to form a *Mittelstellung* between East and West if it wanted to salvage its 'Christian civilization'.[29]

Julius Fröbel had a different political pedigree. He had been a radical deputy at the Frankfurt parliament. In 1848 he published *Wien, Deutschland und Europa* in which he advocated a union composed of Germany, Poland, Hungary and the South Slav and Wallachian lands. Fröbel was encouraged in his speculations by the erroneous belief that nationalism was contrary to the spirit of the age.[30] After a period of emigration in America and after the Crimean War, which he rightly saw would induce Russia temporarily to turn inwards to put her house in order, he published *Amerika, Europa und die politische Gesichtspunkt der Gegenwart* in 1859. According to this, Europe was threatened by the two flanking continental powers. In 1859 he still retained enough enthusiasm for Louis Napoleon to suggest France might take the lead in bringing about the unity of Europe. Indeed, strictly speaking he was calling for the unity of the occident, of all Europe, excluding Russia, rather than a specifically Central European union. But as the perceived threat in the West moved outwards from France or Britain to the Americas, this was a frequent conclusion.[31] The most important of the German federalists, Constantin Frantz was equally impressed by these wider geopolitical considerations.[32]

Whether the wider geopolitical considerations were taken as evidence of the need for a Pan-European or a Central European solution was vital. Where Pan-European solutions prevailed the focus tended to be upon a Franco-German axis. Sometimes Britain would be included, sometimes not. In any event, Pan-European solutions emphasized the Western character of Germany. Central European solutions tended to suggest that Germans, usually in association with the other peoples of East Central Europe, were distinct in their political, economic or cultural life and occupied a middle position between West and East.

These characteristics came to the fore at the end of the century as the idea of Mitteleuropa gained ground. It was far from a breakthrough for the idea. The historian Meyer, with some exaggeration, collected his observations on the period 1870 to 1914 under the heading 'Slender Threads'. There was a flurry of interest in the first half of the 1880s. The Hungarian Guido von Baussern tried to persuade Bismarck of the virtues of a customs union between Germany and Austria-Hungary in 1880. The French economic liberal G. von Molinari sought to talk Bismarck into a wider Central European customs union, including France, the Low countries and Switzerland. Neither met with much success.[33] Others were also showing an interest in the idea. Alongside A von Peez, a longstanding enthusiast for Mitteleuropa, Gustav Schmoller and, briefly, Lujo von Brentano took up the cause. Brenatano's interest is worthy of note since he was generally committed to liberal economic strategies. Brentano had been persuaded that Germany's agriculture could not withstand free trade, but was reluctant to embrace protectionism, if for no other reason than that it would invoke retaliatory tariffs from Germany's trading partners. He found a compromise solution in the idea of a customs union. Hungarian agriculturalists, worried by American competition, showed some enthusiasm and Brentano tried to interest the German Foreign Office, without success.[34]

More official support for the idea emerged in the 1890s as the new Chancellor, Caprivi, embarked on a series of commercial treaties which seemed to point to a solution based upon Mitteleuropa. Indeed, as he presented the first successful treaty to the Reichstag he invoked the idea of a mitteleuropäisch customs union and was followed by representatives of the Social Democrats, National Liberals and the Centre Party.[35] The actual outcome was less dramatic. Moreover, given the inclusion of Russia in the system of treaties, its identity as a mitteleuropäisch union had always had a question mark over it. The head of the foreign trade division of the Foreign Ministry, von Berchem, did advocate an anti-Russian preference system, but this was vetoed by Caprivi.[36] Caprivi was really looking for long-term treaties in order to be able to withstand the pressure for higher tariffs, especially protective tariffs for German agriculture.

The German Mitteleuropa debate was becoming embroiled in a larger conflict over the future development of German society. The key question was: should Germany became an 'industrial state' or try to remain an 'agrarian state'? It was a debate over Germany's social and political structure as much as over its economic policy. Caprivi was certainly not a doctrinaire partisan. But in terms of this debate he stood on the side of industry and comparatively low tariffs. Brentano too swung behind the industrial party, arguing that Germany's salvation lay in the victory of industrialism over reactionary feudalism.[37]

In one sense Caprivi and Brentano were proved right. Especially after 1895, Germany witnessed a surge of German industrial development. The consequence was that she was tied into the world economy, to an extent that undermined the prospects of Central European integration in the long run. For Germany's explosion on to the world market meant, in reality, a turn away from Mitteleuropa. By 1914 of a total of 23.5 billion Reichsmarks of foreign investment, only 3 billion were located in the Habsburg Empire, with a further 1.7 billion in the Balkans. The United States and Canada accounted for more than the Habsburg Empire, with 3.7 billion Reichsmarks of German investment.[38] Trade with the Empire also showed a significant decline. By 1900 the Empire supplied only 15 per cent of German imports and took only 19 per cent of German exports. On the eve of the First World War the figures had declined still further. In 1912 the Empire supplied 8 per cent of German imports and took 12 per cent of her exports.[39]

This shift in Germany's real interests did not exclude a turn to Mitteleuropa away from the wider world. Indeed, the tensions that arose because of greater integration into a world economy fuelled advocacy of Mitteleuropa. This was pronounced in the case of German trade relations with the United States.[40] Moreover, the idea that the world was being divided up into competing regional economic blocs was now so widespread that criticism of it was the exception. An army of propagandists clamoured for a Central European orientation to German foreign and economic policy.[41] Among the groups at work, the Mitteleuropäische Wirtschaftsverein, founded in 1904 by Julius Wolff, envisaged the incorporation of Belgium, Holland and Switzerland as well as the Balkans.[42] While the Mitteleuropäische Wirtschaftsverein worked on technical studies for the benefit of its industrial members, more raucous prophets enjoyed considerable popularity. Theodor Schiemann, who enjoyed favour with the German emperor, set out his guidance for German policy succinctly:

> Central European customs and economic union, a settlement of the colonial question on generous lines, the humiliation of England, the preservation of peace with our allies Austria-Hungary and Italy and the containment of the powerful Russian influence.[43]

The political and economic supremacy of Germans within Mitteleuropa had always meant that any proposal for union in the region would carry with it the implication that the other peoples would play a subordinate role. Even otherwise liberal Germans within the German Empire or the Habsburg Empire had difficulty restraining their sense of superiority and their belief in the civilizing mission of Germans. Now the imperialist rhetoric was rampant. It became more and more difficult for conceptions of a united Mitteleuropa to escape the taint of imperialist hegemony, even where it was not present.

The First World War quickly turned the rhetoric into reality. As early as September 1914, when imminent victory over France was still expected, Chancellor Bethman-Hollweg drafted a war-aims programme whose fourth point was:

> We must create a central European economic association through com-
> mon customs treaties, to include France, Belgium, Holland, Denmark,
> Austria-Hungary, Poland and perhaps Italy, Sweden and Norway. This
> association will not have any common constitutional supreme authority
> and all its members will be formally equal, but in practice will be under
> German leadership and must stabilise Germany's economic dominance
> over Mitteleuropa.[44]

Progress towards this goal was impeded by two factors: the development of the
military conflict and the concerns of Austria-Hungary. Vienna was far from
convinced of the economic benefits, favouring at most a system of preference
treaties. Austria's businessmen were even more unenthusiastic.[45] The plan was
also to be plagued by disagreements about the future of Poland. Both parties
accepted that a revived Poland was necessary but disagreed over whether it was
to be more firmly tied to the Habsburg throne, the so-called Austro-Polish
solution, or to Germany. Even more important was a fundamental difference
about the nature of Mitteleuropa and the place of the Habsburg Empire within
it. This difference was put most bluntly in the wake of a meeting between the
German Chancellor Bethmann-Hollweg and the Austrian Foreign Minister
Burian in November 1915. As part of the follow-up the German State Secretary, Jagow, sent a memorandum summarizing his Government's views. In it he
wrote:

> Due to an increase in political power of other national elements in the
> lands of the Austrian crown, a development has appeared through which
> the Germanic element itself has lost the leading role ... a further strength-
> ening of the non-Germanic elements in Austria would appear to con-
> tradict the basis of our alliance and the foreign interests of both signatories.
> The imperial governement ... urgently submits to the consideration of
> the imperial-royal government that it devise whatever measures seem
> appropriate which will impede the progressive slavicization of Austria and
> return to the Germanic element the leading role which it deserves in the
> interest of Austria as the German Ostmark.[46]

The Austrian reply quite rightly took exception to the presumption of its ally in
seeking to interfere in its internal affairs, defended the role of its non-German
citizens and denied that monarchy was 'merely "a Germanic Ostmark"'.[47] The
conception of Austria as merely a Germanic Ostmark would be the death-knell
of the Empire. What Jagow was doing, along with a host of pan-Germans in
Austria and Germany, was to effectively reopen the decision of 1866.[48] That
year had seen the division of the German people into two competing units, in
one of which Germans were a numerical minority. The assertion of some kind
of unification of the Germanic element carried with it the implication of the
subjugation of the non-Germanic peoples who would fall within its sphere of
influence. In all probability this would have been the outcome of any

Mitteleuropa forged in the war years, but the starting point still makes a difference. Jagow's starting point was the need to strengthen the Germanic element against the threat of slavicization.

It was becoming increasingly difficult for German authors to persuade non-Germans that any conception of Mitteleuropa was something more than propaganda for Germanic hegemony. Friedrich Naumann, in the most famous contribution of the war years, entitled simply *Mitteleuropa,* sought to recommend Mitteleuropa to his co-nationals and to persuade other nationalities that Mitteleuropa did not entail their subjugation. He pleaded for greater German sensitivity to the feelings of the non-Germanic peoples. He claimed that his proposed Central European state would not interfere in religious, educational or linguistic matters.[49] By and large his efforts to assuage the fears of non-Germans were unsuccessful. The exiled Czech leader Masaryk and the British publicist R.W. Seton-Watson launched a journal, *The New Europe,* whose avowed aim was, 'the emancipation of the subject races of central and south-eastern Europe from German and Magyar control - such must be our answer to the Pan-German project of "Central Europe" and "Berlin-Baghdad" '.[50] In fact the Pan-Germans were amongst Naumann's most bitter critics: not that this did anything to mitigate the suspicion which Naumann's book induced among non-Germans.

In the light of the mistrust and differences of interest between Germany and Austria-Hungary, it is not surprising that progress on Mitteleuropa was slow. Talks on unifying tariff schedules did not begin until April 1916. By the end of the year the only substantive achievement was to provoke the Allied Powers into the Paris Economic Conference at which they threatened to continue their economic warfare against Central Europe after the conclusion of hostilities.[51] In fact, as the Verein für Sozialpolitik concluded, apart from the unusual conditions of war Mitteleuropa made little economic sense for Germany.[52] But then the argument was not just about economics. It was, as Jagow's demands made clear, about political hegemony. From this perspective Austria-Hungary was fighting a losing battle. Militarily the weaker partner, she was also becoming financially dependent on her northern ally. These pressures and the presence of a more sympathetic negotiating partner in Berlin, Kühlmann, facilitated an agreement with the Austrian Foreign Minister Czernin. The Austro-Polish solution was revived, Germany was to receive Romania and progress would resume on building Mitteleuropa. At this point, however, the agreement of the politicians was blocked by the German high command. At the end of 1917 Generals Ludendorff and Hindenburg were exercising near dictatorial power in Germany. Ludendorff exhibited a traditional Prussian distrust and dislike of Austria-Hungary. More important, he was fundamentally uninterested in Mitteleuropa. Ludendorff was attracted instead by the open plains of North and Eastern Europe. From this perspective Poland was a bridge to the Baltic, the Ukraine and Romania. The collapse of Russia and the peace treaty of Brest-Litovsk encouraged Ludendorff's ambitions (see Map 3). In the words of the historian Fritz Fischer:

Germany's great Eastern Idea, which went far beyond Brest-Litovsk, prevented the completion of Mitteleuropa which, in the last phase, was dropped by Germany in favour of absolute domination of the *Ostraum* - a goal as old as the Mitteleuropa idea itself.[53]

The First World War had witnessed the triumph of German power over Mitteleuropa and then its sudden collapse. The Austro-Hungarian Empire disintegrated. Austrian Germans looked initially to *Anschluss* with the new Germany, but were denied this option by the Allies. New or revived states emerged from the chaos at the end of the war. And the idea of Mitteleuropa was henceforth associated with the real and imagined imperialist ambitions of Germany. With the exclusion of German-dominated states from much of the region, new problems were added to old ones. The need for some kind of integrating factor was recognized by some, but was incompatible with the desire for independence of the various peoples of Mitteleuropa.

Since the interwar period is usually seen as witnessing the triumph of superheated nationalism, it is worth emphasizing how widespread was the assumption that some kind of regional unity was needed. Among the Allies both French and the American diplomats were initially prepared to support varying degrees of regional integration.[54] The French, in particular, hoped for the preservation of a Danubian federation as a counterweight to Germany, which they also wanted to dismember. These kinds of geopolitical calculations were also found among the leaders of the non-Germanic peoples of the region. One of the most ideologically committed was General Pilsudski of Poland. Pilsudski had been born in Lithuania and was a convinced adherent of the idea of a restoration of the old Jagiellonian Empire. For Pilsudski, geopolitical considerations of building up a state capable of withstanding pressure from Russia and a genuine commitment to a multinational state rubbed shoulders. The General's attitude was revealing for he did not naïvely presume that an Empire which had been long dissolved could simply be restored. Against fellow Poles who argued for the limited territorial annexation of lands inhabited by Ukrainians and Lithuanians followed by a policy of assimilation, Pilsudski pointed to the strength of Lithuanian and Ukrainian nationalism. Though far from fully developed it had, he believed, gone too far to permit that solution. The way forward lay in accepting their independence in the hope of a later federation with Poland.[55] Amidst the exigencies of war, Pilsudski found it difficult to hold to his basic insight and contributed to a worsening of Polish-Lithuanian relations by inspiring a botched coup in Wilno.

In broader geopolitical terms the supposed motive for integration was defence against either German or, to a lesser extent, Russian or Communist ambitions. But ideas of integration based upon geopolitical calculations signally failed. They could not surmount the internal antagonisms between the peoples of the region. Indeed, these antagonisms were reflected in the few partial attempts to organize regional stability. The most enduring of these was the

so-called Little Entente incorporating Czechoslovakia, Romania and Yugoslavia which was formed in 1920–1. Although its French patron saw the system
of alliances as a way of building up a barrier against Germany, there was a strong
intra-regional motive in the alliance. All the members of the Entente had
benefitted from the harsh Treaty of Trianon which the Allies had imposed upon
Hungary. All were consequently prospective targets of Hungarian irredentism.

The other partial success story, the Balkan Entente formed in 1934, also
found its rationale in antipathy to another member of the region, in this case
Bulgaria. Its limits became apparent as soon as the Entente was formed, as each
state sought to ensure that it would not be dragged into a war with one of the
Great Powers because of the Alliance. Since each had something to fear from a
different extra-regional state, the prospects of the Entente were scarcely good.[56]
Geopolitics pointed not to unity but to intra-regional conflict and subservience
to the Great Powers, primarily Germany, Italy and France, each of whom
sought to manipulate its clients in its own interests. The outcome of the attempt
to organize the region without German-dominated states was an abject failure.
The strongest common motive was nothing more precise than a shared vulnerability – and this was insufficient.

The Versailles settlement may have bequeathed a region without German-
dominated states (see Map 4). It had left large numbers of German nationals
strewn across the region. Germans formed one of several minority groups. Of all
the states, only Austria and the much-truncated Hungary were substantially ethnically homogenous. The peace-makers at Versailles attempted to deal with the
intractability of the ethnic map by imposing a system of guarantees for the rights
of minorities.[57] In the place of a federal solution which would, in one way or
another, cede decision-making power to the different peoples of the region, the
Versailles system established a network of internationally supervised legal guarantees. Not suprisingly the latter were ineffective. The general climate was
hardly propitious. Czechoslovakia, for example, proclaimed itself to be a state of
the Czechoslovak nation at a time when it was not clear that there was any such
nation and when there were more Germans than Slovaks in the state. The order
of the day was assimilation, often tinged with coercion. Minorities, often but
not always Jews, provided ready scapegoats for the mounting socioeconomic
difficulties of the region.

The best placed to take advantage of the inevitable inequities were the
Germans. As the largest state by far, the economically most powerful and with
Hitler's rearmament programme the militarily most powerful, Germany could
redraw the map in a way in which no other state could. Advocates of revision
made frequent appeals to the idea of Mitteleuropa. Just as before the war, reference was made to federalism as a way of dealing with the ethnic complexity,
sometimes sincerely, sometimes not and often with a superficiality which made
the proposal look like a threadbare apology for Germanic hegemony.[58]

The most worrying development of the Mitteleuropa idea emerged in the
writings of political ideologists and the geographers. Ever since the end of the

Napoleonic wars German geographers had struggled to find some geographical identity to the idea of Mitteleuropa, to secure geography's title, to define the region and to demonstrate their importance to the role of Germans within the region. The task had never been easy but they sought to balance political and more strictly geographical features, to exhibit the mutual interaction of human activity and the landscape. In the 1920s and 1930s the emphasis became more one-sided. According to the new emphasis, the landscape was the creation of 'specifically talented men who transform nature according to their will'.[59] In other words, the primary category was the nation. Everything else, including the natural environment, was seen through this ethnic and racial prism.

The political ideologists often came to the same conclusion, albeit by a different route. Here the starting point was the difference between Western Europe on the one hand and Mitteleuropa, including the Germanic lands, on the other. The Western nation state, its archetypal political form of parliamentary democracy and its social and economic structure, were all said to be inappropriate to Mitteleuropa. Thus far the argument is shared by many commentators of diverse political persuasions. A more precise stamp was given when it was argued that some peoples, but not others, in the region were capable of creating appropriate state structures.[60] The Germans and occasionally selected others, usually the Magyars, were ascribed the requisite capacity. Just as the geographers saw the landscape of Mitteleuropa as a product of an ethnic or racial category, so too the political ideologists saw its political structure, or at least what they judged to be its appropriate political structure, as a product of a racial category. This fitted in with the extreme politicization of the idea of Mitteleuropa. Mitteleuropa was being defined as a product of political will. The proximity of this to Nazi ideology is clear.

These extreme conceptions were not the only ones available. They were not even held by all German nationalists. The *Auslandseutsche*, the Germans living beyond the boundaries of the German state as citizens of other states, initially looked to the improvement of their position within their respective states. Their leaders, including some who were to become infamous as fifth columnists, inclined towards more archaic but somewhat more tolerant forms of political organization than the Nazis.[61]

These nuances were to be ironed out as the growth of Nazi power and ambition closed off options and forced men to make simpler choices. As Germans were forced to choose they were being led by a man who was deeply influenced by the longstanding antagonisms of Mitteleuropa, but whose perverse vision owed more to Ludendorff's *Ostraum* than it did to Mitteleuropa. Hitler may well have learned his intense racial obsessions from the background of conflict between Czech and German in Bohemia.[62] His solution, alongside the mass murder of Europe's Jews, was the pursuit of *Lebensraum* in an ill-defined East.

The non-Germanic states of Europe were ill-prepared for the ensuing onslaught. Despite the frequently repeated urgency of cooperation, despite the equally frequently asserted need for some kind of economic integration, they remained obdurately divided. On the eve of the Second World War Mitteleuropa had already been transformed. Austria, the rump state of the Empire which had once dominated a large part of Mitteleuropa and also imposed some restraint upon the concentration of power to its north, had been incorporated into the Third Reich by the *Anschluss* of 1938. German industrialists were not alone in seeing Austria as a stepping stone to further expansion in the South East. Czechoslovakia had been dismembered, first by the incorporation of the German-occupied Sudetenland in the same year, and then, in March 1939, by the dismemberment of the remainder of the Czechoslovak state. Her neighbours, Hungary and Poland, took the opportunity to satisfy part of their territorial ambitions.

Much more dramatic changes were still to come. Mitteleuropa would be radically and irrevocably transformed. But Mitteleuropa did not enjoy the ideological, let alone political, importance that it had in the First World War. It is true that Hitler, an Austrian by birth, thought in terms of a constricted kind of Mitteleuropa: that is, of Germany, Austria and a Bohemia which was Germanized and substantially purged of 'alien' elements. Beyond this, however, the dominant elements in Hitler's mental universe were the 'Nordic-Germanic race' and the Ostraum. The former, including Danes, Dutchmen, Swedes and Norwegians, were to exercise an imperial rule over the slavs of the Baltic coast and the Ukraine.[63] Economic planning pointed in the same direction. Although Hitler's Third Reich had deliberately sought to relocate its trade to the south east of Europe, in order to have alternative sources of foodstuffs and raw materials to overseas supplies which would be endangered by naval blockade in wartime, the result had been only partially successful at best. The reality of the Third Reich's economic interests were revealed as her planners turned to consider the New Order of Europe in the summer of 1940. Greater Germany, including the old Austria, was to form the industrial core. Bohemia and Moravia were often added to this. Several north and north-western states came into consideration for particularly close association. Customs unions, preferential systems and even a currency union were mentioned.[64] The Danubian states did not come into consideration for similar treatment. Minister Funk explained why, with customary brutality:

> A Currency or customs union could only be envisaged with a country having a similar standard of life to our own. This was not the case in south-eastern Europe, for instance, and it was not at all in our interest to confer on that area a similar standard of life to ours.[65]

The hard economics of the German war-machine consolidated this judgement. It was western and north-western Europe that supplied the resources for the continuation of the war. According to the calculations of the Reichsbank the per capita contribution of Poland in 1942 amounted to only RM 190. Serbia managed only RM 156. On the other hand the figures for The Netherlands and

Belgium stood at RM 763 and RM 604 respectively.[66] Enthusiasts of Mitteleuropa were still in evidence, most notably in the Mitteleuropäische Wirtshaftstag, an association dominated by German big business, some of whose members even favoured the long-term industrialization of south-eastern Europe.[67] Less practical ideologues still enthused over the possibilities of river-borne trade, seeing the Rhine and the Danube as the economic backbone of the new order.[68] In terms of the guiding ideology and the reality of the Nazi war-machine the emphasis lay elsewhwere.

Despite the ideological downgrading of the idea of Mitteleuropa the Third Reich was to have a profound impact upon its reality, and consequently upon the subsequent development of the idea. The most evident transformation was brought about by the murder of the Jews of Europe. This had a special signifi-cance in Mitteleuropa, for the Jews had played a disproportionate role in the region's urban élites. They constituted an important element of a transnational élite which had done much to give the region its cultural homogeneity.[69] Although the holocaust is evidently distinctive it did form part of a larger pro-gramme of ethnic engineering, of the conversion of people and of their expul-sion and resettlement. This affected Germans too. Himmler, in his capacity as Reich Commissar for the Strengthening of Germandom, was beginning to con-solidate the large numbers of Germans who were scattered throughout the re-gion, displacing other peoples to make way for them. This approach to the ethnic entanglement of the region – that is, compulsory resettlement or simple expulsion – was also advocated by the leaders of the oppressed nationalities. Here the Czech leader Benes was the most active and influential, securing the reluctant or in the case of the Soviet Union enthusiastic, appproval of the Allies for the expulsion of the Sudeten Germans from the future Czechoslovakia.

A broader policy of expulsion was later sanctioned by the Allies. At the end of the war the Czechoslovak state was to treat the Hungarians in a similar fash-ion. The ethnic problem was to be solved by the expedient of expelling foreign elements. In the light of the events of the war years this was easier to carry out in the case of the Germans.[70] The result was that one of Mitteleuropa's defining characteristics, the presence of Germans throughout the region, was substan-tially brought to an end. With the murder of the Jews and the expulsion of the Germans the old Mitteleuropa ceased to exist. The peoples of Mitteleuropa had decided to solve the problems posed by the ethnic complexity of the region by purging the would-be nation states of 'foreign' elements. They were, despite the enormous population movements, far from successful, save in the case of the Germans, though the ethnic map was undeniably simplified.

The experience of occupation naturally affected the ideas of the resistance and of exiles. Among both groups, most prominently among the exiles, support grew for a federation of some or all of the non-Germanic peoples of the region. Under the impact of defeat the Polish and Czechoslovak exile governments drew up an Agreement dated 11 November 1940. In it they expressed their intention to form: 'a closer political and economic association, which would become the basis of a new order in Central Europe and a guarantee of its stability'.[71] Approximately one year later a Central and East European Planning Board was established in New York. Incorporating representatives of trade unions and business as well as of governments, the Planning Board was to formulate a variety of propsals for regional integration. By then joint Czechoslovak and Polish commissions had begun to work on an agreement between their two governments, in implementation of their decision of November 1940. The resulting Agreement was signed 23 January 1942. Days before, on 15 January 1942, a Greek-Yugoslav Pact was signed, as a precursor to a wider Balkan union. Most of the leading exiles looked to a link between these two blocs and wrote of a union or confederation extending from the Baltic to the Adriatic.[72] The connection between these ideas and those of the interwar period is clear. It was an attempt to organize Mitteleuropa without, and against, the Germans.

There was, however, another threat looming in the background. The common assumption was the military defeat of Germany. But what would the attitude of the Soviet Union be?[73] Most of the exiles sought to reassure the Soviet Union that their plans could only be of benefit. They would act as a bulwark against renewed German aggression. Stalin, however, was not convinced. At his insistence the Czechs allowed talks on implementing the 1942 Agreement to stagnate and then collapse. Stalin's suspicion that any confederation would have an anti-Soviet or anti-Russian intent was exaggerated, but not wholly without foundation. As early as November 1940 the organ of the Polish home army, the main resistance force in occupied Poland, declared that: 'The only effective answer to the German and Russian tendency to subject weaker nations to stronger ones is the ancient doctrine of Jagiellonian Poland ...'.[74] In other words, a confederation of states centred on Poland was to act as a defensive bloc against both German and Russian ambitions.

The defeated states, however, would be dependent upon Soviet goodwill for any move towards integration. Britain and the United States lacked the ability, and in the American case the will, to impose solutions in the east against Stalin's wishes. Even if they had had more leverage the varied experience of the war, defeat and occupation by Germany, collaboration with Germany and subsequent occupation by the Red Army, were not necessarily conducive to postwar cooperation. The negative impact of the war was well-summarized by a Polish economist, Leon Baranski. Although broadly in favour of cooperation, he noted that there were many obstacles. The experience of war had, if anything, inflamed nationalist antagonisms between the non-Germanic peoples. Nor did the wartime economy offer much hope:

> There is undoubtedly one controlling centre in Berlin, which supervises each of the several countries for Germany's own advantage and according to uniform principles of economic exploitation. But as between the various countries themselves, relations have disintegrated still further, as will become fully apparent when the central controlling authority is broken

and collapses. German domination will have hampered and not facilitated the creation of any union of European states.[75]

The hopes of exiles and members of the resistance alike were to prove futile. As the chaos and misery of the immediate postwar period subsided the division of Europe between the two superpowers emerged. For a while it seemed as if the region's communist leaders might push through a south Slav or Balkan federation. The Yugoslav and Bulgarian leaders, Tito and Dimitrov, had been pushing for this since the latter years of the war, against the background of considerable ambiguity from Stalin. Finally, after a flurry of activity in 1947 and January 1948, the plans were killed off by Stalin.[76] Similarly, Polish and Czechoslovak agreements on cooperative mining ventures ran into Soviet opposition. Economically, Mitteleuropa, east of the Iron Curtain, would find its trade constrained within a system of inflexible bilateral agreements and heavily skewed towards the Soviet Union.[77]

The idea of Mitteleuropa, discredited by its association with German imperialism, seemed irrelevant to the new world. Hopes for a Mitteleuropa without Germans were revealed as futile. Germans and Jews had largely been eradicated from the ethnic landscape. Mitteleuropa was cut in two by the iron curtain. Baranski's fears about the disintegration of the region were in some ways confirmed. Ethnic antagonisms were held in check only by the overarching force of the Red Army and by population transfers. Where these were not possible the old problems remained. The defeated Hungarians, many of whom were consigned to other states, primarily Romania but also Czechoslovakia and Yugoslavia, enjoyed only the ineffective protection accorded by the supposed recognition of human rights. Hungarian attempts to get agreement on recognition of the rights of national groups were quite unsuccessful.[78] In terms of providing a legal framework for the management of Mitteleuropa's ethnic complexity, the postwar settlement had regressed behind the ideas of even Versailles.

Yet for over 40 years the new dispensation brought peace to Mitteleuropa, albeit in the wake of changes which seemed to render the idea of Mitteleuropa obsolete. All that remained, in the 1950s, was the idea of German unification in association with the creation of an atomic- or nuclear-free zone. Several suggestions were made by both sides which might have led to this outcome. Eden for Britain in 1955, Rapacki for Poland in 1957 and both the Soviet Union and the United States in 1959 suggested some kind of neutralization, and the reintegration of Mitteleuropa. The same ideas recurred throughout the 1960s. Often, hopes for a demilitarized and neutralized central zone were associated with the idea that this zone might become a Third Force, an economic and ideological bridge between East and West. There was, however, a difference between the 1950s and the 1960s. In the 1950s the problem of Germany and the problem of tension and the armaments race between the two systems were intimately linked. It was assumed that a solution of one required a solution of the other. After the twin crises over Berlin and Cuba (1958–62) this ceased to be the case. The existence of two German states became a presupposition which few questioned. The focus turned to arms limitation alone.[79]

Even Mitteleuropa's old socio-economic dilemma seemed to be becoming a thing of the past as the Soviet-dominated half of Europe underwent a process of 'imposed industrialization'. Wartime population losses, immense especially in Poland, followed by industrialization and urbanization, transformed the social structure. Whereas only 31.8 per cent of Poles lived in towns in 1946, almost half did so by 1960 and in 1980 the urban population of Poland constituted 58.7 per cent of the total.[80] All this took place within the context of relative isolation from the world market and the reorientation of trade to the members of Comecon. In practice that meant very high levels of dependence upon the Soviet Union. Meanwhile, the Federal Republic of Germany was firmly integrated into the West and the global market. The old choice between a Western orientation and an Eastern orientation in foreign trade was finally and irrevocably resolved in favour of the West. Economic logic, which had long pointed in the direction of a Western orientation, was now confirmed by political allegiance. No matter how important the Federal Republic might become to East Central Europe, East Central Europe could not be a viable alternative to Western integration for the Federal Republic.

Yet despite these profound changes in the reality of Mitteleuropa, changes which call into question the usefulness of the concept, the idea of Mitteleuropa was to be reborn. Its revival came from two sources. For the first time Italy was to play a leading role. The revival showed a strong cultural bias. As early as 1966 the Istituto per gli Incontri Culturali Mitteleuropei was established and met annually thereafter. These meetings remained focused largely on cultural matters.[81] Over a decade later, in 1977, the Movimento Mitteleurpoeo emerged. This group was more explicitly political. Both groups had in common a dissatisfaction with the interpretation of history through the prism of the national culture and the nation state. The supposition of a national culture or of the nation state as the focus of history was criticized in the first place as suppressing important historical experiences of parts of the current states. In the words of one supporter of these ideas:

> If we follow an uncritical historical and political conception, which is still prevalent today and which underlies the nineteenth-century concept of the nation, then today's nation states are fixed magnitudes. Their historical development follows an internal (national) principle which, despite temporary political instability and external cultural influences, must succeed. The historical approach which operates under this assumption succumbs to the error of anachronistically projecting the contemporary state back into past centuries, of making a postulate of the nineteenth century a universally valid standard of historical reconstruction ...[82]

Despite the strong historical focus, which often induces accusations of nostalgia for the old Habsburg era, lay a specific contemporary implication. The suggestion was that the emphasis should be less upon interstate agreements than upon cooperation between peoples. The criterion should not be what is of advantage to states but what improves the life of individuals.[83] It was no accident that this new emphasis took place in the mid-1970s at the same time as the Conference on Security and Cooperation in Europe brought forth the Helsinki Charter by which, among other things, the signatory states agreed to respect specified human rights.[84] The Helsinki Charter helped to give a new stamp to the idea of Mitteleuropa, one which was less concerned with the formation of states, of federations and confederations or even with economic integration and more concerned with the idea of a certain kind of civilization as distinctive of Mitteleuropa.

The same emphasis was taken up in East Central Europe. The two publications that did most to stimulate the revival of the discussion over Mitteleuropa appearerd in the mid-1980s. The most widely cited was a brief essay by the exiled Czech writer Milan Kundera, 'The Tragedy of Central Europe'. The second was a book by the Hungarian, György Konrad, entitled *Antipolitik: Mitteleuropäische Meditationen*. Both posited a cultural identity distinct from and opposed to the prevailing political realities. In this sense and in others, Konrad's book was very much advocacy of *Antipolitik*. The key theme of Kundera's essay was that in cultural terms East Central Europe belonged to the West, but it was a: 'West that, kidnapped, displaced and brainwashed, nevertheless insists on defending its own identity'.[85] The kidnapper was the Soviet Union. The identity of Mitteleuropa was not so easily defined, either by Kundera or Konrad. Critics were not slow to point out that some of the darker features of Mitteleuropa were strikingly absent from their cultural sketches. Kundera, for example, praised Mitteleuropa's Jews as a key element in its identity but was less forthcoming about anti-semitism, and especially Adolf Hitler's anti-semitism, as a product of Mitteleuropa.[86]

The main focus of the debate inspired by Kundera and Konrad lay further East. For in identifying East Central Europe with the West, they excluded Russia from Europe. This was, after all, the whole point to reject the classification of east Central Europe as a part of the East and hence as being in the same category as the Soviet Union. Strictly speaking the antipathy to the Soviet Union and the political system it had foisted upon the region at the end of the Second World War was matched by an accusation levelled at the West. The Soviet Union had kidnapped East Central Europe, and the West had quickly forgotten that the crime had ever taken place. At the heart of this two-pronged criticism stood the symbol of Yalta, the meeting at which the victorious wartime Allies had supposedly divided up the continent. In the words of Konrad: 'Yalta is the military solution of societal questions, a superficial and arbitrary series of decisions taken without asking those affected.'[87] In the interwar period, ideas of the unity of East Central Europe had had a predominantly anti-German emphasis, though in Poland at least the anti-German element was almost always complimented by an anti-Russian element. As the idea of Mitteleuropa was taken up again in the mid-1980s Germany remained divided, unification was not considered to be a serious possibility and the term had been turned around to face eastwards.[88]

Even in 1985, four years before the collapse of the Berlin wall, the symbol of Europe's division, the unification of the two German states was not on the agenda. The events of 1989, especially the collapse of the symbol of the postwar division of Germany, the Berlin wall, changed the agenda with alarming speed. Within a year the unification of the two German states was an accomplished fact. The prospect and then the reality of German unification gave great encouragement to advocates of Mitteleuropa. It caused similarly great apprehension in the capitals of other states, both east and west. German unification threatened to revive the old disequilibrium which had plagued Mitteleuropa before 1945. The fear arose in part because of the simple size, the combined economic output of a united Germany. It also arose, and this was probably more important, because of fears about future German policy. The alarm bells rang throughout Europe, loudest of all in Paris. Michel Debre, a former adviser to President De Gaulle, raised the spectre of Rapallo, the Treaty of 1922 between Germany and Russia which was widely taken at the time as a sign of an eastward turn in Germany's foreign policy.[89] The Soviet Union, itself in the process of transformation, sought for a while to revive its options of the 1950s: that is, for a united Germany outside the global system of alliances.[90] That meant a united Germany which did not belong to NATO.

But the Soviet Union had neither the ability nor the will to veto unification if its wishes were not met. Gorbachev finally ceded the point in July 1991, with good grace. The enlarged Federal Republic of Germany would retain its membership of the North Atlantic Alliance. Chancellor Kohl's insistence that the united Germany would retain the Federal Republic's Western commitments extended to Germany's role within the European Community. Indeed, Kohl sought to accelerate integration within the Community as an explicit guarantee that a powerful, united Germany would be a 'European Germany': that is, one safely contained within wider, supranational power structures. Fears that the opening up of eastern markets would involve a reorientation of Germany's foreign economic policy were met with the same strategy. The more precise worries of Germany's eastern neighbours, Poland and Czechoslovakia, concerned, above all, the stability of the postwar borders (for Poland) and minority and property rights (for Czechoslovakia). Chancellor Kohl was at first equivocal, pandering to domestic critics, but eventually overruled oppositon and signed treaties on these outstanding isssues.[91]

The Federal Republic has already begun to act as an advocate of the cause of its Central European neighbours.[92] It is the largest supplier of aid to the region, supplying some 32 per cent of the total. It argued for the rapid conclusion of association agreements between the European Community and Czechoslovakia, Poland and Hungary.[93] Kohl has shown some understanding of the need of the East Central European states for at least firm prospects of admission to the European Community itself, stating in the Bundestag debate on the Maastricht

Treaty that Poland, Hungary, the Czech Republic and Slovakia must have the prospect of membership in the 'forseeable future'. He added that it was unacceptable for Germany to constitute the eastern border of the European Community and insisted that Poland lies not in Eastern Europe but in Mitteleuropa.[94] But there are also limits to Germany's ability and desire to exert influence over or on behalf of her eastern neighbours. The strains of integrating the former German Democratic Republic have imposed a severe burden and will continue to do so for the foreseeable future. Indeed, Germany has complained about the failure of other countries to play a full part in aiding the transformation in the region.[95] The internal difficulties of the Community have added to doubts about its ability to incorporate new members.

There were other echoes of the vicissitudes of Mitteleuropa in the Bundestag debate on the Maastricht Treaty. The Foreign Minister, Klaus Klinkel, criticized those who suggest that the fall of the Iron Curtain had mitigated the need for European integration. The latter, he insisted, was not a product of the East-West conflict but of 'centuries-long civil war in Europe'. The Minister President of Hesse took up a broader, but related, theme. Referring explicitly to Germany's position in the centre of Europe, and hence her exposure to waves of migration, he called into question the assumption that the boundaries of national identity and the territorially defined state must coincide.[96]

From the perspective of Germany's East Central European neighbours any kind of East Central European cooperation serves primarily to facilitate the achievement of their prime goal – admission to the main institutions of western integration, that is the European Community and NATO, or, as a temporary substitute, the Western European Union. Yet renewed interest in cooperation predated the events of 1989. As far back as 1978 cooperation began within the framework of the Alpine-Adriatic group, linking together regions of states on both sides of the ideological division. These were consolidated in November 1989 as Hungary, Austria, Italy and Yugoslavia agreed to expand their cooperation. Soon joined by Czechoslovakia the group became know as the Pentagonal, and, after later expansion, the Hexagonal and subsequently the Central European Initiative. In reality it consisted of a series of working groups, each chaired by one of the member states, with representatives from regions of states outside the core members sometimes attending.

This loose form of organization reflected the limited or transitional ambitions of the group. For Hungary, Czechoslovakia and Yugoslavia, it represented only one of many openings to the West. There are more concrete plans, for the improvement of transport and for turning Triest – once the major port of the Habsburg Empire – into a centre of regional activity.[97] The underlying limitations of East Central European cooperation – even when bolstered by the incorporation of Austria and Italy – are clear to all concerned. The Pentagonal was no substitute for the European Community. This does not mean that it is insignificant. It can act as a forum and amplifier for the interests of each member, of Austria's concern with environmental matters, or of Hungary's attempts to gain recognition for the rights of minorities.[98] Nor does it mean that the common historical experience of these countries, parts of which are former members of the Habsburg Empire, does not play some role in facilitating cooperation, at least where more pressing issues do not intervene. Any assessment of this intiti-ative depends heavily upon understanding its explicit limits. In the words of Géza Jeszenszky, Hungarian Foreign Minister, the initiative:'prove[s] that it is possible to establish close cooperation among countries and regions of the area without the need to raise it to the level of political integration or any type of bloc.'[99]

The same reservation applies to another initiative in regional cooperation, the Vísegrád group incorporating Poland, Czechoslovakia and Hungary, which became the focus of attention as the Hexagonal ground to a halt with Yugo-slavia's disintegration. This initiative took its name from the Vísegrád Summit in February 1991 which formed part of an *ad hoc* response to the prospective dismantling of the Warsaw Pact.[100] Again the explicit aim was limited. At the Cracow Summit of October 1991, the resulting declaration emphasized: 'Europe as a single and indivisible territory' and gave pride of place to develop-ing and cementing links with the European Community and NATO.[101] Initial suggestions of developing an economic dimension to their cooperation had not been fruitful. However, a decline of intra-regional trade pushed the states to reconsider this option. Despite considerable scepticism, the Vísegrád group – soon to be enlarged to four members by the division of Czechoslovakia – did reach agreement on a free trade zone which was signed on 21 December 1992.[102]

Yet even if the agreement is duly implemented there will be severe limits to regional economic integration, as opposed to integration within a broader European framework. This became clear in discussions for a Central European Payments Union, designed to facilitate intra-regional trade. Although the idea enjoyed some support it was never likely to repeat the success of the European Payments Union of the 1950s on which the idea was modelled. The share of intra-regional trade as a percentage of total trade was simply too small to make it a significant option.[103] Politically and economically East Central Europe is de-pendent upon the West and the broader institutions of the European Commu-nity, the Council of Europe, the CSCE and NATO.

These regional initiatives and the insistent search for integration within es-tablished bodies dominated by western states is evidence of the persistence of the region's vulnerability. Of the latter there can be no doubt. The break-up of Czechoslovakia into two states and the disintegration of Yugoslavia amidst bru-tal slaughter are sufficient proof of that. Despite the efforts of many Mitteleuropäer the predominant path through the region's ethnic complexity has been marked by a series of expulsions and populations' transfers. The sav-agery of the 'ethnic cleansing' in the former Yugoslavia is but the latest mile-stone. The outcome is a greatly simplified ethnic map.[104] Two nations at least, Germany and Poland, are no longer agitated by the old minorities problem.[105] For most of the rest of the region, however, ethnic entwinement remains significant. The problem is sufficiently substantial to enable us to speak of the reality of Mitteleuropa. But this Mitteleuropa is equally different from that of the nineteenth century, or even of the Mitteleuropa of the interwar period. The disappearance, for all practical purposes, of Jews and Germans means that Mitteleuropa as a political or cultural project no longer has the same meaning that it once did. To put it another way: the problem of ethnic entwinement is still there, but one possible kind of unity – one based upon German and Jewish elements – is not. The prospects for the remaining intermixed peoples despite the current bloodshed in the Balkans with all its attendant problems for the existing states, are not wholly black. The underlying resentments between Czechs and Germans, between Hungary and Romania on account of the large Hungarian minority in Romania, are still there, but in neither state is territorial revision the underlying bedrock agenda. The point is worth stressing, for in the interwar period territorial revision was precisely that: an underlying, widespread presupposition of foreign policy.

It is so no longer, though that is no guarantee that in the case of Hungary at least the risk of hightened tension is absent. At the end of the day it was not simple ethnic entwinement that was the problem. It was, at least once the spirit of nationalism had extended its arthritic grip over the region, fear that one's nation could be wiped off the map. As the Hungarian political philosopher István Bibó argued, the idea of the 'death of a nation' could not be taken seriously in Western Europe. In East Central Europe, however: 'one need not actually go the length of extirpating or expelling a nation, here for the perception of danger it is sufficient to hear strong and violently expressed doubts that a given nation exists at all'.[106] Despite Yugoslavia this fear is less prevalent than it was. It will abate to the extent that peoples are protected by international guarantees of the rights of minorities or by the security provided by their own state.

There is a further factor which is important here. Mitteleuropa was defined at the outset of this Introduction in part by its distinctive socioeconomic plight. For East Central Europe, including the new Länder of the Federal Republic of Germany, the pain of transition to a new socio-econmic system is severe. But the intervening years, not least those of Communist rule, have transformed the region. Its states were industrialized, however badly, however inadequately in comparison with international standards of productivity. That in turn means that it no longer makes sense to argue in terms of the states of this region requiring a distinctive political structure by virtue of their social structure. Arguments are still advanced that political culture, the lack of a democratic tradition, may lead to more authoritarian forms of rule. But the justification is usually that these countries have need of a transitional period, of authoritarian stability. The goal is democratic government modelled on Western Europe. In short, the argument is that East Central Europe is burdened by its history, not that it is and should remain fundamentally different from Western Europe.

The most signifcant development, however, concerns the disequilibrium of the region. Again, continuity and radical discontinuity are both evident. The weakness of the small states of East Central Europe is as strong as before. Germany, especially a united Germany, as well as, prospectively at least, a revived Russia still loom over the region like superhuman colossi. But there the similarity ends. Germany's position is different in the first place by virtue of the expulsion of the Germans at the end of the Second World War. Aside from the extreme right there can be no more talk of gathering in Germans within a mitteleuropäisch Reich. Even the old goal of *Anschluss*, the union of Germany-Austria and the German state to the north has disappeared from the agenda. Furthermore, Germany, as her leaders tirelessly reiterate, is now firmly wedded to a European Community. It is the Community that is the goal of the states of East Central Europe. Regional cooperation, in the form of the Central European Initiative or the Vísegrád group, is a stepping-stone to the Community and the other European organizations, a means of coordinating policy to be sanctioned and guaranteed by those European organizations, or it is a form of pragmatic cooperation which explicitly eschews any 'political integration or any type of bloc'.

What then is left of Mitteleuropa? As a complex of problems, of vulnerability associated with ethnic entwinement, political and economic disequilibrium, and socio-economic weakness, Mitteleuropa remains a reality. Yet Mitteleuropa cannot survive on its own. Paradoxically, cohesion within the region will be dependent upon the extent to which cooperation between the states and peoples of the region is facilitated and regulated within the wider European framework.

## NOTES

1 Andrej Krasinski, 'Mitteleuropa', in H.-P. Burmeister, F. Boldt and Gy. Meszaros (eds), *Mitteleuropa, Traum oder Trauma* (Bremen, 1988), p. 38.

2 Alan Palmer, *The Lands Between. A History of East-Central Europe since the Congress of Vienna* (London, 1970), p. 1.

3 Felix Gilbert, 'Mitteleuropa – The Final Stage', *Journal of Central European Affairs*, Vol. 7 (1947), p. 58.

4 N. Davies, *Heart of Europe. A Short History of Poland* (Oxford, 1986), pp. 306–11

5 On the significance of the German presence see Robin Okey, 'Central Europe/Eastern Europe: Behind the Definitions', *Past and Present*, No. 137 (1992), pp. 105–6, 108–9 and Chapter 2 of this volume.

6 Since the term Mitteleuropa is used here to include the lands of the Germans and hence the Rhineland which undisputably belongs to the economically advanced West, I shall use East Central Europe to refer to the area East of the Elbe. I shall also include under East Central Europe the entirety of the Habsburg Empire, including Bohemia. This has the disadvantage of incorporating the most economically advanced part of the Empire, an area which in terms of these rough economic comparisons is evidently Western. Despite this innacuracy it is better to keep the number of geographic categories small, and to acknowledge the exceptions within them, than to seek to map all of the distinctions. To follow the latter approach would confuse as much as it would clarify.

7 Jeno Szucs, 'The Three Historical Regions of Europe', *Acta Historica Academiae Scientiarum Hungaricae*, Vol. 29 (1983), p. 160.

8   Aleksander Gella, *Development of Class Structure in Eastern Europe* (Albany, 1989), p. 86. For the economic impact of this development see Peter Hanak, 'Central Europe:A Historical Region in Modern Times', in George Schöpflin and Nancy Woods (eds), *In Search of Central Europe* (Cambridge, 1989), pp. 58–9.

9   Ibid., pp. 65–6.

10  Gregory M. Luebbert, *Liberalism, Fascism or Social Democracy. Social Classes and the Political origins of Regimes in Interwar Europe* (Oxford, 1991), p. 259. Care should be taken not to counterpose this pattern too rigidly to a homogenous West. Agricultural employment in Spain, for example, stood at 56 per cent and in Italy at 56.2 per cent, both higher than Hungary. Czechoslovakia had only 40.3 per cent in agriculture, though the Eastern, Slovak part of the country was similar to the general East Central European pattern. Ibid., p. 287.

11  The phrase 'The Politics of Population Pressure' is a chapter heading in Z. A. B. Zeman *The Making and Breaking of Communist Europe* (Oxford, 1991). Both that chapter and the succeeding one give illuminating examples of the mentalities and conflicts engendered by population growth in the region. For the weakness of land reform, apart from in the Baltic states, see Werner Conze, 'Die Strukturkrise des Östlichen Mitteleuropas vor und nach 1919', *Vierteljahrehefte für Zeitgeschichte*, Vol. 1 (1953), pp. 319–37. For the strategy of imposed industrialization see Witwold Morawski, 'Society and Strategy of Imposed Industrialization: The Polish Case', *The Polish Sociological Bulletin*, No. 4 (1980), pp. 69–81.

12  On early usages see Heinz Gollwitzer, *Europabild und Europagedanke* (Munich, 1964), pp. 241 and 263, Helmut Rumpf, Mitteleuropa. Zur Geschichte und Deutung eines politischen Begriffs', *Historische Zeitschrift*, Vol. 165 (1942), pp. 513–14. According to the American historian Henry Cord Meyer, however, the term was not common until after 1914: H. C. Meyer, *Mitteleuropa in German Thought and Action* (The Hague, 1955), pp. 112–13. Though it did enjoy its heyday after 1914 Meyer exaggerates his point.

13  Quoted by Robert A. Kann, *The Multinational Empire. Nationalism and National Reform in the Habsburg Monarchy 1848–1918*, Vol. 2, *Empire Reform* (New York, 1964), pp. 18–19. Krasinski's idea is clearly influenced by memories of the Jagiellonian Empire, a Polish-Lithuanian federation founded in 1385 which at its height extended from the Baltic to the Black Sea. Opposition to the Germans and subsequently the Russians was crucial to the self-appointed role of the federation and had a lasting influnce upon Polish political culture. On this, see, Davies, *Heart of Europe* and O. Halecki, *A History of Poland* (London, 1955).

14  For Palacký's response see R. W. Seton-Watson, *A History of the Czechs and Slovaks* (London, 1943), pp. 186–7. Robert A. Kann, *The Multinational Empire. Nationalism and National Reform in the Habsburg Monarchy 1848–1918*, Vol. 1, *Empire and Nationalities*, p. 74, warns against assuming that the nationalist idea was clear-cut at this time.

15  Kann, *Multinational Empire*, Vol. 2, p. 139.

16  This does not mean that the issue was of purely intra-German significance. The European-wide implications of the relationship between the Germans is forcefully described by Wolf Gruner, *Die Deutsche Frage* (Munich, 1985).

17  W. O. Henderson, *The Zollverein* (London, 1968) p. 181, points out that List was wrong on this point. German industry prospered without substantive protection.

18  W. O. Henerson, 'Mitteleuropäische Zollvereinspläne', *Zeitschrift für die gesamte Staaatswissenschaft*, Vol. 122 (1961), pp. 133–7.

19  Kann, *Multinational Empire*, Vol. 2, pp. 75–6.

20  On Bruck's proposals and the ensuing negotiations see Henderson, *Zollverein*, pp. 196–213. Meyer, *Mitteleuropa*, pp. 16–19, counts Bruck as a 'Precursor of Mitteleuropa'.

21  Kann, *The Multinational Empire*, Vol. 2, pp. 32–3.

22  Rudolf Wiener, *Der Föderalismus in Donauraum* (Vienna, 1960), pp. 99–100.

23  This is emphasized by Kann, *Multinational Empire*, Vol. 2, p. 143. Yet the Hungarian federalist Oscar Jászi described Fischhof as 'the deepest political thinker of the period, noble and clear-sighted'. See Oscar Jászi, *The Dissolution of the Habsburg Monarchy* (Chicago, 1929), p. 102. See also the favourable judgement of Fischhof in this volume by Steven Beller.

24  Cited in Hans Mommsen, *Die Sozialdemokratie und die Nationalitätenfrage im habsburgischen Vielvölkerstaat* (Vienna, 1963), p. 335.

25  On Renner's ideas see Kann, *Multinational Empire*, Vol. 2, pp. 157–67, and Mommsen, *Die Sozialdemokratie und die Nationalitätenfrage*.

26  Quoted in ibid., p. 322.

27  Kann, *Multinational Empire*, Vol. 2, pp. 244–5

28  Ibid., p. 163.

29  Geoffrey Barraclough, 'Europa, Amerika und Russland im Vorstellung und Denken des 19. Jahrhunderts', *Historische Zeitschrift*, Vol. 203 (1966), pp. 300–2.

30  Gollwitzer, *Europabild und Europagedanke*, pp. 206–7, Kann, *Multinational Empire*, Vol. 2, pp. 78–9.

31  Barraclough, 'Europa, Amerika und Russland', p. 304; Gollwitzer, *Europabild und Europagedanke*, pp. 310–11.

32  On Frantz see the analysis in this volume by Walter Weitzmann.

33  On von Baussern see Meyer, *Mitteleuropa*, p. 59 and Jean Nurdin, *L'idée d'Europe dans la pensée allemande à l'epoque bismarckienne* ((Berne, 1980), pp. 429–30).

34  James J. Sheehan, *The Career of Lujo Brentano* (Chicago, 1966), pp. 108–10.

35  Gustav Schmoller, 'Die Handels und Zollnäherung Mitteleuropas', *Jahrbuch für die Gesetzgebung, Verwaltung und Volkswirtschaft in dem Deutschen Reich*, Vol. 40 (1916), pp. 531–2.

36  Peter Theiner, '"Mitteleuropa"-Pläne im Wilhelminischen Deutschland', in Helmut Berding (ed.), *Wirtschaftliche und politische Integration in Europa im 19. und 20. Jahrhundert* (Göttingen, 1984), pp. 130–4.

37  In general see Kenneth D. Barkin, *The Controversy over German Industrialism 1890–1902* (Chicago, 1970). On Brentano, see Sheehan, *The Career of Lujo Brentano*, pp. 126–33. Caprivi envisaged Germany as an exporter of industrial goods with secure European markets. See Immanuel Geiss, *De Lange Weg in der Katastrophe* (Munich, 1990), pp. 187–9.

38  Meyer, *Mitteleuropa*, p. 67.

39  Peter J. Katzenstein, *Disjointed Partners. Austria and Germany since 1815* (Berkeley, 1976), p. 98.

40  On the importance of this see R. F. von Hase, 'Die deutsch-ameri-kanischen Wirtschaftsbeziehungen, 1890–1914, im Zeichen von Protektionismus und internationaler Integration', *Amerikastudien*, Vol. 33 (1988), pp. 329–7.

41  This did not stop the same propagandists from calling with equal vigour for

the pursuit of Weltpolitik: that is, the development of naval power and the acquisition of overseas colonies. Fritz Fischer, *War of Illusions: German Policies from 1911 to 1914* (London, 1975), p. 33.

42 Hartmut Kaelble, *Industrielle Interessenpolitik in der Wilhelminischen Gesellschaft. Centralverband deutscher Industriller 1895–1914* (Berlin, 1967), p. 156

43 Fischer, *War of Illusions.*, p. 39

44 Fischer, *Germany's Aims in the First World War* (London, 1967), p. 104

45 Gary W. Shanafelt, *The Secret Enemy: Austria-Hungary and the German Alliance 1914–1918* (Boulder, Colorado, 1985), pp. 73–4.

46 Stephen Verosta, 'The German Concept of *Mitteleuropa* 1916–1918 and its Contemporary Critics', in Robert A. Kann, Bela K. Kiraly and S. Fichtner (eds), *The Habsburg Empire in World War 1* (Boulder, 1977), p. 210. On the meeting and its implications, see also Fischer, *Germany's Aims*, pp. 208–14.

47 Verosta, 'The German Concept of *Mitteleuropa* 1916–1918', pp. 210–13.

48 Shanafelt, *The Secret Enemy*, p. 74.

49 Friedrich Naumann, *Central Europe* (London, 1916), pp. 108, 255–60.

50 Quoted in Hugh and Christopher Seton-Watson, *The Making of a New Europe. R.W.Seton-Watson and the Last Years of Austria-Hungary* (London, 1981), p. 179. For divergent assessments of Naumann's book see Meyer, *Mitteleuropa*, pp. 194–217, which is sympathetic, and Verosta, 'The German Concept of *Mitteleuropa* 1916–1918', pp. 204–8.

51 Fischer, *Germany's Aims*, pp. 255–6.

52 Meyer, *Mitteleuropa* , p. 171.

53 Fischer, *Germany's Aims*, p. 510.

54 In January 1918 Wilson was prepared to accept some kind of federal reform of the Habsburg Empire: Shanafelt, *The Secret Enemey*, p. 182. According to S. Marks, 'Allied leaders hoped for a separarte peace with Austria Hungary and were prepared to subordinate national self-determination to that aim.' *The Illusion of Peace* (London, 1976), p. 4.

55 M. K. Dziemanowski, *Joseph Pilsudski. A European Federalist, 1918–1922* (Stanford, 1969), pp. 98–9. For brief surveys of the tradition see also P. S. Wandycz, 'The Polish Precursors of Federalism', *Journal of Central European Affairs* (1953), pp. 346–55, and Oscar Halecki, 'The Problem of Federalism in the History of East Central Europe', *Polish Review* (Summer 1960), pp. 5–19.

56 L. S. Stavrianos, *Balkan Federation. A History of the Movement Toward Balkan Unity in Modern Times* (Hamden, 1964), pp. 245–6. A fuller account is given in the more optimistic R. J. Kerner and H. N. Howard, *The Balkan Conferences and the Balkan Entente 1930–1935* (Westport, 1970).

57 For a list of the relevant treaties, including reciprocal agreements between specific states, see *The Treaty of Versailles and After* (New York, 1968), pp. 116–19.

58 Paul Sweet summarised the problem as follows: 'men were federal with their minds, nationalist with their hearts.' 'Recent German Literature on Mitteleuropa', *Journal of Central European Affairs* Vol. 3 (1943), p. 23

59 Quoted by Hans-Dietrich Schultz,'Deustchlands "natürliche" Grenzen. "Mittellage" und "Mitteleuropa" in der Diskussion der Geographen seit dem Beginn des 19. Jahrhunderts', *Geschichte und Gesellschaft*, Vol. 15 (1989), p. 273.

60 The argument summarised here is a composite. Individual authors varied in where they placed the emphasis. See P. M. R. Stirk, 'Authoritarian and

National Socialist Conceptions of Nation, State and Europe', in P. M. R. Stirk (ed.), *European Unity in Context. The Interwar Period* (London, 1989), pp. 125–48; Sweet,'Recent German Literature on Mitteleuropa', pp. 1–24.

61  John Hiden, 'The Weimar Republic and the Problem of the Auslandsdeutsche', *Journal of Contemporary History*, Vol. 12 (1977), pp. 273–89.

62  Zeman, *The Making and Breaking of Communist Europe*, pp. 110–13.

63  'Hitler im Führer Hauptquartier, 17./18. 9. 1941', in Wolfgang Michalka (ed.), *Das Dritte Reich. Band 2: Weltmachtanspruch und nationaler Zussamenbruch 1939–1945* (Munich, 1985), pp. 185–7.

64  See for example 'Denkshrift von Botschafter Ritter, Auswärtiges Amt, über einen von Deutschland beherrschten Grosswirtschaftsraum, 1.6.40.', *ibid.*, pp. 133–4.

65  'Meeting at Reich Economic Ministry: Reorganization of European Economy. 22 July 1940', W. Lipgens (ed.), *Documents on the History of European Integration*, Vol. 1 (Berlin, 1985), p. 63. On these issues see the contribution by A. McElligott in this volume.

66  Waclaw Dlugoborski, ' Die deutsche Besatzungspolitik und die Veränderung der sozialen Struktur Polens 1939–1945', in Waclaw Dlugoborski (ed.), *Zweiter Weltkrieg und sozialer Wandel* (Göttingen, 1981), p. 351. Poland was more important as a source of labour, supplying 22 per cent of male foreign workers in the Reich in 1943 and 30.7 per cent of female foreign workers. J. Noakes and G. Pridham (eds), *Nazism* (Exeter, 1988), Vol. 3, p. 909.

67  Manfred Ansdorf, 'Ulrich von Hassells Europakonzeption und der Mitteleuropäische Wirtschaftstag', *Jahrbuch des Instituts für deustche Geschichte*, Vol. 7 (1978), pp. 387–419.

68  Matthias Ziegler, 'Um die Gestaltung Europas', *Nationalsozialistische Monatshefte* (April 1939), pp. 291–5. The Rhine-Main-Danube canal linking the North Sea and the Black Sea was finaly completed in 1992, amidst doubts about its economic viability. See *The German Tribune* (14 August 1992) and *Financial Times* (25 September 1992).

69  Most commentators are agreed on the significance of the Jews for the region. See, for example, Jacques Rupnik, 'Central Europe or Mitteleuropa?', in Stephen R. Graubard (ed.), *Eastern Europe ... Central Europe ...Europe* (Boulder, 1991), pp. 243–4, Milan Kundera, Die Tragödie Mitteleuropas', in E. Busek and G. Wilflinger (eds), *Aufbruch nach Mitteleuropa* (Vienna, 1986), pp. 140–1. For a more substantial analysis see the contribution by Steven Beller in this volume.

70  On these events see the appropriately titled chapter, 'The Great Migration of Peoples', in Zeman, *The Making and Breaking of Communist Europe*. A critical survey of Allied policy is given in Alfred M. de Zayas, *Nemesis at Potsdam. The Anglo-Americans and the Expulsion of the Germans* (London, 1977). The literature on this subject is extensive.

71  'Polish-Czechoslovak Agreement, November 11, 1940', in Stavrianos, *Balkan Federation*, p. 307.

72  On these developments see W. Lipgens (ed.), *Documents on the History of European Integration*, Vol. 2 (Berlin, 1986).

73  On this and the limits of Britain's commitment see Chapter 4 of this volume.

74  Lipgens (ed.), *Documents on the History of European Integration*, Vol. 1, p. 628. The title Home Army was adopted in February 1942, Prior to that the organization of armed resistance went by the name of Organization for Armed Struggle.

75  Lipgens (ed.), *Documents on the History of European Integration*, Vol. 2, p. 394.
76  On this see Piotr S. Wandycz, 'Recent Traditions of the Quest for Unity. Attempted Polish–Czechoslovak and Yugoslav–Bulgarian Confederations 1940–1948', in Jerzy Lukasczewski (ed.), *The People's Democracies after Prague* (Bruges, 1970), pp. 69–93.
77  Josef M. van Brabant, 'Zur Rolle Mitteleuropas im Rahmen des Rats für Gegenseitige Wirtschaftshilfe', *Osteuropa Wirtschaft*, Vol. 21 (1976), pp. 1–20.
78  On this issue see R. N. Berki, 'Postwar Misery in Eastern Europe: Glosses on an Hungarian Perspective' and M. Fülöp, 'The Hungarian Draft treaty for the Protection of Minorities', in Peter M. R. Stirk and David Willis (eds), *Shaping Postwar Europe. European Unity and Disunity 1945–1957* (London, 1991), pp. 53–67 and 68–76 and Stephen D. Kertesz, *Between Russia and the West. Hungary and the Illusion of Peacemaking, 1945–1947* (Notre Dame, 1984).
79  For the interpretation in this paragraph see Eckart Conze, 'Vom Herter-Plan zum Genscher-Plan', *Europäische Rundschau*, Vol. 18, No. 4 (1990), pp. 65–77. For the survival of the ideas through the 1960s see Francis S. Wagner (ed.), *Toward a New Central Europe* (Astor Park, Florida, 1970).
80  George Kolankiewicz and Paul G. Lewis, *Poland. Politics, Economics and Society* (London, 1988), p. 26. Only Romania had a lower level of urbanisation in the 1980s. See Statistisches Bundesamt, *Country Reports. Central and Eastern Europe 1991* (Brussels, 1991), p. 39.
81  See Walter Zettl, 'Mitteleuropa-Tarockanische Utopie oder Heimweh nach dem Völkerkerker', *Europäische Rundschau*, Vol. 14, No. 3 (1986), pp. 93–8.
82  Moritz Csaky, 'Österreich und die Mitteleuropaidee', *Europäische Rundschau*, Vol. 14, No. 2 (1986), p. 100. See also Angelo Ara, 'Das Erbe Mittel-europas in Italien', *Europäische Rundschau*, Vol. 15, No. 3 (1987), pp. 127–38.
83  Wendelin Ettmayer, 'Mitteleuropa-belastet die Geschichte?', *Europäische Rundschau*, Vol. 15, No. 1 (1987), pp. 108–10.
84  The idea of a Conference on Security and Cooperation in Europe forms a link between the debates of the 1950s on Mitteleuropa as a demilitarized and neutralized zone and the debates of the 1970s. Both elements – military security and civil rights – were present in the Helsinki Charter. The combination helps to explain the interest shown in Mitteleuropa by sections of the German Green movement.
85  Milan Kundera, 'Die Tragödie Mitteleuropas', p. 134.
86  For a summary see Egon Schwarz, 'Central Europe – What it is and what it is not', in Schöpflin and Wood (eds), *In Search of Central Europe*, pp. 143–56 and also the comments in Rudolf Jaworski, 'Die Aktuelle Mittel-europadiskussion in Historischer Perspektive', *Historische Zeitschrift*, Vol. 247 (1988), pp. 529–50.
87  György Konrad, *Antipolitik. Mitteleuropäische Meditationen* (Frankfurt am Main, 1985), p. 65.
88  For examples of the debate see the second half of Schöpflin and Wood (eds), *In Search of Central Europe*. Tony Judt, 'The Rediscovery of Central Europe', in Graubard (ed.), *Eastern Europe … Central Europe … Europe*, pp. 23–58 provides a scathing assessment of the Western interest in the Mitteleuropa idea.
89  Quoted in Renata Fritsch–Bournazel, *Europe and German Unification* (Oxford, 1992), p. 129.

90  On the inherent implausibity of this option see the remarks of Brigitte Seebacher-Brandt, Ibid., p. 133.

91  For a summary of these developments see Harald Müller, 'German Foreign Policy After Unification', in Paul B. Stares (ed.), *The New Germany and the New Europe* (Washington, DC, 1992), pp. 146–50.

92  As, for example, Kohl promised Czechoslovakia at the signing of the German-Czechoslovak Treaty in February 1992. *Financial Times* (28 February 1992).

93  Reinhard Stuth, 'Germany's New Role in a Changing Europe', *Aussenpolitik*, Vol. 43, No. 1 (1992), p. 29.

94  *Das Parlament* (1 January 1993).

95  At the Anglo-German Königswinter Conference, Volker Rühe, newly appointed as Minister of Defence, declared, 'Until now, Germany has done much more than its allies – indeed too much – for eastern Europe. It is up to the West as a whole to make good its promises to help.' *The Guardian* (2 April 1992).

96  *Das Parlament* (1 January 1993). Eichel was arguing for accepting as a citizen whoever lived permanently within the boudaries of the state. For an alternative view see Kurt Heissig, 'Eurokraten und Völkerbewusstsein. Deutschlands mitteleuropäische Aufgabe', *Criticon*, No. 126 (July/August 1991), pp. 167–9. According to Heissig the Western concept of nationality is alien to Mitteleuropa, and to Germany as a mitteleuropäisch state. The argument is that Western European concepts follow the American model in seeking to fuse and mix cultural traditions in a new synthesis. Mitteleuropa, however, should seek to guarantee each nation and culture its own integrity and space. Not mixture, but co-existence should be the slogan.

97  On the Pentagonal see Erwin Suchparipa, 'Die Pentagonale', *Europäische Rundschau*, Vol. 18, No. 3 (1990), pp. 25–34 and Rudolf Stamm, 'Die Pentagonale als Beitrag zur Annäherung in Europa', *Europäische Rundschau*, Vol. 19, No. 2 (1991), pp. 35–41. Italy had initially seen the group as a possible counterweight to Germany, but seems to have been reassured by the strengthening of the CSCE and attempts to strengthen the European Community.

98  Even here, though, Hungary's aim is to have these rights sanctioned by the CSCE or the Council of Europe. See the interview with Ivan Baba, Deputy State Secretary for Central and Eastern Europe, regional cooperation and national security, in *East European Reporter,* Vol. 5, No. 4 (July/August, 1992), pp. 55–7.

99  'The State of Hungary's Foreign Policy', *Current Policy*, No. 38 (1991), Minstry of Foreign Affairs, Budapest.

100  This judgement is taken from Rudolf L. Tökes, 'From Visegrad to Krakow: Cooperation, Competition and Coexistence in Central Europe', *Problems of Communism* (November-December 1991), pp. 100–14.

101  *East European Reporter*, Vol. 5, No. 1 (1992), p. 44.

102  On this see Karoly Okolicsanyi, 'The Visegrad Triangle's Free Trade Zone', *RFE/RL*, Vol. 2, No. 3 (January 1993), pp. 19–22. Significantly, the Hungarian Ministry of Foreign Affairs described it as 'the first step on their [the three countries] common road to European integration'. *Newsletter*, 616/1992 (22 December 1992).

103  See John Williamson, *The Economic Opening of Eastern Europe* (Washington, 1991), pp. 33–4.

104  It is important to emphasize the cost of this. These population transfers have always been marked by savagery and considerable problems in incorporating those expelled into new areas. See the important article by Hans Lemberg, '"Ethnische Säuberung": Ein Mittel zur Lösung von Nationalitätenproblemen', *Aus Politik und Zeitgeschichte*, No. 46/92 (6 November 1992), pp. 27–38.

105  But they do both face problems of how to deal with high levels of immigration. It is this which lay behind President Walesa's speculation at the March 1992 Vísegrád meeting on the need for military cooperation to counter mass migration! Republic of Hungary, Ministry of Foreign Affairs, *Newsletter*, 1992/94.

106  Quoted by Berki, 'Postwar Misery in Eastern Europe', p. 57. The same point is made by Kundera who turns it into a defining characteristic of being a small nation. 'Die Tragödie Mitteleuropas', p. 141. This same fear underlay the Pan-Germanic concern about the *Auslandsdeutschen* and, in even more extreme form the racist vision of Hitler and the prophets of the Nordic idea. On the latter see Hans-Jürgen Lutzhöft, *Der Nordische Gedanke in Deutschland 1920–1940* (Stuttgart, 1971).

Chapter 1

# Constantin Frantz, Germany and Central Europe
## An Ambiguous Legacy

### Walter R. Weitzmann

'Und es mag am deutschen Wesen
Einmal noch die Welt genesen.'

[And German spirit may one day
Save our world from its decay.]

Emanuel Geibel, 'Deutschlands Beruf'
[Germany's Vocation]
(1861)

A century after his death, Constantin Frantz's name may be found as an occasional footnote in a text but his work is rarely read and only a few of his sixty-odd books are easily obtained. None have been translated. A cantankerous loner in his own lifetime, unyielding in his views, he was forgotten even before he died and his work had little impact on his own or later generations. Originating in German romanticism and idealism, his ideas seemed antiquated even as he wrote and his concrete proposals were surpassed by events. Like the proverbial prophet without honour in his time or country, Frantz wrote for the future. At a time when the German problem seemed to have been solved, he insisted that the Second Reich created by Bismarck was a mere 'provisorium' that could not last. The German problem was the problem of Europe and its peoples, and could not be solved through the construction of a 'closed national state.' In its stead, Frantz proposed a federal union of German states linked through permanent alliances and confederacies to the states surrounding Germany on its eastern and western borders. He was the most insistent proponent of a German-led Central European Federation, which he hoped would eventually lead to a European-wide confederation of states.

He has been hailed, therefore, by some, as a prophet for our own day. But as we shall see, this enthusiasm must be tempered somewhat. Frantz came to his solution from the rather parochial perspective of pre-industrial Germany and he surrounded it with a great deal of intellectual baggage, much of which partook of what has been called the 'German ideology'.[1] Frantz conceived of Mitteleuropa and Germany as successors of the Holy Roman Empire of the German Nation making them practically synonymous, and he wrapped his grand design in the mantle of a philosophy of Christian revelation. His vision of a Europe free from internecine, national strife, led by the example of a confederation of German and Central European states, points only vaguely in the direction of our own European Community enlarged by the inclusion of the successor states to the Soviet empire.

But his work also demonstrates the ambiguities that have traditionally adhered to proposals for Central European federation. During the First World War, for example, Friedrich Naumann, who had developed a German version of social imperialism, proposed that Germany and Austria extend their wartime alliance into a 'single nation of brothers'.[2] This greater Germany would have included not only the nationalities of the Austrian empire, but would also have reigned over the smaller, independent states of Serbia, Romania and presumably Poland. After the war we find a proliferation of proposals by German industrialists and nationalists aiming at German penetration of Central Europe, to create new markets and political alliances. Whether flag would follow trade, or the reverse, depended on the special interests making the proposal. Within nationalist circles in Weimar Germany, there were also planners of a *Grossraumwirtschaft* – a market covering a large region united by a customs union or preferential tariffs – that would give Germany the continental equivalent of overseas colonies. The idea of a *Grossraum* became especially popular in the 1930s and 1940s, when political theorists like Carl Schmitt propagated the term.[3] The racial fanatics within the NSDAP converted the concept into the notion of 'living space', an ominous term implying the biological replacement of Eastern Central European peoples by German 'colonists.' At the same time, French statesmen, looking to shore up their political and economic influence in the vacuum created by the collapse of empires, supported plans for a Danubian federation that would exclude the German states and serve as a barrier to their influence.[4] Earlier, throughout the nineteenth century, Czech and Polish theorists had proposed Slavic schemes for some sort of Central European Union which would have excluded both Germany and German Austria.[5]

The geographic, political and cultural concept of Mitteleuropa thus varied considerably through time, and was determined in large measure by the origin and the national perspective of its advocates. Constantin Frantz, unhesitatingly, must be ranked among those who saw the region lying between France and Russia as falling naturally within the culture zone of German influence. He fervently believed and argued that it was Germany's vocation to organize the multiplicity of peoples and historic traditions into a transnational federated state that would enhance the power of Germany and German culture and at the same time serve as a model for the successful coexistence of different nationalities under one political umbrella.

Frantz repays re-reading, not so much for the concrete suggestions his works contained, as for the insights they provide into the problematic character of solutions for the organization of Central Europe and for an appreciation of the ambiguous legacy Frantz's unresolved pan-Germanism left to his successors.

Constantin Frantz was born on 12 September 1817 in Börneke, near the former episcopal seat of Halberstadt, which in the late Middle Ages had been in the imperial district of Lower Saxony but had passed to Magdeburg/Prussia in 1657. His mother was of Huguenot descent, his father was a protestant pastor. His background was typical of the non-commercial bourgeoisie, the *Bürgerstand* of preindustrial Prussia, who sent their sons to universities in the hope of pro- curing a job in the Prussian civil service.[6]

Despite his religious background, Frantz, like his father and father-in-law, was a freemason and did not leave his lodge until 1859 or 1860.[7] Perhaps this accounts for his preference for closely knit societies and groups. In 1859 he thought his plan for a Central European federation stretching from North Cape in Norway to Faro in the Portuguese Algarve could be achieved by a band of courageous statesmen who in the spirit of freemasonry would dedicate them- selves to fight against 'the lawlessness overrunning Europe.'[8] In 1860, Frantz suggested to Julius Fröbel that what was needed to reform society was a commu- nity, like 'a masonic lodge', where educated men could work out the necessary plans. Fröbel's friend, Kapp, who admittedly had an anti-Catholic phobia, sus- pected Frantz of 'Jesuit connections'.[9]

Frantz attended the *Gymnasium*, the German preparatory school for higher education, in Halberstadt, then the Universities of Halle and Berlin. His chosen subjects were mathematics and physics but he also attended lectures by Friedrich Schelling on philosophy and by Leopold von Ranke on modern history. To Ranke he owed his understanding of the European state system, and he might well have absorbed Ranke's teaching that all states are equal in the eyes of God.[10] To Schelling he owed his belief in Christian revelation as the key to understand- ing human history, his conception of history, and his insistence that mankind's mission in the realm of secular history was to fulfil God's plan of salvation.[11] During his university years he mingled with a group of radical-liberal young Hegelians, who under the name 'The Free Ones' (*Die Freien*) grouped them- selves around the journal *Athenaeum*. The ideas he discussed must have been those on which the young Marx sharpened his critical pen.[12] Beginning from a similar starting point – German idealism and romanticism – Frantz, however, turned in a very different direction.

His ideological pedigree spans the entire spectrum of German thought in the first half of the nineteenth century. His ideas owed much to political romanticism, although he rejected its adoration of the state and severely criti- cized the conservatives of the historical school for ignoring social issues and attempting to restore dead institutions that could not be revived. In these matters he was closer to Viktor Aimé Huber, an advocate of a corporate system based on estates. Huber wrote in 1827: 'I see more possibilities for true liberty under a so-called absolute monarchy which lacks general representation but [instead] has competent communal governments that limit state rule, than under our present representative bureaucracies.'[13] He would have been in total agreement. Frantz also shared many views with other conservatives such as Heinrich Leo who, like Frantz, stressed the uniqueness of German development, rejecting foreign models and insisting that only what had grown on native soil (*urwüchsig*) and had historical roots was worth preserving and developing.[14]

Frantz was also a child of German idealism. He never shed the fundamental categories he absorbed from this prevailing philosophical current, although he abandoned his earlier Hegelianism to become an ardent admirer and advocate of Schelling's idealism. Born a generation later, he never hid his admiration for the 'war of liberation' waged against Napoleon, and for Freiherr vom Stein and Count Hardenberg, the non-Prussian architects of the Prussian reform movement.[15] Frantz used them as examples to show that the centre of German thought and culture lay in the heartland of Germany, not in Prussia.[16] Although he criticized their tendency to rely on foreign models, they represented to Frantz the direction reform must take: greater independence and autonomy to the regions and the corporate entities; self-government of urban and rural counties, and an army rooted in the people (*volkstümlich*). His interest in social reform was stimulated by reading Lorenz vom Stein's book on French utopian socialism, the writings of the French utopians themselves, and above all the work of Georg Winkelblech (Marlo), leader of the General German Workers' Association, founded in 1848 to represent the interests of German journeymen. Marlo's 1848 work reflected the reaction of artisan journeymen against the threat the new free market system posed to their stable, though declining, existence. Against competitive capitalism, Marlo demanded the regulation of the 'organization of work' – a phrase that Frantz borrowed and integrated into his own social thought.[17] Finally he absorbed the growing tendency towards political realism for which von Rochau coined the term *Realpolitik*.[18]

Financed by Johann Eichenhorn, the reactionary Minister of Religion and Education who employed him in his ministry, Frantz took a study trip in 1847/48 to East Central Europe, traversing much of it on foot, learning Czech and Polish, acquainting himself with the non-German areas of Prussia and Austria at first hand, and preparing himself for a career in the Prussian government. He summarized his findings in a memorandum to the Prussian government in which he proposed a more Polish-friendly policy to the minister, and in a pamphlet which first expounds his conception of federalism as a way to link East Central Europe, through Germany, to Europe. The international legal form this political constellation would take, would be 'federalist'.[19]

As a Prussian civil servant, with ambitions for a career as a foreign-policy adviser, Frantz, in the 1850s, wrote pamphlets defending the Prussian state against liberal reforms and against those who wished to see Prussia 'merge into Germany'. To Frantz, this was a fatal loss of identity in the creation of a German unitary state. In much of his writings he echoed the conservative line, arguing, however, against both the attempts of the conservative camarilla, surrounding

Friedrich Wilhelm IV, to restore feudal and patrimonial rule, and the ministerial bureaucrats whose main concern was to muddle through without the vision to take bold initiatives. Vision and action, however, were what the young Frantz yearned for and which he himself tried to express in his own works. Impatient with the bureaucratic and cautious approach of Manteuffel, the minister who paid his salary, Frantz was naturally attracted by Bismarck's aggressive stance against liberalism and by his activism in foreign policy.[20] In letters and personal interviews, Frantz tried to convince Bismarck to intercede on his behalf for a permanent position in the Foreign Office. There is no evidence that Bismarck did so.[21] In 1852, impressed by Louis Napoleon's *coup d'état,* he wrote a highly favourable analysis of Bonapartism, indicating a preference for caesaristic coups when 'organic society' had been shattered by revolution and paralysed by parliamentary incompetence.[22]

Having run foul of the Prussian censor, and having offended conservatives with tracts that were considered critical of the camarilla around the king, Frantz was exiled into consular service in Spain in 1852.[23] Already irritable and difficult, he returned in 1856, resentful of the multiple and expensive moves that his Iberian consul had put him through, demanding compensation for what he thought he was owed and alienating his employer, Minister President Manteuffel. He turned down the offer of a consular post in Smyrna, refused an academic appointment at Breslau and instead chose to remain in Berlin on a preretirement subsidy, which provided him with the leisure and financial security to raise a family and devote his time to writing. He was undoubtedly waiting for the day when his political fortunes would turn, for he remained convinced throughout his life that the movement of politics would be in his direction, believing that the world was about to see 'the dawning of a new world view that would be composed of German elements'.[24]

The contours of Frantz's mature thought can already be seen in the works of this highly productive period. The books he wrote were more ambitious in their scope and more theoretical in their treatment than his earlier pamphlets. His Prussian phase was ending; he now concentrated on the construction of a theory of the state in *Prologomena to a Physiology of the State.* In *Examination of the European Balance of Power,* Frantz traced the development of the European state system and criticized the impasse to which it had led. *The Military State* depicted Prussia as a militarist, colonial state whose function would be not to lead but to defend German unity, and in *Thirty-three Propositions on the German Confederation,* he proposed a programme to activate the German Confederation and thereby unite Germany on a federalist basis.[25] In *Quid Faciamos Nos,* he pointed the way to a Germanic alliance that would include the Scandinavian states and England and lead to an enlarged Central Europe. This work created something of a sensation. It argued against the Manteuffel policy of an alliance of Germany with France and Russia. According to Frantz, it cost him his career and pension.[26]

From these and later works a vision emerged that would form the centre of

Frantz's ambitious plans for Germany and for Europe in an era of global politics. His view of the state would develop and change as he came to see it as subsidiary to a higher form of political authority he called the *Reich*. This was to be the ultimate political form standing above the varying forms of social organization and political association that would be united under its umbrella. Above all he would develop the notion, so common to his contemporaries, that the salvation of Europe's ailments could only come from a revitalized Germany. Frantz felt that he was living in a period of transition when what historians called modern history was already moving into a post-modern era of 'newest history'. 'The old world,' he wrote, 'wants to give itself a new form, but does not yet know what it is she wants. She only knows that she does not want the old. She presses forward without a definite goal, towards dissolution.'[27]

The old structures were collapsing. In international politics the pentarchy, whatever its value might have been in 1818, was played out. The Crimean War had shown the strains in the alliance that the war against Napoleon and the revolution had inspired. Now the pentarchy had become an obstacle to the free movement of states and the pursuit of new constellations of forces and alliances.[28]

Frantz's search for new international alliances was motivated by his concern to find new freedom of action for the German Confederation and his concern for German unity and German power. The former, he thought, was an absolute prerequisite for the achievement of the latter. German power was to be exerted, however, for higher than national ends. Harnessed to the service of a higher mission derived from Christian revelation, it was destined to lead mankind through history to the final goal of redemption.[29]

The fall of the Roman Empire had been followed by medieval civilization which he saw as the pinnacle of German achievement. The creation of the Holy Roman Empire, to which Frantz always added 'of the German nation', had provided an umbrella under which the different structures of feudal Europe could flourish and develop in unity and diversity. Since its dissolution, however, Europe had lost its providential path. The reception of Roman law and the adoption of natural rights' theories, both of them contrary to German tradition, glorified secular power and became the basis for the nation state. The unity of occidental Europe was shattered in the aftermath of the Reformation. The old Empire was now gone forever, as was the feudal order that had supported it, but the function the Empire had performed to harmonize competing interests and provide the necessary harmony and peace still needed filling. The idea of the medieval *Reich* had to be realized in new and modernized form. Just as it had been the Germanic spirit that had created the old *Reich*, so a return to German traditions would create the new one. The new *Reich* that would rise, as a sort of metastate, above the existing political units could only be the result of German initiatives.

Frantz saw himself not as the restorer of the past but as the prophet of the future. He showed little sympathy for the *ancien régimes* that had replaced the medieval Empire. They had been absolutist, bureaucratic and patrimonial. Their glaring faults had led to revolution. In Germany, they had created a group of territorial states whose petty, selfish concerns kept Germany from playing the key role in the proper organization of occidental Europe. The reaction to the faults of the *ancien régime*, moreover, had spawned erroneous theories of natural rights, of nationalism, of capitalist greed. A new revolution in thought would be needed to heal the break and to resume the organic course of European history.[30] To this Frantz dedicated his voluminous writings.

Frantz described his method as 'ideal-realism'. Critics might describe this as a way of cloaking real political interest in a mantle of idealistic conceptions. And there was certainly much of that in Frantz and other ideologues of a German mission. But on the level on which he perceived it, it meant two things: first, stripping political institutions, like the state, of the mystical aura which romantics had placed around them, and second, through this realistic analysis enable statesmen to move from the plane of ideas to the plane of action.

Following Leo's suggestive essay, Frantz constructed a sociological as well as a naturalistic theory of the state. Its origins shrouded in mystery, the state was a necessary condition for social existence and therefore coeval with family, clan, tribe or society. It could not be created through human will or social contract. Anticipating German phenomenology, Frantz described the state as having many aspects, depending on how one viewed it: it had an organic side, it had a will to express its individuality and power, it had an architecture of related parts, and, not to be neglected, it had a spiritual aspect supplied by its human directors. For the state itself, seen as a product of nature, as well as an instrumental mechanism of power, was amoral and Frantz never tired of denying to the state any direct divine purpose or legitimation.[31]

Frantz's view of the state was based on the world view he had appropriated from Schelling's *Ages of The World*: there was the realm of nature, or necessity; the realm of history, or freedom; and the timeless, otherworldly, realm of divine grace. Secular institutions, like the state, were natural and historical, never divine, for only man, as God's creation, was connected to both the realm of nature and the realm of grace. 'History is the arena of human freedom. It is a realm of its own belonging neither to the realm of nature nor the realm of grace.' Thus only the inhabitants of the state could impart to it a moral purpose and direction.[32]

The main thrust of Frantz's political theory, however, was to deny the theoretical and historical basis for the constitutional, representative state that was emerging. The state was a mechanism of power. Since much of its function was to maintain, defend and extend the state's territory, its military arm was a key part of its legal architecture. Frantz, therefore, made the army into a fourth branch of government, adding defence to the executive, legislative and judicial branches. As might be expected the executive and defence branches were seen as primary, for these two branches, he thought, would represent the collective needs of the individuals embedded in their social structures (*gegliederte Gesellschaft*) much better than any elected representatives. Frantz believed in a social monarchy that would revive the dynastic institutions, supported by popular, local institutions, like a regional militia. Opposed to codified law which would provide a uniform law to all regions of Germany, Frantz belittled the importance of the judicial branch. As for the legislative, its agencies were to be primarily the guardians of the historic rights enshrined in the geographic regions of Germany, and be composed of representation from corporate bodies like chambers of commerce or agriculture and economic and professional interest groups (*Stände*). 'What a fallacy it is,' he wrote, 'to believe that the state should be based on a law. In actuality, it is based always on realities, i.e. on the real elements that are given by land and people and shaped by history.'[33]

Frantz's attention turned increasingly from the state and its government to the society that formed its substructure. He compared society to an ocean, spreading its energies horizontally in all directions and requiring a point of concentration that could focus its collective will. Government was seen as a rock rising vertically from the sea, standing like the proverbial Prussian *roche de bronze* amidst the swirl of individual interests, and providing the needed direction of social energies for the common good. Although recognizing that there was bound to be a continuous conflict between government (state) and society, he thought that it could be resolved by decentralizing their functions. The relationship of government (the state incorporated in the person of the monarch) to society was to be regulated by the principle of subsidiarity.[34]

Each region and corporate body was to be autonomous within its own legitimate sphere of activity and competence. This constituted the basic principle of federalism that Frantz applied to both domestic and intra-national relationships. In effect this meant, however, that state power remained unlimited in policy decisions relating to war and peace, the maintenance of domestic order and all other matters of national concern. Social and economic interests were to be represented regionally and nationally by chambers of interest groups and representatives from occupational associations, reaching from the local level up to a *Ständeparlament* that would 'advise' the government. In the 1880s Bismarck had also suggested a parliament of economic interests to parallel the political parliament created by the constitution. In the years of the Weimar Republic, the demand for a *Ständestaat* of organized occupational interests was to become the alternative to parliamentary democracy favoured by right-wing parties; in Austria under clerical fascism, there was to be a short-lived attempt to implement it.

In Frantz's system political decisions were more a matter of administration than of legislation.[35] Families, communities, counties, provinces and territorial states would continue to develop what custom and experience had created. Representative bodies, made up of interest groups and regional bodies, would only be allowed to address matters that the lower bodies who selected them could not themselves resolve. At best the state bureaucracy would have supervisory tasks over local and estate affairs. The corporate bodies of which society was composed would be autonomous and independent in the administration of their own affairs.

Limited to their own spheres of action, the manifold social structures would not be able to rise above their own interests to the higher plane of national tasks and concerns. The role of the state was to focus the social energies of its people and direct them to national or transnational tasks. It would wage war, provide and regulate coinage, weights and measures, transportation, communication and international trade and set out national goals and priorities.

Frantz's model of the self-sufficient social unit was the family. It was not only the 'prototype of the social order but the prototype of federalism as well. [That is why we] speak of the "marriage union,"' wrote Frantz.[36] Without the need of constitutions or abstract notions of equality, the members of the family each contributed according to their natural talents which their gender differences and level of maturity dictated. Although the male and female principles were natural opposites, in the family they were joined in perfect complementary union. As such the family provided an example of how complementary opposites, through the acceptance of differentiated functions, could rise above these contradictions in a higher synthesis that would replace egotistical conflicts with cooperation and dedication to a common purpose. Frantz adamantly opposed the emancipation of women, seeing in it the application of the same erroneous principle of abstract rights that he so abhorred in political theory and practice. He predicted it would result in a disastrous decline in population and in the eventual destruction of the family.[37]

In his political prescriptions, Frantz sought to find associational forms that would implement in civil society the 'synthetic principle' he had found in the family. Like husbands and wives in the family, government and its subjects were to supplement and complement each other. Since the male principle represented the authority of the state, and the female principle the passive principle of society, political power in the monarchy – his preferred form of government – would naturally remain in the hands of those qualified by birth or vocation.[38]

A major contribution to conservative thought, and vital to his principle of federalism, was Frantz's insistence that the management of 'internal' affairs and the efforts to maintain or extend the state's territory, were part of one continuum. At a time when German theorists made a sharp distinction between domestic and foreign policy, Frantz preached that there was no such dividing line. Foreign policy in its best and ultimate sense was the application of the federalist principle to the society of states. He sharply condemned the reigning political theories that drew a sharp line between the two spheres of action and applied to them different sets of rules. To Frantz, domestic and international law must both respond to the same overriding principles of justice; what were now seen as 'external' affairs should become transnational relations. The political units of the world system of states should be governed by domestic law when dealing in matters in which they were sovereign, but in their relations with other states they were to be regulated by internationally binding agreements. The combination of these two legal forms would characterize the new political system of federalism. A Germany united and organized along federalist lines would be able to construct a wider Central European federation without incurring fears of its smaller neighbour states being deprived of their unique national character.

But before Germany could organize Europe, it had to reform itself. Throughout the 1850s and 1860s Frantz's efforts were directed toward effecting German unity. His many books and pamphlets on how the German Confederation was to be reformed and activated to create a politically unified German Reich were quickly outpaced by events.[39] Frantz based his proposals on his interpretation of German history which saw its development as determined by its origin. In Ottonian times the core of the German kingdom had been its five stem duchies. Austria was then a border march, called the Ostmark, and the lands of Brandenburg-Prussia, outposts in colonial border lands settled by Slavs, into which Germans poured as 'civilizers' and 'colonizers'. Each of the units of this German kingdom had developed its unique character, function and vocation within Germany and Europe. Western and Southern Germany were the areas in which the original stem duchies had created the German medieval Reich. Prussia was the military and militaristic power, destined by its history and social organization to provide the military spearhead of German power and to extend and defend its Eastern borders against Russian invasion.[40] Having acquired its diverse territory less by conquest and more by inheritance and marriage, Austria had historically formed a state of many nations and was to continue in this role. Prussia had denied its historic past and its future destiny by absorbing the Western provinces of the Rhineland in 1815. This had corrupted its character by destroying its homogeneity and introducing a 'contradiction' into Prussian development.

The unification of Germany was to be achieved by developing not eliminating these historic characteristics. Whatever its weaknesses, the German Confederation had at least preserved these differences. It was to be strengthened by placing a greater concentration of power in the *Bund* executive with a triadic composition that was to reflect the federalist nature of the Confederacy's membership. The result would be a larger league of German and Central European states that was to be made up of three more or less sovereign states, joined together through a variety of international treaties and agreements. The small and middle states would federate into a German state which Frantz called 'the narrow union,' in a form that modern terminology might call a *Bundesstaat*. To this federal state would be joined the two separate states of Austria and Prussia. Together this triad would form a 'wider union', or a *Staatenbund*.[41] Together with their non-German possessions, these three political entities would control Central Europe. The Rhenish provinces were to be separated from Prussia and joined to the narrow union. This would not only create a more equitable power balance in the entire Confederacy but also restore Prussia's 'historic character', directed to the East. It should be noted that it would also take from Prussia its industrial areas which were the hotbeds of national-liberal agitation. Austria and Prussia would now presumably lose their European power status and henceforth, linked, but not dissolved into, the wider Confederacy, act through and with Germany. A strong German power would have been created. Prussia would have regained its historic mission of becoming the military spear and shield of western Germany. Austria would bring into the German Confederacy its Slavic and Magyar possessions and serve as the civilizer of South Eastern Europe. 'If America declaims "westward the star of empire", our slogan,' wrote Frantz, 'should be "ex oriente lux."'[42]

The union he envisaged would not be accomplished through parliaments or nationalist movements such as the *Nationalverein* that had been formed in 1858 to push for a *kleindeutsch* Germany united under Prussian leadership. The initiative, Frantz believed, must come from ruling dynasts of Germany, especially those of the small and middle states. They alone could mediate between the rival powers, each trying to establish control. To bring his plan into action, in 1860 Frantz proposed the calling of a Diet of Princes (*Fürstentag*) to draw up the articles of the Confederation.[43] Three years later, on the suggestion of Julius Fröbel, who was then working for the Austrian government, the Austrian Emperor formally called for such a Diet. But boycotted by Prussia and rent by internal divisions, the Frankfurt meeting led to nothing.[44] Germany's dualism was to be resolved not by reform or by agreement but through the trial of arms.

Frantz always believed that the German *Reich* that Bismarck built would not last. In 1893, disillusioned, more isolated than ever, Frantz left Berlin, which he considered to be the centre of Jewish influence and the hated capital of the false *Reich*, and withdrew to the Blasewitz, a suburb of Dresden. Symbolically, he had turned his back on his native Prussia and its Germany and had become a Saxon by choice.[45]

In the 1860s Frantz had considered particularism to be the main obstacle to German unity. After the creation of the Prussian dominated German *Reich* of 1871, the enemy for Frantz was centralization. He stressed that concentration, which he felt was necessary, was the opposite of centralization, which he opposed. To the 'false' German *Reich* of 1871, he opposed the true *Reich* that would link past and present and resolve particularism, national enmities and international conflicts, in the higher form of occidental European unity. The extension of the federalist principle from primary groups to an association of political entities, in the form of the *Reich,* now took centre stage in his writings. In 1867, he wrote to Richard Wagner that in the *Prolegomena* he had not yet grasped the higher notion of the *Reich*.[46] In his foreword to *Naturlehre*, published in 1870, he announced that although his book intended to explore the true nature of the state, it would culminate in showing how the state itself could be transcended by a new synthetic concept of the *Reich* which would combine the sovereignty inherent in states and the functions of an international organization, creating both a horizontal and vertical form of political organization.[47] It would be the form by which first Central Europe and then the rest of occidental Europe could be united.

Russia was to be driven back to the lands she had held before the partition of

Poland in the eighteenth century. Frantz disapproved of the partitions, considering them 'crimes of history', but although both Austria and Prussia had benefited from them, he considered Russia the main culprit. The acquisitions of that period had been Russia's gateway to Europe. As a semi-Asiatic power, she was to be driven out of Europe, having had no part in its history, and directed towards Asia where her true mission lay.

Poland, however, was not to be restored to her *status quo ante*. The arguments Frantz used, spurious though they might sound to modern ears are typical of his thinking, combining religious, historical and realpolitical considerations. The Polish state had lost its spiritual legitimacy by abandoning the historic task of christianizing Eastern Europe to the Teutonic Knights. Modern nationalist attempts to reconstitute a Polish state were mistakenly confounding nationality and statehood. The state 'if it is to have any promise of permanence must be the product of slow organic growth rooted in historic fact'. It could never be based on nationality.[48] Contemporary nationalism represented not organic development but 'revolution'.

A reconstituted land-locked Polish state would inevitably come into conflict with Prussia in its search for an outlet to the sea. Its success would lead to the subjection of the culturally superior German population in the areas of mixed ethnic composition and would constitute a 'turning back of history'.[49] The Polish people, oppressed for centuries by an indolent nobility and exploited by its Jews, needed to mature before it was ready for statehood. The downfall of the former Polish imperium should be seen as 'the historic confirmation of the existence of a moral world order'.[50] It deserved to fall and the injustice of the partitions, Frantz argued, consisted only in that its executors had been self-appointed without the moral right to carry out the will of providence.

The attempts by Prussia to Germanize its Slavic possessions, however, had been a serious error. The Slavs had their own linguistic culture in which they might well take pride. They should be allowed to nurture and develop it. To that end they should be permitted to have their own cultural institutions, including a university. Indeed, Frantz thought, the federalist form of political affiliation which he proposed would allow the full development of national expression.[51]

Instead of the objectionable restoration of a unified and independent Poland, Frantz proposed the revival of Congress Poland and of Lithuania, both under Prussian suzerainty.[52] They would have their own constitution and administration but would be joined in personal union to the Prussian crown. Poland was to be ruled by a Viceroy, the Grandduchy of Lithuania by a governor. Prussian Poland was to be given greater autonomy and become a Grandduchy, as well. Galicia was to remain under Austrian rule. Politically eviscerated, the Polish people were to be given cultural freedom and self-administration, while also benefiting from the political and economic power of their German neighbours and their culturally superior offerings.[53] Together with the former Russian possession and the Slavic parts of Prussia and Austria, German power would be extended into Central Europe. From there, Austria could launch her expansion into South Eastern Europe and fulfil her mission of carrying occidental civilization through the Danubian lands down to the Bosporus.

Admittedly, the ideas of so complex a union that would include three separate political German states, as well as the entities carved out of former Russian and Turkish territories, organized in a structure that was to combine both domestic sovereignty and international law seemed even to Frantz incomprehensible (*unfassbar*) in its complexity. The mind had to leap forward, beyond the state idea to the idea of the *Reich* which alone could accommodate the diversity of forms his visionary concept comprehended.[54]

It was this idea of the *Reich* as the ultimate form that humanity could achieve in the realm of secular history that capped his political sociology, his theory of states, his idea of German unity, his concept of a Central European federation. He derived it from his study of German history and from the growing conviction that the key to all collective life, beginning with the family and extending through civil society and the 'society of nations' lay in the application of the principle of 'federalism'. Federalism to him was 'nothing less than the Germanic principle ... The federative principle expresses both the libertarian instinct of the Germanic peoples and their impulse towards expansion.'[55]

To Frantz, the Christian occident was Germanic in origin and Germanic in spirit and development. Throughout its history, as shown in the old Holy Roman Empire of the German nation, Germany had been inextricably linked to Europe, had never been national but always transnational. This was its historic character and this was its destiny: to lead occidental Europe once again to a new greatness, combining the strength of its diverse peoples into a political union that could resist the encroachments of the rising world states of America and Russia, and hold its own in an era of global power.

The concept of the *Reich* was a well established idea in the mainstream of conservative and historicist thought in Frantz's day. Already imbued with an aura of legend and mystique which it would maintain into the twentieth century, it took on a meaning that carried beyond any translation as 'empire' or 'imperium'.[56] What Frantz did was to join it to his other basic concepts, the vocation of Germany in creating a European constellation of nations, and the federalist form it must take.

Thus the medieval Holy Roman Empire of the German Nation was to be revived albeit in a modern, very different, form. 'What is needed is to create a federalist land area from the Scheldte to the Duna, from the Swiss Alps to the Pontus.'[57] Transcending nation state and territorial divisions, this new *Reich* would stretch from the Dutch lowlands to the Bosporus.

From his 1859 idea of a Germanic alliance that would depend on its Anglo-German axis, Frantz's thought had moved eastward. He had dropped the idea that England had to be a vital part of this political constellation, but still believed that Switzerland, Holland and Belgium would find it to their advantage to affiliate themselves, in one form or another, with the West German 'closer union', for not only would their economic future depend on it, but their historic past as former members of the medieval *Reich* predestined them to this affiliation.[58] Their association would not only stimulate German progress but would benefit these countries as well, for 'in the final analysis, what else are the German Swiss, the Dutch and even the Flemings, than branches of our common tree which in isolation can only expect to wither and to die'.[59]

As a conservative Frantz often expressed the view that his ultimate vision would come about through evolution rather than revolution. But having never developed a theory of change, he was increasingly forced to rely on a cataclysmic event, like war, to bring things into motion. In 1864 he wrote, 'Only a war – a *Bundeskrieg* – will create German unity for us.'[60] In 1859 he declared all too prophetically, 'Only on the walls of Paris can a lasting peace for occidental Europe be constructed.'[61] In 1873, he exclaimed triumphantly, 'The defeat of France is a sure sign of Germany's reawakening.'[62] In 1882, referring to the need to drive Russia out of Central Europe, he stated his view that 'only a war in a grand style can lead to success.'[63] And as late as 1890, when according to his admirers he had reached his most pacifist position, he preached the necessity of a war against Russia.[64] Just as he looked for a *Klammer*, a cement that could hold the diverse interests and states together, and found it in a 'crusade under the banner of Christianity', he also looked for a *Hebel*, a lever that would move inertia-ridden governments to action. If the cement was Christianity in its most active form, the lever was to be war.

Although unpredictable events would offer opportunities for action that could not be foreseen, Frantz realized that to effect his plans, a 'revolution in thought', would have to take place to reverse the current direction of European thought.[65] Rejecting the liberal assumptions of contemporary political theory, Frantz called for a 'metapolitics', a synthetic and 'Christian politics' rising above particular interests that would be able to create the metastate which his *Reich* idea represented.[66]

Frantz's defenders claim that he spoke for Europe, that he was a good European first and a German last.[67] And it is true that his later works show a greater emphasis on the universal, on humanity as a whole. But even then it must be noted that to Frantz 'Germany was humanity'.[68] Although Frantz presumed to speak for Europe, his concept was quite parochial. He saw it through the tunnel vision of his German perspective. The solution to the European problems of power politics, the growing nationalism encouraged by the formation of closed nation states, the 'armed peace' which he feared would eventually erupt in general war, all lay, according to Frantz, in Germany.

For German unity to come about, Austria and Prussia had to stop acting as European powers in their own right and act with and through Germany. This would invariably transform the pentarchical European state system: the smaller states around Germany's borders who now had no voice could, and surely would, chose to associate themselves with a power built along federalist lines. No longer threatened with being swallowed up by a major nation state, they would gladly put themselves under the protection of and affiliate themselves with the German Confederacy. Faced by a Central European league of states backed by German power, Russia would turn eastward, as she had done in the past. Closed nation states like France or Italy which represented the spirit of revolution would either be closed out of this European federation, or, in time, when their internal nationalism and centralism had run its course, join the federated European *Reich*. In the meantime, France and Italy would be directed to seek other avenues of expansion in North Africa and the Levant.

Led by Germany, there would arise in the heart of Europe a power able to stand up to Russia on one side and the United States of America on the other. Just as Frantz had prodded the German *Bund* to become 'activated,' so his proposals were meant to prod the European state system into change and motion. What was needed was to isolate France, Italy and Russia, through the construction of the Central European Federation. In time, a wider European unity could be envisioned.

This united occidental Europe was to include 'those peoples who in medieval times had formed the territory of occidental Christianity [*Abendland*]. It would include not only Western Europe as such but also Germany, Hungary, Poland and the Baltic coastal lands, including Finland.'[69] The reconstituted *Abendland* would have a civilizing mission in the South East Europe. Not only was it the duty of Christian peoples to civilize lesser cultures, but a crusade against the Turks, 'under the banner of the cross', led by Austria might well provide the cement that would unite all of Christian Europe.[70] In any case, as Frantz never ceased to repeat, war against Russia would certainly be necessary to drive her out of East Central Europe. A number of opportunities had already been missed to utilize the lever of war to unite Germany and bring about the desired Central European Union. In 1854, had she acted in concert with Austria, Prussia could have joined the war against Russia and thus saved future wars. In 1859, Prussia and the other German states could have helped Austria in the war against Sardinia and France. There was still time for Prussia to launch three armies against Riga, Warsaw and Vilna to create the Polish duchies that were to be part of the Central European Reich. The defeat of Russia in a major war was the *sine qua non* for all his designs.

Having defeated Russia and driven her back behind the Duna in the north, the Dniestr in the centre, and the Prypiat River in the South, the way would be clear for Europe to regain the territories that had been part of its medieval territory. The primary agent of this reconquest would be a federalist Germany.

Federalism, to Frantz, was German in origin and spirit. As the land of the middle, a federalist Germany would show the way to other European nations. United by the common crusade against Russia and the Turkish heathen, Europe would be held together by the renaissance of the occidental spirit. With the elimination of nationalist rivalries, the armed camps of states would turn their swords into ploughshares – literally so, for Frantz believed in physiocratic fashion that agriculture was the only sure basis of a sound economy – there would arise a Europe strong enough to survive the threat of the world powers on its wings.

Frantz developed his analysis of global politics in a work to which he gave the title *World Politics,* a term he did not create but which he developed more fully than any one had before.[71] In Frantz's analysis there were only two true world powers – the United States and Russia, – for he believed that the possession of a large territorial base was the prerequisite for global power. Therefore, he considered the British Empire to be artificial and impermanent; France, which was striving for a claim to global might, would be denied it if Germany ever found unity. Russia's power, on the other hand, was based on its vast land mass and the military might its huge population could provide.[72] The rise to power of the United States was the result of the vast resources of free land that were available for cultivation. It was an advantage that land-poor Europe did not have. For Frantz, who valued agriculture over manufacturing, this was a major determinant of power.[73]

Frantz was afraid that the rise of these massive world powers would threaten the existence of the Old World. He argued for the federation of Europe not only on the basis of idealist considerations, but also on the basis of the need to compete with the new world powers. Unless Germany united it would be 'ground between the millstones of France and Russia'. And unless Europe joined together, its historic claim to lead mankind would be extinguished. On the not too distant horizon Frantz foresaw a cataclysmic war that would begin in Europe but encompass the entire world.[74]

A Europe sorely challenged by the incursion of a semi-Asiatic Russia and the economic might of a democratic America could survive only by joining together in federative union. There was hope for the future. America's success had been based on the availability of unlimited free land and the individualism it engendered; the closing of its frontiers would eventually rob her of these advantages. Individualism would lead to an asymmetry of rich and poor that would threaten her democratic institutions. Faced with sufficient internal problems she would lose her initial advantage over the Old World. As early as 1850 Frantz predicted that the United States would be torn apart by civil war. Thirty-two years later, in *Weltpolitik,* he reiterated his belief that America's success would be short-lived provided that Europe could rise to the challenge.

A Germany united under the banner of federalism and converted into an international structure called the *Reich,* leading Central Europe and eventually all of Europe to a new world position of eminence; a renewal of the mission of occidental Europe, under German leadership, to christianize and civilize the world; the unity of all mankind united under the banner of Christianity – these were Frantz's final goals and they were to begin with the federalist reformation of Germany and Central Europe.

Frantz was never quite clear what the exact borders of his Central European metastate would be.[75] This was because the he believed only war, not geopolitical planners, ultimately decided final boundaries. At times he spoke of a region from the 'Scheldte to the Bosporus'. But at other times he included the Scandinavian and Iberian countries, delineating an area reaching from the North Cape to Faro, from the Scheldte to the Pontus. If he was vague about the geographic limits of Central Europe, he was even vaguer about the future all-European Union. Both Italy and France were 'seedbeds of nationalism', which for Frantz was 'revolution'[76] and he was inclined to exclude them as unassimilatable to his federalist *Reich*; moreover he always believed that strong centralized states that might challenge German leadership should not be included in any federation. Late in his life, he seemed to hold out hope that France, the 'hereditary enemy' of Germany, once she was humbled and her pride broken by war,[77] might join a federated Europe. As the Bismarckian *Reich* continued, he became more pessimistic that the ultimate goals of his work would be achieved in his lifetime, but he remained confident that history's progress would eventually vindicate his vision.

Although Frantz was a repetitive thinker, his work was neither consistent nor systematic. He vacillated between a pacifist attitude stemming from his growing distaste for militarism and war, which he identified with the power of the centralized state, and his pan-German imperialism, associated with his never-relinquished belief in the German *Sendung*. The inherent and basic contradictions in Frantz's thought no doubt account for different interpretations of his work, especially by those who select from the vast body of his publications those aspects they wish to emphasize. But Frantz was above all what would today be called a holist and his work must be taken as a whole, not as parts to be selected at will. The exploration of these contradictions allow us to see more clearly the ambiguities of his legacy, and the problematic nature of his proposals for a Central European Federation.

Although he preached local autonomy, the decentralization of power and administration, and the granting of language rights to each ethnic minority, he seems to have ignored all this when discussing (or more accurately, refusing to discuss) Austrian conditions. Bismarck had already accused him of this omission in 1852 and maintained that Frantz had fallen under the influence of Fürst von Schwarzenberg whom he had met while on his study trip through Austria.[78] But this refusal to come to grips with Austria's struggle to keep its German minority in the saddle remained with Frantz throughout his life, long after he had abandoned his hope that Austria would be more helpful than Prussia in reforming and activating the German Confederation.

Austria was a centralized and anti-federalist state under Schwarzenberg; the constitution of 1861 provided only vague promises for national identity and self-expression, and legislation to implement them ran into such resistance in the national parliament that governments that advanced such a programme, usually fell. Except for Galicia whose Polish nobility managed to gain a favoured position among the ethnic groups of the Empire by supporting every governmental coalition that ensued, and Hungary, whose Magyar élite got a blank check in the Compromise of 1867 to rule and oppress its subject races, the Slavic and Italian

populations of the Empire remained disadvantaged. Far from being the labora-
tory of ethnic accommodation that Frantz had thought her to be, Austria became the 'prison of nationalities', the stage for national conflicts that would
eventually rend her asunder. As the eleven recognized national minorities
pushed for greater language rights and educational opportunities as avenues to
political and economic power, the German minority of the mixed regions of the
crown lands of Cisleithania resisted all efforts to decentralize ethnic power.

Yet there is not a word in Frantz's works about this struggle which was
already all too evident during the years when he was writing his treatises on
world politics, federalism and Central European politics. His silence on the
matter suggests either acquiescence or accommodation. In any case it bodes ill
for the multi-ethnic international society he wished to create in Central Europe,
for in his conception Austria was given the main task of spearheading the drive
towards the South East and of organizing the South Slav area of the Balkans.

Although Frantz preached against founding states on ethnic principles and
rejected what he called the 'closed nation state', he never deviated from his view
that German culture, German spirit, German history provided a claim of superiority and precedence over less advanced peoples. They were to be given cultural
autonomy but it would be under German tutelage and hegemony. Frantz clearly
believed that they would find it to their advantage to absorb the advanced
science and technology of German culture. Their mores, languages and traditions would be preserved, but Germany would constitute the core; the non-
Germanic members would be the periphery of Frantz's European world system.

The means-ends relationship had always troubled Frantz's conscience. In
1860, during his Kissingen meeting with Julius Fröbel, he had discussed the
moral dilemma it posed, and admitted that he thought the end at times did
justify the means.[79] Despite his moralizing tendency, Frantz generally resolved
the dilemma in favour of ends. And when he complains that a just polity cannot
be built on unjust foundations, the measure of justness is derived from the final
cause, not the other way around. He himself showed little sensitivity when it
came to clearing obstacles or punishing perceived enemies of German interests.
The Poles should not have a state of their own because they had forfeited this
right. Russia's Asiatic nature excluded her from being treated as a European
power. France in declaring war on Prussia in 1870 had forfeited her rights to the
northern border areas which should be annexed by Germany. The peace that
would initiate the federation of nations in the heart of Europe had to be dictated
'on the walls of Paris.'

As a conservative, Frantz believed in evolutionary development. His wish for
a federative *Reich* would not come at once but would be a step-by-step process.
But at other times Frantz searched desperately for the lever that could be applied
to the fulcrum of politics to bring about a change in direction. The two levers
that most suggested themselves were war and revolution, the latter in the form
of a coup, not from below. In 1852, in his pamphlet on Louis Napoleon, Frantz
had already shown his preference for Bonapartist caesarism when directed

against bourgeois politicians in the National Assembly. Prussia's neutrality had prevented a united action on the part of Austria to seize the opportunity to drive Russia back to its prescribed borders at the time of the Crimean War. And although Frantz was fond of rephrasing the Latin *vis pacem, para bellum* to *vis pacem para pacem*,[80] when it came to opportunities to clear Central Europe of competitors to German power, Frantz enthusiastically advocated the use of force. Russia had to be beaten, France humbled, alliances with states of equal or greater strengths were to be avoided. There is a great deal of truth in the statement by Frantz's biographer, Eugen Stamm, that Frantz's thought was a combination of 'pacifism and imperialism'.[81]

A great obstacle to the achievement of his federalist Europe was his basic intolerance of the Alien, the Other, as shown by his Russophobia, the rejection of Muslim culture as Asiatic and barbaric, and his ever-present anti-semitism. His German tunnel vision, his identification of German spirit and German mission with Christianity caused him to exclude all those who stood outside his vision of the *Abendland*. Far from being a mere aberration, as some have claimed,[82] his anti-semitism was consistent with his exclusionary view and it permeated almost every work he wrote. Some of his champions and even some of his critics soften it by noting that it was not 'racial anti-semitism'. But it surely was virulent enough to go far beyond the general distaste for Jews shown by many of his contemporaries. If much is made of Treitschke's complaint that 'Jews were Germany's misfortune', what of Frantz's descriptions of them as 'tapeworms' feeding on Germany's entrails?[83] His Jew-hatred was more than just a hatred of the modernity they represented; it was personal and unrelenting, an *idée fixe* that he inserted into his works at every opportunity. Germans could get along with a pliable people like the Slavs, Frantz thought, but Jews could not be assimilated because their nationality was inextricably connected to their religion. They had Asiatic minds and they would always be parasitic aliens in a Christian Europe.[84] Europe had both an external and an internal 'eastern question'. The former could be solved by joint action against the Turks; the latter involved solving the Jewish question.[85] He did not favour violence, but like many anti-semites contributed to its incitement by predicting widespread pogroms in Germany and all of Europe, if the 'judaisation' of society was not reversed. He proposed undoing emancipation and denying Jews citizenship rights. Instead, a special set of laws was to be created which would deny them access to certain professions, treat them as 'guests' of their host country and, for that privilege, charge them special taxes. It was the revival of the medieval ghetto, with expulsion to be the future goal.[86]

A major motive for Frantz's proposal to make Posnania a Grandduchy was to stop the influx of Polish Jews into Prussia, since they would no longer be citizens of a Prussian province. What first attracted him to Richard Wagner, an admirer of Frantz's '*Reich* Germanism', was the composer's diatribe against 'Jewish music'. Racial anti-semites like Schlemann and compatriots in the circle around Wagner's *Bayreuther Blätter* appreciated him as much for his anti-semitism as for his federalism. When Fröbel invited him to Kissingen to meet some political friends, Frantz agreed 'as long as they are not Jews.'[87] Towards the end of his life, his anti-Jewish language became even more intemperate as he absorbed the sharper tenor of the anti-semitic wave that swept through Germany in the 1880s. He now saw Jews as a sort of fifth column, coming out of Asia and undermining European civilization from within.[88]

The rejection of all that was not within the narrow limits of his conception of occidental Christian Europe and his patronizing attitudes toward non-Germanic peoples seriously tarnish his reputation and sow doubts about the ultimate value of his work. For without the sort of tolerance for ethnic diversity *and* equality that Frantz completely lacked, any idea of a lasting federation of diverse ethnic groups was completely Utopian. What he believed in, somewhat naïvely, was that so long as they were permitted to practise their own mores and customs through regional autonomy, the non-German populations of his *Reich* would accept the German cultural and political leadership which was to be its guiding spirit.

It is a commonplace of intellectual historians that it is dangerous to trace a line of descent from an idea to its eventual realization. One would have to agree with Freiherr von Aretin that no thinker can determine the path his ideas will travel and one cannot make a theorist 'responsible for the ideas his theories breed'.[89] But there is no avoiding the hard fact that if one wanted to give a thumbnail sketch of Frantz one would have to describe him as corporatist (occupational and interest groups as the basis of representation); imperialist (in the sense that it is the German mission to liberate and organize Central Europe); anti-capitalist (in the peculiarly German way that differentiates between 'speculative' and 'productive' capitalism and advocates a return to pre-market mechanisms); antisemitic (in a most radical form even for his day); reactionary and yet modernizing – seeking a 'third way' that would be neither capitalist nor socialist, but 'economically federalist'. Frantz must therefore be seen less as an originator, than a reflector of ideas originating in his lifetime, ideas which he absorbed and wove into his own fabric, but which had a life of their own that went beyond and in many ways in the opposite direction to his final goals.

The difficulty in evaluating Frantz lies in the fact that some of his ideas, expressed as they were in Christian terms in the years of Bismarck's Germany, would take on very different contours and meanings in the decades to follow. For Frantz *Weltpolitik* meant the need for Germany and Europe to recognize that new powers were rising on their wings that would threaten European hegemony unless the occident united to meet the challenge; to Kaiser Wilhelm II, the term meant German overseas expansion and challenging English sea power. Frantz's pre-capitalist corporatism became the hallmark of fascist and early Nazi theory. The idea of a German mission to regenerate Europe, expressed as a call to restore order and legitimacy by Friedrich Gentz in 1819, and taken up by Frantz, was cruelly transformed and distorted by Hitler in his vision of a New European Order. Blood and soil were to be functional substitutes for Frantz'

Christian *Sendung*. The dream of a multi-ethnic federalist union of Central Europe was perverted by the Nazis into a programme to expand Germany's biological living space eastward. Genocide became a plausible solution for making the new Europe 'free of Jews' once the avenues of expulsion had closed. Welded to nationalism and racism, a radical pan-Germanism redefined the nobler concepts of a German mission to regenerate Europe. Hitler's slogan 'Europe for the Europeans' would become a cloak for brutal conquest.[90]

## NOTES

1  First, by Karl Marx, *The German Ideology*, and more recently, by George L. Mosse, *The Crisis of German Ideology* (New York, 1964); Fritz Stern discussed three of the thinkers in this tradition under the title *The Politics of Cultural Despair; A Study in the Rise of the Germanic Ideology* (New York, 1965); Armin Mohler, *Die konservative Revolution in Deutschland 1918– 1932. Grundriß ihrer Weltanschauungen* (Stuttgart, 1950), gives a sympathetic survey of twentieth- century representatives of the 'Germanic Movmement'.

2  Friedrich Naumann, *Central Europe* (New York, 1917), p. 39; Jacques Stern, *'Mitteleuropa' von Leibniz bis Naumann über List und Frantz, Planck und Lagarde* (Stuttgart, 1917). See also Henry Cord Mayer, *Mitteleuropa in German Thought and Action, 1815–1945* (The Hague, 1955).

3  On Carl Schmitt, see the somewhat apologetic biography Joseph W. Bendersky, *Carl Schmitt.Theorist for the Reich* (Princeton, NJ, 1983).

4  Joachim Kühl, *Föderationspläne im Donauraum und in Ostmitteleuropa* (Munich, 1958).

5  J. Kren, 'Palacky's Mitteleuropavorstellungen 1848–1849', in V. Precan (ed.), *Acta Creatonis: Independent Historiography in Czechoslovakia* (Bucharest, 1980), pp. 119–46.

6  Biographical information on Frantz can be found in 'Gustav Adolph Constantin Frantz', *Deutsche Allgemeine Biographie*, Vol. 47 (Leipzig, 1911), pp. 716–20; 'Constantin Frantz', *Neue Deutsche Biographie*, Vol. 5 (Berlin, 1961), pp. 353–7; Ottmar Schuchardt, 'Konstantin Frantz. Ein Gedenkblatt zu seinem 100. Geburtstag', *Thüringisch-Sächsische Zeitschrift für Geschichte und Kunst*, Vol. 7 (1917), pp. 155–74, and Eugen Stamm, *Konstantin Frantz: Schriften und Leben 1817–1856* (Heidelberg, 1907).

7  Eugen Stamm, *Konstantin Frantz, 1857 bis 1866. Ein Wort zur deutschen Frage* (Stuttgart, 1930), pp. 4, 14, 97.

8  Constantin Frantz, *Untersuchungen über das europäische Gleichgewicht* (Berlin, 1859; Osnabrück, 1968), p. 178.

9  Julius Fröbel, *Ein Lebenslauf. Aufzeichnungen, Erinnerungen und Bekenntniße*, Vol. 2 (Stuttgart, 1891), p. 53.

10  In his later works Frantz criticized Ranke for focusing on the 'power cult' of states and ignoring the 'moral and social circumstances of peoples'. Constantin Frantz, *Die Weltpolitik unter besonderer Bezugnahme auf Deutschland*, Vol. 2 (Chemnitz, 1882/83; Osnabrück, 1966), p. 171.

11  He devoted two of his works to the explication of Schelling's thought: *Grundzüge des wahren und wirklichen Idealismus* (Berlin, 1843); and *Schellings positive Philosophie*, 3 Vols. (Cöthen, 1879/80).

12  Eberhard Quadflieg, 'Dokumente zum Werden von Constantin Frantz', *Historisches Jahrbuch der J. Görres Gesellschaft*, Vol. 53 (1933), p. 321; Eugen Stamm, *Ein berühmter Unberühmter* (Konstanz, 1948), pp. 28–9.

13 Cited in Rudolf Elvers, *Victor Aimée Huber. Sein Werden und Wirken*, Vol. 1 (Bremen, 1872/74), p. 296

14 Leo was a professor of history at the University of Halle, which Frantz attended, and in 1833 had published the sociologically oriented *Studien und Skizzen zu einer Naturlehre des Staates* (Halle, 1833). This was republished and edited by Kurt Mautz (Frankfurt am Main, 1948). Frantz undoubtedly was familiar with Leo's work and appropriated much of it. See also Georg v. Below, 'Heinrich Leo' in Hans von Arnim and Georg von Below (eds), *Deutscher Aufstieg* (Berlin, 1925), pp. 69–75.

15 Constantin Frantz, *Die Religion des Nationalliberalismus* (Leipzig, 1872; Aalen, 1970), p. 159.

16 Constantin Frantz, 'Die preußische Intelligenz und ihre Grenzen' (1874) in Constantin Frantz, *Blätter für deutsche Politik und deutsches Recht; Gesammelte Aufsätze aus den Jahren 1873–1875* (Munich, 1880). See also Wilhelm Mommsen, *Stein, Ranke, Bismarck. Ein Beitrag zur politischen und sozialen Bewegung des 19. Jahrhunderts* (Munich, 1954).

17 An abridged version of Lorenz von Stein's 1850 work appeared in 1964 under the title *The History of the Social Movement in France, 1789–1850*, edited and translated by Kaethe Mengelberg (Totowa, NJ, 1964); on Winkelblech, see Karl Marlo, *Untersuchungen über die Organisation der Arbeit oder System der Weltökonomie*, (Tübingen, 1884: 2nd edn); E. Biermann, *Karl Georg Winkelblech (Karl Marlo) Sein Leben und sein Werk* (Leipzig, 1909); Ralph H. Bowen, *German Theories of the Corporative State* (New York, 1947), p. 64, briefly mentions Frantz whom he erroneously describes, however, as a 'catholic political writer.'

18 August Ludwig von Rochau, *Grundsätze der Realpolitik, angewendet auf die staatlichen Zustände Deutschlands*, (Berlin, 1859: 2nd edn) was much more liberal in his views than Frantz and was influential in turning the liberals of 1848 into admirers of Prussian power and a *kleindeutsch* solution. See also Leonard Krieger, *The German Idea of Freedom* (Boston, 1957), pp. 353–6.

19 Constantin Frantz, *Polen, Preußen und Deutschland* (Halberstadt,1849). This was republished with the addition of Frantz's unpublished *Denkschrift des Verfassers zur Polenfrage aus dem Jahr 1848*, edited by H. E. Onnau (Siegburg, 1969).

20 In *Die Quelle alles übels, Betrachtungen über die preußische Verfassungskrise* (Stuttgart, 1863), p. 94, he described Manteuffel in most unflattering terms: 'His maxim was to accept everything, to give in to all, to blunt all proposals, to let matters drift without exerting a will of his own, to see the task of government in the maintenance of order, regardless of what this order looked like or what its inner worth might be.' In 1874 he went even further and accused Manteuffel of having been 'in league with the Jews'. *Der Nationalliberalismus und die Judenherrschaft* (Munich, 1874), p. 7.

21 In letters to Manteuffel and Ludwig von Gerlach (23 October 1852 and 6 November 1852 respectively), he expressed appreciation for Frantz's perspicacity but warned that his ideas were often 'fantastical' and should not be taken too seriously. Otto von Bismarck, *Werke in Auswahl*, Vol. 1 (Stuttgart, 1962), pp. 495–8.

22 Constantin Frantz, *Louis Napoleon* (Potsdam, 1852; Sonderausgabe Darmstadt, 1960).

23 In particular, *Die Staatskrankheit* (Berlin, 1852).

24 Letter to Cotta (5 May 1863), in Udo Sautter and Hans Elmar Onnau (eds), *Constantin Frantz, Briefe* (Wiesbaden, 1974), p. 35.

25  *Vorschule zur Physiologie der Staaten* (Berlin, 1857); *Untersuchungen über das europäische Gleichgewicht*; *Quid faciamus nos?* (Berlin, 1858); *Der Militärstaat* (Berlin, 1859); *Dreiunddreißig Sätze vom Deutschen Bund* (Berlin, 1861).

26  Letter to H. von Wolzogen (3 December 1887) in U. Sautter (ed.), *Briefe*, p. 146.

27  Frantz, *Die Quelle alles übels*, p. 61.

28  Frantz, *Untersuchungen über das europäische Gleichgewicht*, p. 35f. and *passim*.

29  The intellectual history of this concept is well laid out in Karl Löwith, *Weltgeschichte und Heilsgeschehen* (Stuttgart, 1953).

30  Constantin Frantz, *Der Föderalismus* (Mainz, 1879; Aalen, 1962), p. 422.

31  Constantin Frantz, *Der Untergang der alten Parteien und die Parteien der Zukunft* (Berlin, 1878; Frankfurt am Main, 1970), p. 149.

32  *Ibid.*, p. 144.

33  Frantz, *Die Quelle alles übels*, pp. 148–9.

34  Frantz' view here paralleled catholic social theory. The principle of subsidiarity became the focal point of the 1931 papal encyclical *Quadragesimo Anno*.

35  Constantin Frantz, 'Der preußische Landtag von 65', *Deutsche Vierteljahrsschrift*, Vol. 29, No. 1 (1866), pp. 64–5.

36  Frantz, *Der Föderalismus*, p. 110.

37  Frantz devoted the entire Chapter 3 of *Der Föderalismus* to the disastrous effects of women's emancipation. Although he argued against the family as the primeval unit from which the state originated, as catholic theorists implied, he saw the family as a model of the sort of complementary collaboration, of brawn and brain, of heart and mind, of different rights and responsibilities that his preferred 'structured society' would follow. His basic view of the family was first developed in a youthful, utopian pamphlet, *Versuch über die Verfassung der Familie: ein Mittel gegen den Pauperismus* (Berlin, 1844).

38  Frantz, *Die Naturlehre des Staates*, p. 165.

39  The clearest formulation of how he thought the unity of Germany should come about can be found in Frantz, *Dreiunddreißig Sätze vom Deutschen Bund* and *Die Wiederherstellung Deutschlands* (Berlin, 1865; Aalen, 1972).

40  This characterization of Prussia runs through all of Frantz's mature works. It is most fully expressed in his *Der Militärstaat*, where Prussian militarism is still viewed positively;  in 'Theorie der deutschen Frage', *Deutsche Vierteljahrsschrift*, Vol. 29, Nos. 2–3 (1866), pp. 1–62; 179–258, it received more critical treatment.

41  Frantz rejected these terms because they connoted opposites; he sought ways to synthesize the concepts.

42  Frantz, *Die Weltpolitik*, Vol. 1, p. 139.

43  Frantz, *Dreiunddreißig Sätze vom Deutschen Bund*, pp. 38–9, 108–15 and *passim*.

44  Fröbel, *Ein Lebenslauf*, Vol. 2, pp. 259–60.

45  Karl Buchheim, 'Constantin Frantz als Wahlsachse,' *Historisches Jahrbuch* (West Germany), Vol. 94 (1974), pp. 243–6.

46  Frantz, letter to Richard Wagner (8 February 1867), in U. Sautter (ed.), *Briefe*, p. 61.

47  Frantz, *Die Naturlehre des Staates*, pp. xiv–xv.

48  Konstantin Frantz, 'Gefahr aus dem Osten', published posthumously in Ottmar Schuchardt (ed.), *Die Deutsche Politik der Zukunft*, Vol. 1 (Berlin, 1899), p. 150.

49  *Ibid.*, pp. 32, 36.

50  Ibid., p. 38.
51  Ibid., p. 160.
52  Frantz, *Die Weltpolitik*, Vol. 2, pp. 63–4.
53  Ibid., p. 65.
54  Frantz, *Der Föderalismus*, p. 315.
55  Frantz, *Die Weltpolitik*, Vol. 3, pp. 49–50.
56  Frantz letter to R. Wagner (21 January 1860) in U. Sautter (ed.), *Briefe*, p. 60. A recent historical treatment of the Holy Roman Empire describes it as 'based on a constitution which, without precluding the development of a national consciousness, specifically rendered impossible (or at least extremely unlikely) the development of a monolithic state power that could be dangerous to the freedom of its own peoples – as that was conceived at the time – or to the independence and integrity of other countries'. John G. Gagliardo, *Reich and Nation. The Holy Roman Empire as Idea and Reality 1763–1806* (Bloomington, Indiana, 1980), pp. ix–x. Describing the German radical conservative outlook, Armin Mohler writes, 'The idea of the nation state is alien to German political thought … German nationalism conceives of the nation not in its west-european sense, but rather as a psychological state of being. Insofar as concrete state forms are discussed, they are in the form of the Reich or imperium, both of which transcend the character of the mere nation state.' Mohler, *Die konservative Revolution in Deutschland 1918–1932*, p. 23.
57  Frantz, *Die Weltpolitik*, Vol. 2, pp. 69–70.
58  Frantz, *Untersuchungen über das europäische Gleichgewicht*, p. 173.
59  Frantz, *Der Föderalismus*, p. 317.
60  Constantin Frantz, *Der dänische Erbfolgestreit und die Bundespolitik* (Berlin, 1864), p. 61.
61  Frantz, *Untersuchungen über das europäische Gleichgewicht*, p. 399.
62  Constantin Frantz, *Was soll aus Elsaß-Lothringen werden?* (Munich, 1873), p. 3.
63  Frantz, *Die Weltpolitik*, Vol. 2, p. 59.
64  Frantz, 'Gefahr aus dem Osten', p. 150.
65  This phrase can be found in almost every one of his works. For examples, see *Der Untergang der alten Parteien*, p.199; *Deutsche Antwort auf die orientalische Frage* (Leipzig, 1877), p. vi; *Der Föderalismus*, p. 371.
66  Constantin Frantz, *Bankrott der herrschenden Staatsweisheit* (Munich, 1874), pp. 68, 70–1. By metapolitics, Frantz meant a 'Christian' politics standing above party interests, states and nations, and representing the ultimate interests of all humanity.
67  Karl Friedrich Kindler, '"Ein berühmter Unberühmter": Konstantin Frantz', *Politik und Soziologie*, No 5 (1972), p. 21.
68  Constantin Frantz, *Das Neue Deutschland* (Leipzig, 1871), p. 47.
69  Frantz, *Die Weltpolitik*, Vol. 1, p. 124.
70  Franz, *Deutsche Antwort auf die orientalische Frage*, p. 49.
71  Heinz Gollwitzer, *Geschichte des weltpolitischen Denkens*, Vol. 1 (Göttingen, 1972). Fröbel and Frantz are discussed on pp. 472–83.
72  Frantz, *Die Weltpolitik*, Vol. 1, pp. 109; 97–101.
73  Ibid., pp. 57–8.
74  Constantin Frantz, 'Großmacht und Weltmacht', *Zeitschrift für die gesamte Staatswissenschaft*, Vol. 44 (1888), pp. 675, 712–19.
75  In that sense, 'his work remained a torso'. Georg von Rauch, 'Einheit und Grenzen Europas bei C. Frantz und H. Martin', *Europaarchiv*, Vol. 4 (1949), p. 2665.

76  Constantin Frantz, *Unsere Politik* (Berlin, 1850; 3rd edn), p. 63.
77  Frantz, *Deutsche Antwort auf die orientalische Frage*, pp. 377–8.
78  Bismarck to Minister Manteuffel (12 and 13 July 1851), *Ausgewählte Werke*, Vol. 1, pp. 425–6.
79  See Fröbel, *Ein Lebenslauf*, Vol. 2, pp. 76–7.
80  Frantz, *Der Untergang der alten Parteien*, p. 110.
81  Stamm, *Konstantin Frantz, 1857 bis 1866*, p. 109.
82  So Heiko Flottau, who describes Frantz's anti-semitism as an 'inexplicable mental confusion'. [*Verwirrung*], in 'Constantin Frantz. Theorien über Deutschland', *Süddeutsche Zeitung* (Munich), Saturday/Sunday edition: (9/10 September 1967), p. 7. Wilhelm Foerster, the pacifist, called it an 'inexplicable misstep' [*Verirrung*], cf. Max Häne, *Die Staatsidee des Konstantin Frantz* (Gladbach, 1929), p. 272; Ilse Hartmann, *Constantin Frantz. Der Föderalismus als universale Idee* (Berlin, 1948) viewed it a 'serious faux pas' [*Entgleisung*]; P. F. H. Lauxtermann, *Constantin Frantz. Romantik und Werk eines politischen Außenseiters* (Groeningen, 1978), pp. 193f., dismisses it as having played 'a subordinate role' in Frantz's work; this is also the view of Peter G.J. Pulzer, *The Rise of Political Anti-semitism in Germany and Austria* (New York, London, 1964), pp. 77–9.
83  Frantz, *Deutsche Antwort auf die orientalische Frage*, p. 92.
84  Ibid., pp. 93–5; Frantz, *Die Weltpolitik*, Vol. 3, p. 119.
85  Frantz, *Der Föderalismus*, pp. 406–9.
86  Frantz, *Die Weltpolitik*, Vol. 3, pp. 110–18.
87  Fröbel, *Ein Lebenslauf*, Vol. 2, p. 76.
88  Constantin Frantz, 'A. Wahrmund. Der Kulturkampf zwischen Asien und Europa' (review article), *Bayreuther Blätter*, Vol. 2 (1888), pp. 360–8. In the unceasing struggle between Asia and Europe, it was the Jews who acted as Asia's agents. In Wahrmund's book, Frantz saw his anti-semitism 'scientifically' confirmed by the author's racialist ethnology.
89  Geleitwort', U. Sautter (ed), *Briefe*, pp. viii–x.
90  Lothar Gruchmann, *Nationalsozialistische Großraumordnung. Die Konstruktion einer 'Deutschen Monroe Doktrin'* (Stuttgart, 1962), p. 12.

Chapter 2

# Germans and Jews as Central European and 'Mitteleuropäisch' Elites

*Steven Beller*

Until the middle of this century there were two national or ethnic groups which were well enough represented throughout Central Europe to claim the title of being 'mitteleuropäisch' or Central European. Both Germans and Jews were dispersed across the face of the region in a way in which no other ethnic group was: Germans more to the north and west; Jews more to the east, where they were often seen as, and often were, representatives of German culture, or even the German interest. For a long time the two groups were closely allied, providing the source for much of what was best about the 'Central European' spirit, and the modern high culture for which Central Europe is now so highly praised. Yet their fates divided from the late nineteenth century onward and led to tragedy for both groups, from which neither they nor Central Europe, has ever really recovered. The question I wish to address here is how each group performed its function as a Central European or 'mitteleuropäisch' elite, and how, in turn, this influenced their, and our, understanding of what Central Europe was, and is.

The basis of the German position in Central Europe in the nineteenth and early twentieth centuries was the existence of two German empires, which together dominated the political map of the region. In the north, the Prussian kingdom, subsumed from 1871 in the German Empire, occupied much of what is now Poland, both in terms of historically and ethnically German territories which were 'polonized' after 1945 (chiefly Silesia and large parts of Pomerania and East Prussia) and areas, such as Posen and West Prussia, which were heavily Polish in population, though under Prussian and hence German rule. In the south-east corner of the Baltic, Königsberg, now Kaliningrad, provided an ancient centre of German culture. Within the Russian Empire itself, especially in the Baltic provinces and the Kingdom of Poland, Germans played an important role as entrepreneurs, the city of Lodz being perhaps the best example. In the northern tier of Central Europe, however, the German presence was unambivalently focused on Prussian regional dominance.

In the southern tier, by contrast, the political underpinning of the German presence was provided by the nationally hugely ambivalent empire of the Habsburgs. In many respects the Austrian empire could be described as a German empire. Until 1866 it had maintained a central role in German affairs, had indeed been the leading German power among the colourful array of states of various size which had made up first the Holy Roman Empire of the Germans, and subsequently the German Confederation. Even after Austria's eviction by Bismarck, the alliance with Germany from 1878 created the impression of a continuing close connection with German affairs.

Then again, the dynasty was clearly and unabashedly a German dynasty, although this had never prevented it from looking beyond narrow national interests to fulfil its universal and Catholic pretensions. After all, the idea of pursuing national interests had only emerged as a part of political thought long after the Habsburg dynasty had already been ruling various possessions in Europe and beyond for some centuries, including at one time or another the Spanish American empire, The Netherlands and most of the Italian peninsula. Ruling most of Central Europe was, in terms of the dynasty's own history, rather small beer. Nevertheless, Franz Joseph's claim that he was 'ein deutscher Fürst' pointed to the fact that the national group with which the Habsburgs identified most remained a German one, even if that was in effect restricted to the princely families of the ancient Holy Roman Empire.

The Habsburgs, moreover, had been instrumental in making German the administrative language of their dynastic state during the eighteenth century. Maria Theresa and Joseph II had introduced German, in place of what was perceived as outmoded medieval Latin, as the language of administration not with any idea of 'germanization' of the various peoples under their rule, but rather as part of a modernization of the administration made imperative by the new, more cut-throat world ushered in by Prussia's invasion of Silesia in 1740.[1] It was thus for reasons of dynastic power and *raison d'état*, not for national aggrandisement, that what was to become known as the Josephist bureaucracy operated in German.

The adoption of German as the language of administration (except Hungary) and hence the effective language of state produced the greatest of those ambivalences that marked Austrian German identity. In effect it created a large category of individuals, whether bureaucrats, army officers, or indeed any member of the governing élite, whose language and hence cultural heritage was German, but whose prime loyalty was not to the German nation – whatever that meant – but rather to the Habsburg state or, even more narrowly, the dynasty itself, as was the case with the army's oath of loyalty.[2] This sort of national ambivalence derived partly from the supranational nature of the dynasty, as discussed above, which had trickled down to its servants at all levels. The high Austrian nobility, for instance, was shot through with a large international element, dating at least from the time of the Thirty Years' War, when Catholic adventurers from all over Europe had flocked to serve the leading family of the Counter Reformation. It was thus very 'Austrian' for the longest-serving of Franz Joseph's premiers, Count Taaffe, to be descended from a Catholic Irish mercenary.

The German language of bureaucracy and army made the state appear a German one, and the Germans appear to be the *Staatsvolk*. Yet many Habsburg Germans were more Habsburg than German, having a higher loyalty to the state they served, which, as we shall see, often pursued policies that conflicted with perceived German national interests within the Monarchy. The national standing of the Germans in the Monarchy was made even more complicated by there being a large, as it were, genuinely German population, concentrated in the western half of the Habsburg lands, in the area of what is now the Austrian Republic, and also having more recent, but nevertheless long-established areas of settlement on the edges and dotted around the Bohemian crownlands of Bohemia, Moravia and Austrian Silesia. The Bohemian Germans, though loyal to the state and dynasty, were also not 'invented' Germans as many in the Josephist bureaucracy were, but were as German as their co-nationals in the contiguous German Empire.

To add a final level of complexity, the provincial Germans, whether in the 'hereditary lands' of the Alpine region, or the German areas of Bohemia and Moravia, which have been given the somewhat misleading shorthand of the Sudetenland, differed in the 'authenticity' of their Germanness from the population of the imperial capital of Vienna. This, as one commentator put it, was far from being 'dyed-in-the-wool' German, but was rather composed of all the nationalities of the Monarchy, especially the Czechs, who had acquired their German (of sorts) on the streets and in the artisan shops of Vienna and continued to wear their Germanness very lightly, or so it appeared from the provinces.[3] In the Habsburg Monarchy, therefore, the 'real' Germans were often not in the governing élite of this Central European empire, and the German-speakers who ran it, and who lived at its centre in the imperial capital, were often not 'really' German.

It was in this 'German' empire which in so many respects was only ambivalently German that Germans played their most Central European role. Unlike their northern conationals, who were able to rely on the fact of Prussian-German dominance, they had to act as one player among many, even if a central player, in the variegated ethnic, linguistic and above all national palette that was Habsburg Central Europe (see Map 2).

Partly as a result of German being the *de facto* state language, and therefore the effective lingua franca of the region, German could be heard in almost all parts of the empire. Academic and scientific conferences would naturally adopt German as the common denominator, even if a majority of the participants were not themselves native German-speakers.[4] Even the meetings of the Slav Congress of 1848 in Prague were held in German, for this was the only language which educated Czechs, Poles, Croats and the like actually shared, no matter the ideological embarrassment this might cause.[5]

The other reason why German could be heard in most parts of the empire was that there were German-speakers living there. Overall, Germans comprised around a quarter of the population of Austria-Hungary at the turn of the century, and approximately 36 per cent of the population of Cisleithania (the Austrian part of Austria- Hungary).[6] The main concentration was in what is now the Republic of Austria, but one of the most influential, richest and best-educated parts of the Austrian German population lived in the Bohemian crownlands, where German entrepreneurs had been at the forefront of the industrial revolution in Central Europe and provided the economic powerhouse of the Monarchy. This is not perhaps surprising, because historically Germans, as merchants, artisans and generally town-dwellers (burghers) had been imported into the region by various monarchs, German and non-German (Wenceslas of Bohemia being a famous example of the latter), in order to increase, or even in many cases start economic activity. Hence the German mid-nineteenth-century domination of most of the significant urban centres of Habsburg Central Europe. One result of this was that when industrial activity took off in Central Europe, it did so in the German-populated regions of Bohemia and Moravia, centred on 'German' cities such as Budweis, Brünn, Reichenberg and Prague. The subsequent attraction of Czechs to these economically booming areas, and the demographic threat perceived from their migration to the 'German' areas, was to prove one of the main bones of contention in the chronic German-Czech conflict, which did so much to paralyse Habsburg politics in the final decades of the empire.

In the other parts of Cisleithania there were also German populations, which were, though, declining in relative and absolute terms because of economic and political factors. In Galicia (Austrian Southern Poland) the German population suffered relative and then absolute declines by 1910. This was largely because of the switch of allegiance of Galician Jews from 'German' to 'Polish' between the censuses of 1900 and 1910. Other causes were both the emigration of German settlers – descendants of colonists from the reign of Joseph II – to the neighbouring, Prussian provinces of Posen and West Prussia, and the assimilation of many German farmers into the Polish population. The 'polonization' process, as well as the emigration of German merchants, officials and artisans, was also greatly encouraged by the *de facto* granting of autonomy to the Polish aristocratic ruling class of the province by 1870.[7]

In the Bukovina, whose balanced ethnic diversity prevented the domination of any one national interest as in Galicia, the German presence retained its position, and indeed was enhanced by the capital, Czernowitz, becoming the seat of a German university. In the Bukovina the Jewish population, unlike its Galician counterpart, was not forced to switch to a Polish allegiance and so remained 'German'. Jewish and Christian German-speakers, taken together, comprised over 48 per cent of Czernowitz's population in 1910.[8]

It was in Hungary, however, that some of the most interesting and widely scattered forms of German settlement had taken place. Germans remained in the late nineteenth century the third largest national group in Hungary (after the Magyars and Romanians), more populous, at around two million, than either

Slovaks or Croats. Yet here too the Germans came under heavy demographic pressure, declining in relative and absolute terms by 1914, from 12.5 per cent of the population in 1880 to just under 10 per cent in 1910.[9]

One of the major problems in maintaining the integrity of the German population in Hungary was the wide dispersion of Germans over the kingdom. Unlike Croats, Slovaks or Romanians, but similar to Jews, Germans could be found in small communities in all areas of Hungary. Germans were present in 381 of Hungary's 413 districts (comitate). This meant that, though widespread, in few areas did they reach a critical social or political mass which enabled them to resist successfully a Magyar political nation intent on making Hungary a properly Hungarian (Magyar) state.

Part of the reason for this dispersed pattern of settlement, and another reason for the weakness of German interests in Hungary, was the great diversity of reasons why Germans were in Hungary. The Germans in the 'seven towns' (Siebenbürgen) of Transylvania, known as 'Saxons' had emigrated there in the Middle Ages, whereas the German settlements in 'Swabian Turkey' in Southern Hungary were the result of mainly Southern Germans (hence 'Swabian'), being systematically settled in the largely devastated region in the wake of the Habsburg reconquest of the area from the Turks at the end of the seventeenth century.

There was similarly a town-country divide, whereby the German burghers in Hungarian towns had been there for many centuries and were an integral part of Hungarian society. Before the age of nationalism, as in the rest of Central Europe, the Germans constituted the urban element of Hungarian society, and as such constituted part of the Hungarian 'nation'. The German farming settlements, on the other hand, had largely been established during the course of the eighteenth century, and were thus much more communities unto themselves, following classic colonial patterns. To these two main immigration groups could be added the wave of economic entrepreneurs, many of them Jews, seeking economic opportunity in the virtual 'Wild West' left in the wake of the Turks, and technicians and skilled workers who came to set up and staff the factories – largely in Budapest – when the Hungarian economy began to take off in the 1860s and 1870s.[10]

The extent to which the urban population of Central Europe had been and continued to be German, in many cases until the very last years before 1914, should always be kept in mind when discussing the German Central European role. In many of those areas without a German 'national reservoir' the German presence in the urban centres was slipping in the face of demographic, economic and overtly political pressure from the other national groups. The most noteworthy, for Germans notorious, cause for concern in the Bohemian lands was that of the provincial capital of Prague, where a two-thirds German-speaking majority in 1847 had been converted by 1910 into an official German presence of little over 8 per cent, and only just over 6 per cent of the population of Greater Prague. Budweis had been clearly German in 1850, by 1880 there was a precarious German control over a population in national balance, but by 1910 the German element was down to 38 per cent of the population. Brünn, the major industrial centre in Moravia, sometimes called the 'Austrian Manchester' appeared to offer a counter example, where the German proportion of the city's population actually increased from 60 per cent to 66 per cent between 1880 and 1910. Here as well, however, the broader trend was ominous for the German interest, as the Czech presence in the greater urban area had greatly increased, turning a German majority into a slight German minority of 47 per cent by 1910.[11]

In Hungary the process was even more pronounced, due to the greater success of the Magyar leadership in gaining their national political goals. Nevertheless, what is as remarkable as the transformation of Hungarian cities into Magyar-speaking ones is the previous extent of the German urban presence, and its continuance up to 1914. By 1910 only 9 per cent of the Hungarian capital's population claimed to be German. In 1880, however, the corresponding figure had been over 34 per cent, and this itself was a steep decline from the position in 1851, where the combined populations of Ofen (Buda) and Pest were comprised in a slight majority by Germans.[12] Moreover, in the educated élite of Budapest, recent calculations have suggested that something in the order of two-thirds of graduates of Budapest's universities were, in their ethnic origins if not in their language, not Magyar and over half were German or Jewish.[13]

In many of Hungary's other cities, the German presence remained far more conspicuous than in the capital. In the former capital of Pressburg (Pozsony, now Bratislava) Germans had also lost their majority position by 1914, but as late as 1900 50.4 per cent of the city's population had been German. Ödenburg (now Sopron) still had a German majority in 1910. To the south, Temeschburg (now Timisoara) was half German in 1900, as was Esseg, which gained unwelcome notoriety recently as Osijek. In many other towns all over Central Europe, even though the Germans might now comprise a small minority of the population, they could still look back on urban traditions which more often than not had German origins. In this sense, the apparently absurd German claim, that Budweis, even if its population was now in majority Czech, was a German city, 'an old possession of the Germans', had a certain logic to it, and could have served for many of Central Europe's other urban centres.[14]

Another way of looking at the same phenomenon of the urban dominance of Germans in Habsburg Central Europe is provided by the percentages by nationality of the population of the cities in Cisleithania over 25,000 in population. Although this percentage was also lessening at the end of the nineteenth century, it had stood at 62.8 per cent in 1880 and remained at 57.2 per cent in 1910.[15] Germans were the only recognized nationality that was 'overrepresented' in the cities of Cisleithania.

This dominance of the urban scene (caused largely by the 'German' character of Vienna) was paralleled by the disproportionate concentration of the wealth and income of the Habsburg Monarchy in German hands, especially in Cisleithania. During the arguments from 1905 about how to apportion the seats in the new

*Reichsrat*, voted by universal male suffrage, it was calculated that although Germans comprised only 35.8 per cent of the population they contributed 63.4 per cent of the direct state taxes.[16] The Germans were clearly in control of the Austrian economy to an extent quite disproportionate to their demographic numbers. Much of this apparent German dominance of the economy arose from the concentration of ownership in 'German' Vienna, where 67.7 per cent of Austrian share capital resided in 1912. Even so, there does seem to have been a real German economic overweight. Even in Bohemia, where the Czechs had developed a relatively sophisticated economy and society by 1914, Germans still had more savings in the Sparkassen than Czechs, despite being only around 40 per cent of the population; and it was claimed, probably correctly, that Germans paid more tax revenue in the province than the majority Czechs.[17]

In economic terms the Germans were certainly the élite in Austria. Perhaps not to the same extent, the Germans also comprised the largest proportion of the educated élite of the Austrian half of the Monarchy. In 1857, when Jews are counted with Germans, the 'German' presence at the six universities in what was to be Cisleithania stood at just under 50 per cent of the total.[18] In 1910 Germans still comprised just over 40 per cent of all students at institutions of higher learning. The next largest groups, the Czechs and Poles, stood each at just over 20 per cent. The situation was almost identical in secondary schools by 1912/13 with Germans comprising 42 per cent, the Czechs 22 per cent and the Poles 21 per cent of all children at secondary school.[19] This was only a slight over-representation from the population proportion of 36 per cent, but it does underline the dominant position of Germans, especially if it is considered that the premier educational institution of the Monarchy, the University of Vienna, was a bastion of 'German culture'.

Similar questions of prestige and influence should also shape our view of general German cultural hegemony in the region. The role of German as the language of international and academic communication has already been mentioned, but associated with this was the fact that high culture, especially that imported from the West, tended to be mediated through the German language and the German-language press. When it is seen that 68 per cent of all periodicals in Cisleithania in 1873 were in German, and that still in 1913 fully 55 per cent of all periodicals remained so, then it should also be realized that within this figure lies an even greater German dominance, due to the greater prestige and influence of newspapers such as the *Neue Freie Presse*, or *Die Zeit*.[20]

The German national *Besitzstand* (property) in Austria was thus most considerable, far beyond what the population figures might suggest. The question confronting Austria's Germans in the second half of the nineteenth century was what to do with this 'possession' of theirs in the face of their numerical disadvantage; in their response they proved to be far more 'mitteleuropäisch' than Central European. To understand what that means, we need briefly to survey the political development of the German position until the Monarchy's demise in 1918.

In the Vormärz period Germans had been the dominant group in the Monarchy, though not as Germans, but rather as servants of the Habsburgs. Obversely, with Austria being the senior member of the German Confederation, there had been no clear split between Germans in Austria and Germans in other German lands; Austrian Germans had thought of themselves as an integral part of the German nation, and the educated classes on the Austrian side of the black-yellow border posts looked to their fellow Germans for the liberal political thought and action that would free them from the yoke of Habsburg absolutism. In one aspect, therefore, educated Germans who formed the radical vanguard of dissent within the Monarchy saw the Habsburg state as an obstacle to their liberal aspirations for a constitutional and German state, while other sectors of the German populace, especially in the border areas, continued to see the Habsburg dynasty as their primary object of loyalty, and, moreover, the guarantee of the continued German predominance in the region.

These contradictions in the German approach to the Habsburgs were made plain in the revolutions of 1848, where those Germans who viewed their national, German cause as inherently a liberal one, aimed at overthrowing dynastic oppression of the (German) people, could support the Hungarians' bid for independence, whereas large parts of the German populace in Ofen (Budapest) and Pressburg, with prior loyalties to the Habsburg state rather than any liberal idea of Germandom, were among the opponents of Kossuth's revolution. It was only during the course of the 1848 revolution that the supreme awkwardness of the Germans' situation in Central Europe became evident, as the problems of how to combine the German parts of the Habsburg domains in the new, large German state envisaged at Frankfurt while preserving the Habsburg empire as a vehicle of 'civilization' (the spreading of 'German culture') in the non-German parts of Central Europe proved insuperable. The supreme ambivalence of German liberals, wanting both liberal, constitutional political systems, and yet also wanting to retain German hegemony in the region, fatally compromised their position, as it was to do from then to the end of the Monarchy. The way in which they largely applauded Windischgrätz's action against the Czechs in Prague, the first success of the Counter-Revolution, but seen by Germans as a defence of German national interests, is an indication of the problematic nature of their situation.[21]

The full import of this was never realized, as Franz Joseph's imposition of a neo-absolutist regime cut short the play of contradictions between the liberal and national aims of the German liberal revolutionaries. By the time German liberals had regained enough power to influence the course of policy, Austria was no longer in the same position in German affairs as in 1848 when Vienna had still been the unofficial German political capital. During the period of neo-absolutism in the 1850s the Germans were probably at their most powerful and omnipresent as representatives of the Habsburgs, helping the state to enforce its will throughout the realm, including the Hungarian kingdom. At the same time this had been at the expense of the political, and hence liberal, national agenda of the self-appointed leadership of the German (bourgeois) political nation. Moreover, the period of neo-absolutism had ended with military and financial disasters which culminated in the exclusion of Austria from first Italian (1860) and then German affairs (1866).

The Compromise between the Emperor and Hungary in 1867, along with the subsequent, informal deal with the Polish nobility in Galicia (*de facto* autonomy in the province in return for political support for the government in the new Austrian parliament in Vienna), left Austria's Germans generally cut off from their co-nationals in the soon-to-be-formed *Reich* (1871), and the Germans in Hungary and Galicia cut off from the core German populations in the west of the Monarchy, with the sort of deleterious consequences for the strength of the German presence there already mentioned. The granting of a liberal constitution in 1867, an electoral geometry plainly favouring the Germans, and a denial of a position for the Czechs equal to that of the Hungarians or even the Poles, were scant consolation for this disastrous change in the German position in the Monarchy. The creation of Prussian-dominated '*Kleindeutschland*' at the expense of Frankfurt's preferred '*Grossdeutschland*' was a blow not only to Habsburg prestige and influence, but also to German interests in those (Austrian) territories thus excluded.

On the other hand the post-1867 settlement did appear to give the (German) liberals control of what was left of the Monarchy. In the circumstances the best that they could do was maintain the German position and the influence of 'German culture' in that part of Central Europe still under direct control from Vienna. The influential editor of the *Neue Freie Presse*, Max Friedländer, himself a Jewish convert born in Breslau in Prussian Central Europe, formulated this by envisaging Austria historically as the equivalent to Germany, or Latin America to Spain, or North America to England, 'a second Germany'. The formation of this equivalent of a German colonial empire might have been only partially realized, but the position which had been achieved should be protected against the encroachments of both Habsburg and Slav plotting.[22]

In the era of German liberal dominance 1867–1879 it was clear to the German liberal leadership that the need to maintain the German position in the Monarchy extended far beyond any narrow, German national interests, but rather was necessary for protecting the cause of freedom itself. In the Central European context, these representatives of the German Bürgertum (middle classes) saw that class as the main hope for liberal civilization in the region. One among them, August Weeber, went so far as to claim that, if the Liberal Party was 'mostly German' it was not exclusively so, and its opposition to the Slav parties was due simply to the Slavs' siding with the 'forces of reaction'.[23] Indeed, in the German liberal world view, German was synonymous with liberal and progressive. To support the German cause therefore was not merely a national gesture, but also an ideological one. Even when, in 1899, such an identification was extremely hard to justify in reality, the oracle of German liberalism in Austria, the *Neue Freie Presse*, by now edited by two German Jews from the

Bohemian lands, Moritz Benedikt and Eduard Bacher, continued to maintain it in the realm of wishful thinking. As an editorial celebrating Goethe's 150th birthday, put it: 'It is a comfort to think that, despite the difficulty of fighting simultaneously for Germandom and liberty, being liberal and thinking liberal is not a fashion, but rather the realization of the human ideal, and truly German.'[24]

Initially there was some substance to these claims, as the Germans were by far the wealthiest and most educated, and hence most politically 'progressive' of the national groups in the empire, and indeed those from the other nationalities who had received an education or had amassed wealth had often adopted German as their culture, simply because it was the culture and language of education, sophistication and the social 'betters' of Habsburg society. However, the economic and social development of the region led not to greater accretions to the German middle classes, but rather to the formation of middle classes of each of the nationalities, a process often directly inspired by German, Herderian ideology.

By the 1870s, therefore, German claims to be the only true representatives of the liberal cause of the propertied middle-classes appeared ever more questionable in the light of the development of liberal middle class parties for the other national groups, above all the Czechs. What allowed the Germans to continue thinking themselves the protectors of the liberal verities was that the Czech national leadership, in order to overcome German resistance to the assertion of Czech national rights, allied with the 'forces of reaction' and the Habsburg interest, against the cause of progress and freedom, at least as defined by the German liberals.

Franz Joseph had attempted to break the stranglehold of the German liberals' power in Cisleithania first with the Hohenwarth ministry of 1871, but it was only in 1879 that he succeeded in arranging for a ministry, under his close friend Count Taaffe, which successfully loosened the apparently guaranteed grip of German liberals on power in the *Reichsrat*. The German political leadership saw this disaster as a temporary setback to what was the natural party of progressive government, but it proved a permanent defeat. The German liberals were never again to have the sort of dominating role in Austrian affairs that they had from 1867 to 1879, spending almost all the subsequent life of the Monarchy in the political wilderness of opposition.

On the other hand, from a foreign-policy perspective, the German interest in Central Europe was greatly enhanced by the contemporaneous Austro-German alliance of 1878, which, if it prevented undue meddling by Prussian Germany in Austrian affairs, was also to put great limits on how far the Habsburg authorities could compromise the German national Besitzstand in Cisleithania to satisfy the demands of the other nationalities. If relatively minor German interests in Hungary and Galicia could be sacrificed with equanimity, the alliance with Germany was part of the reason why the much larger German interests in the Bohemian lands could not.

We should also note that the regime that ousted the Liberals in 1879 was still dominated by Germans. The central Habsburg administration was still German, as were the regime's clerical and conservative supporters, and the Bohemian high nobility. It was just that, in the complex world of Habsburg politics, these groups put their ideological loyalties to Church and Crown above their supposed loyalty to nation. If the German Liberals could justify their nationalism on the ideological grounds of their defence of the liberal cause, their conservative opponents within the German camp could throw over national interests for similarly ideological reasons. Germans, though 'non-national' Germans, remained in charge.

After 1879, on the other hand, and despite declarations to the contrary, the Liberals became increasingly the representatives not of the constitutional state, but of a national group. What is worse is that within the German camp the crisis of 1879 led to the breaking up of the party into a liberal wing and an openly nationalist one under Georg von Schönerer, who advocated the break-up of the Central European Monarchy in favour of a *Grossdeutschland*, inclusive of the Bohemian lands. In advocating Anschluss one faction among the Germans became a disintegrative force in the Monarchy, when before they had always been viewed, by themselves at least, as an integrative and constitutive one, indeed the constitutive force of the Habsburg empire, as Staatsvolk. The German interest in the Monarchy was thus split into at least three groups. the German nationalists, the German Liberals and the German clericals and conservatives, with only one of the groups, the German Liberals, preserving the idea of a Central European empire under (liberal) German hegemony. The nationalists' adoption of racial anti-semitism produced a further split in the German camp between 'Aryan' and Jew.

By the next great crisis in the Monarchy's history, the Badeni Crisis of 1897, the German situation had become even more complicated by the emergence of more splinter parties in the 'national' camp as well as two ideologically innovative parties, on the left and right, the socialists and Christian Socials, as major players on the state level. By 1897 Germans were thus not only on the defensive when it came to their political and cultural, even economic, position within the Monarchy, but also hopelessly split along ideological grounds, unable to fulfil their chosen role as the hegemonic group in Cisleithanian politics.

The outcome of the Badeni Affair, in which riots outside and inside the Austrian parliament by Germans and Czechs over the language to be spoken by officials in the Bohemian lands brought the Monarchy to the verge of revolution, was in the short-term quite favourable to the German position. The language ordinances were rescinded and the momentary uniting of almost all German parties behind the preservation of the national Besitzstand put a marker down on how far the Habsburg authorities were able to sacrifice German interests to satisfy other nationalities. In the long-term, however, the results were far less sanguine, as the successful defence of German national interests was paid for by the German liberal establishment twofold.

The defence of German interests alone meant the abandonment of the ideological,. liberal agenda, as illustrated by their having to accept the non-functioning of the Austrian parliament, and the governing of the Monarchy from 1897 virtually until its demise by officials in Beamtenministerien, a form of albeit relatively tolerant and liberal, absolutism. In addition the rallying around the German cause at the expense of any national accommodation played into the hands of the more extreme nationalist elements, which came in the early twentieth century to dominate the agenda of the 'German' grouping of the Nationalverband. The extent to which this further compromised the liberalism of the German camp can be measured by the passive acceptance by Liberals in the Nationalverband of the anti-semitism of their fellow 'Germans'.

The retreat of German liberals from the governing party of the Monarchy to just one interest group among many was made even more apparent by the introduction of universal suffrage in 1906, where the German parties were faced with having to accept grudgingly what might otherwise have been viewed as a triumph of progress, and squabbling with the other nationalities and the Habsburg authorities to achieve a proportion of mandates above the purely 'mathematical' of head-counting, which took account of their greater contribution to the imperial budget.

It might be noted here that neither of the great beneficiaries of this democratization, the Christian Socials and the Socialists, though both laying claim to supranationality, could solve the nationality issue, because both were ultimately too 'German'. Neither was able to gain or maintain a multinational following which would justify their description as truly Austrian parties. The Christian Socials were never to break out of their powerbase in the hereditary lands, and the Socialists, despite their internationalism, split on national lines in 1911. Even 'supranationally' minded Germans came unstuck in Habsburg politics.

Behind the scenes, however, there were at least two factors working in the Germans' favour. The first was the fact that the central officialdom which ran the Monarchy from 1897 onwards remained, even though it was ostensibly nationally neutral, a German-speaking one, in which a Josephist tradition of efficient, centralized administration – which used German as its language of mediation – continued to be strong. Despite all proposed concessions to the Czechs and others on a local level, this centrality of German was never seriously threatened, and meant that the German position in the Cisleithanian state was maintained, because the 'Staatssprache' remained in practice German. The Germans could thus do without a predominance in the gridlock of representative politics because they continued their hold on un-representative politics, in the higher echelons of the bureaucracy and armed forces, and in the board-rooms of the banks, industrial companies and cartels which dominated the Austrian economy.[25]

The second factor working in favour of the Germans was the increasing closeness of the Habsburgs with their German ally in foreign policy, and Germany's burgeoning power and prestige. In many ways this development was very deleterious to Habsburg interests, narrowing options and causing problems in traditional Austrian markets in the Balkans. For Austrian Germans, however, the power and ambition of Germany could also be seen as a final line of defence against Czech or Slav pretensions in the Monarchy, either in political argument or, ultimately, in political practice. The frequently cited comparison in the liberal press between the 'world language' of German, with 50 million speakers, and the Czech language, with merely 5 million speakers, had within it the perspective of a Central Europe dominated by Germans in which the borders between Germany and Austria-Hungary were only the accident of history.[26] This reliance on the power and numbers of Germans outside the Monarchy, if only to make a rhetorical point, marked the weakness of the German position within the Monarchy, and presaged the thoughts of Mitteleuropa, which, whether in its relatively liberal form proposed by Friedrich Naumann, or the illiberal one adopted by the German high command during the First World War, envisaged a Central Europe dominated by Germans (in Germany or without) and not Austrians.

As Austria became more dependent on the Germans, the German interest in Austria could rally ever more behind a Habsburg regime which was once again pursuing German interests often against its will. The clearest example was provided by the aftermath of the annexation of Bosnia-Hercegovina, the Friedjung Affair, in which the German nationalist (and Jewish) liberal, Heinrich Friedjung was brought in to condemn Slav 'treachery' only to see the evidence provided him turn out to be a Foreign Ministry forgery. Ironically the initial policy had been intended to increase Austria's diplomatic independence from Germany, but the end result was that Austria was made even more reliant on German goodwill to preserve the pretence of great-power status. By the eve of war in 1914, leading elements in the Austrian high command were exclaiming German nationalist positions, even though the army under them was one of the few remaining genuinely supranational institutions in the Monarchy.[27]

The same ambivalence marked Austrian policy, and the attitude of Austria's Germans in the war. The initial enthusiasm for the war among the Germans in the Monarchy uncovered in many wishes for a truly hegemonic position in Central Europe, along the lines of Mitteleuropa. Those who leaned to the Austrian perspective deeply resented the arrogance of the *Reich* Germans in their dealings with them, and they resented even more the fact that the *Reich* Germans had to keep bailing out the Austrian forces on first the eastern and then the Italian fronts.

With the death of Franz Joseph and the succession of Karl, this gave rise to ideas of an independent policy of the Austrians, in the form of a separate peace with the Allies. Ultimately this was scotched, however, not by the Germans discovering this policy, but, prior to that, Karl's own foreign minister, Czernin, throwing in his lot with the Germans, on the gamble that they would achieve total victory. This was so, even though by then it was clear that, with a German victory, Austria would become a virtual vassal of the German *Reich*. The German discovery of Austrian 'perfidy' sealed this prospect, but it was one which the Austrian political élite, in the person of Czernin, had already chosen for it. Austria, it seems, would have disappeared as an independent power in Central Europe, whether it had won or lost the war, and partly this was due to the attitude of its German élite, whether national or not, who ultimately preferred a German-dominated Mitteleuropa to a multinational Central Europe.[28] In this the German élite was following a long tradition in Austrian German liberal politics, but – by now – with any pretence at liberalism left out.

The German role in Central Europe to 1918 was thus a decidedly ambivalent one. While under one aspect the Germans were clearly the dominant nationality, in the Habsburg Monarchy they were on the defensive by the late nineteenth century, and many among them were more attached to dynastic than national interests. While their initially liberal leaders purported to offer German leadership to all groups in the region in order to secure a liberal and constitutional polity, this was compromised by the unwillingness of the other groups to go along with the Germans, and the tendency of the latter to identify liberal interests with German ones rather than the other way around. German as a language may have provided the region with its means of communication, but the Germans, whether nationalist, liberals or Habsburg loyalist Austrians, were at least partly to blame that the language they spoke was not the language of mutual understanding and reconciliation, but of arrogant dominance. Never quite able to decide as a group whether it was a nationality among others in a multinational state or the nation of state, with all the responsibilities that entailed, the German élite ended up with the worst of both worlds: a nation of state without a state – for what was the post-1918 Austrian republic but the imperial capital with some provinces and mountains tacked on? The heart of the 'German nation' in Austria, the group which had been at the heart of first German liberalism and then German nationalism, lay, with the deepest irony and with awful historical consequences, outside 'German Austria', in the German areas of the new Czechoslovakia, the 'Sudetenland'. By the time that problem would be settled it would have become a German and not an Austrian problem, and the core of a renewed, radicalized attempt to substitute a form of Mitteleuropa for the – by that point largely failed – vision of a liberal, democratic and pluralistic 'Central Europe' cherished by Masaryk and the Western powers.

The Germans, then, made only questionable 'Central Europeans', tempted as they were by 'mitteleuropäisch' dreams of a German-dominated region. Central European Jewry, on the other hand, has often been seen as the group who came nearest to being truly 'Central European'. Particularly in their function as the cultural mediators of the region, they have been seen by Milan Kundera among others as the cosmopolitan element who cemented all the groups of the region together and thus enabled the specifically Central European cultural identity to be born.[29] As we shall see, there is much in this picture with which I agree. It should be pointed out, however, that the Jews were not a neutral element in the nationality question of Central Europe, but were often the most vocal and high-profiled supporters of the 'historic' German and Magyar nations, to such an extent that commentators such as Oskar Jaszi, himself a Hungarian Jew, accused them of being among the main fomenters of German and Magyar nationalism.[30] This simply shows that the Jewish 'Central European' role is almost as complicated and ambivalent as that of the German one. Ultimately, however, their position in the region, their history, and their social and cultural background made them in general much more Central European' than the 'mitteleuropäisch' Germans, and this was precisely because they clung more firmly to certain (German) liberal traditions than their German counterparts.

In numerical terms Jews were only a small minority in Central Europe, at under 5 per cent in the Habsburg Monarchy and a mere 1 per cent in the German Empire.[31] Yet Jews were to be found in as many, if not more, corners of Central Europe as the Germans. Demographically they were concentrated to the east, in Prussian and Russian Poland, Galicia, the Bukovina and Eastern Hungary. Jews were the most urban group in the region. Centres such as Pressburg, Brünn, Bielitz and Kosice all had sizeable Jewish populations of between 7 and 15 per cent. Some towns in Poland, such as Brody or Buczacz, had Jewish majorities, and even the larger Polish cities, such as Warsaw, Cracow, Lodz and Lvov (Lemberg) had Jewish populations approaching one third the total or over around 1900.[32] In terms of their influence as a Central European elite, however, it was the urban Jewish communities in the major cities to the west, in Vienna, Budapest, Prague and Berlin, which were the most note-    worthy.

In Berlin the Jewish community (144,007 in 1910) was only roughly 4 per cent of the city's total population, but was dramatically over-represented in the city's élite of 'education and property' with a great impact on the city's eco- nomic and cultural life.[33] This was also the case in the Habsburg 'capitals'. In Budapest the Jewish population (203,687 in 1910) already comprised 23.1 per cent of the city's overall population, which, when combined with the traditional emphases of Jews and Magyar gentry, had the result that most of the commercial life of the capital, and a large slice of its cultural and intellectual life, was run by Jews.

The direct demographic presence of Jews in Vienna, the Habsburg capital, lay between that of Berlin and Budapest, at 8.6 per cent in 1910 (with a Jewish population of 175,318).[34] A closer look at the nature of the Jewish presence in Vienna will indicate what the real Jewish influence behind this bare statistic was on Viennese and Central European life at the turn of the century. Jews com- prised roughly 30 per cent of male students at the capital's elite secondary schools, the Gymnasien. Moreover, roughly a third of all self-employed males in commerce in the city were Jewish, as were around a half of all physicians, law- yers and journalists. Jews were also very well-represented in the financial and industrial elite, which ran Austria's economy from Vienna. The combined effect of their great over-representation in the Gymnasien and their prominent posi- tion in the 'capitalist' sector and the liberal professions meant that, according to the evidence from the Gymnasien records, Jews comprised something approaching two-thirds of the 'liberal bourgeois' sector of the educated elite. This might explain why, in the various cultural and intellectual movements and circles of 'Vienna 1900', individuals of Jewish descent were so numerous as to have, in many instances, comprised a sizeable majority.[35]

This is merely one illustration of the phenomenon which could be seen throughout Central Europe: that the impact of Jews on the cultural, social, economic and political life of the region far outweighed their relatively small numbers. Prague, the fourth 'capital' under consideration, provides in many ways an even more dramatic demonstration of this. In 1910 Jews comprised, at just over 29,000, 6.3 per cent of the population of 'Greater Prague', and a somewhat higher percentage of the city itself. In Central European terms, however, what was more significant was that Jews represented nearly a half of all those proclaiming German as their national language. Moreover, if the attendance at German primary and secondary schools is any indication (89 per cent and 83 per cent respectively of all Jewish pupils in Prague schools), the actual number of Jews 'loyal' to German culture if not prepared to identify with Germans politically was actually much higher than the numbers revealed by the census, making Jews approximately two-thirds of those Praguers in the German cultural sphere.[36] It is hardly surprising, therefore, that the Prague of Franz Kafka (himself a German writer from a 'Czech Jewish' family) was largely a Jewish one.

The Prague example also illustrates the fact that, even though their political loyalties might change, Central European Jewry largely remained culturally loyal to the German heritage of the emancipation. The predominant form of modern Central European Jewish identity was culturally a German one. This is clear, and unquestionable, in the Jewish experience in the lands of the German Empire. In the Habsburg territories it is far from being so obvious. By 1910 official census returns in Austria and Hungary placed German third in rank behind Polish and Magyar as the Jews' language of everyday use (in Austria) or mother tongue (in Hungary). Only under a quarter of Austro-Hungarian Jewry still claimed German as their language.[37] It would thus appear that Habsburg Jewry, if it had started out as having acculturated through German, had dramatically diversified nationally, and was well on the way, depending on one's perspective, to being a genuinely Central European because multinational group, or to being yet another Habsburg supranational group split apart along national lines, thus losing its integrative and hence 'Central European' character.

This appearance of Jewish national diversity was largely deceptive. This was so in the case of Jewish adherence to Polish in Galicia,which was more the result of political shenanigans than a true adoption of the Polish tongue by the province's Jews. They continued to speak their own language of Yiddish as they had done for centuries. The problem was that Yiddish was not recognized as a separate language by the Austrian authorities. Forced to choose a linguistic identity apart from Yiddish, Jews had in large measure claimed German as their language until the Polish authorities in power in Galicia started putting political pressure on the Jewish leadership, resulting in the apparent collapse of German among Galician Jewry noted earlier. Among Bukovinan Jewry, which shared many characteristics with their Galician co-religionists, there was no such collapse. They remained firmly in the German linguistic column.

Something similar appears to have happened in the Bohemian lands. In Silesia and Moravia the Jewish identification with German held up to a remarkable extent. In Bohemia, however, Jewish patterns of settlement (often in micro-communities in Czech-speaking areas) and the often violent nature of the Czech-German conflict, as well as the often blatant anti-semitism of German leaders, conspired to produce a steep decline in Jewish allegiance to German identity. By 1910 German-speaking Jews were apparently outnumbered by Czech-speaking Jews in both the province and its capital, Prague.[38] Here again, however, the sudden 'conversion' around 1900 masked a deeper phenomenon, the fact that Jews had a group identity of their own, and if they did not speak Yiddish as their Galician counterparts did, a great many of them were bilingual, often speaking Czech to their customers and German at home. Their political and cultural 'nationality' were thus optional. Politically many preferred to be 'Czech', but culturally, as the school figures mentioned above suggest, many 'Czech' Jews remained German.

The one national group apart from the Germans which did successfully lure many Habsburg Jews from any German loyalty – political or cultural – was the Magyars. The reasons for this partly arose from the sort of considerations discussed above in the Polish and Czech examples: the installation of the Magyars as the new wielders of power after 1867, with resulting pressure on Jews to 'magyarize'. Yet there were others which made becoming part of the Magyar nation particularly attractive, not least of which was the embrace by the Magyar political elite of Jews as important economic partners in the development of the Hungarian state, and the liberal ideology which went with it. Jews had thus in 1848 been supporters of the Hungarian cause of national emancipation even before they became members of the Magyar-speaking nation. Moreover, as in Prague, the bilingualism of many Hungarian Jews, especially in Budapest, meant that they could be both Hungarian patriots, identifying their mother tongue as Magyar, while also being literate, and often more than literate, in German. György Lukács can, in this sense, serve as a suitable Hungarian parallel to the Czech Jew, Franz Kafka. Jewry in both Prague and Budapest, even though they were 'nationally' Czech and Hungarian, remained closely connected to the German literary and cultural world, and this was even more so in the more elite sectors of those communities. The Prague Jewish establishment remained firmly in the German camp, and the Jewish establishment in Budapest, while fiercely loyal to the Magyar cause, as Jaszi notes, retained their cultural and commercial links with the German world. They did so, notably, through either reading 'liberal' Viennese newspapers such as the *Neue Freie Presse*, or subscribing to their own German-language daily, the *Pester Lloyd*. The Praguers had their equivalent in the *Prager Tagblatt*. Both these newspapers were vital media for communicating the latest economic and cultural trends, and both were owned, edited and staffed largely by Jews.

Although only a quarter of Habsburg Jewry was officially German by 1910, therefore, the Jewish elite still retained a largely German cultural identity, and when, in the Hungarian case, it had ceased to be the prime identity, German remained the language and culture which knitted Central European Jewry together. Habsburg Jewry, to the extent that it had been modernized (remembering Galicia), remained a product of its emancipation and modernization through German culture. As such, the course of the Jewish role in Central Europe closely parallels the German one in general, but there were, from the beginning, significant differences, which became ever more significant as the nationality conflict heated up, to the point where Jews became at once one of the main targets of 'mitteleuropäisch' Germans, and – out of necessity – a rare source of real attempts to create a truly Central European solution to the region's problems.

The key to the Jewish role in Central Europe is that the leading sectors of Central European Jewry were the product of a century-long emancipatory process, based squarely on the ideology of the German Enlightenment and German liberalism. It was the *Haskalah* (Jewish Enlightenment) of Moses Mendelssohn and his German Jewish followers which informed the attempts of Central European Jewry at their emancipation from the late eighteenth century until their eventual success in 1867–71. Out of this process arose an emancipatory ideology which equated liberation with self-improvement and emphasized the moral aspect of education and culture (*Bildung*). It also indulged heavily in the individualistic pathos of the idea of *Menschheit* (humanity). As such it came to identify all that was liberal, progressive and beneficial with the German enlightened culture and thought on which it was based, an identification which was made all the more powerful by seeing in that culture the 'essence' of traditional Jewish values such as education, ethics and individual responsibility. This is why the Jewish identification with 'German culture' proved so strong in Central Europe, because it was the liberal version which Jews saw; and this is why Jews proved particularly enthusiastic supporters of German liberalism, in both Germany and Austria, because not only had this political movement emancipated them, it also appeared to project their own values on to the wider 'Gentile' world.[39]

While they had this firm cultural and ideological commitment to the cause of German liberalism, however, the Jewish establishment in Austria also saw that Jewish German identity was different from the normal German identity. An editorial from 1870 in *Die Neuzeit*, the organ of the liberal Jewish establishment in Vienna, usually a staunch advocate of the German-Jewish identity, nevertheless claimed a supranational identity for Jews in the Monarchy. As Jews they had no historical identity with any one national group, let alone a national identity of their own. As a purely religious group they were without nationality, and were thus the only pure Austrians in the Austrian state. On the other hand, their experience had taught them that culturally and ideologically their 'political mission' was to support the German liberal cause. In other words, Jews should be Germans because Germans were liberals. Jewish national loyalty to the German cause thus rested on ideological and cultural criteria, and the German character of the liberal cause in Central Europe.[40]

This emancipation-based identity proved tenacious. Even when it came to be clearly in Jews' own best interests to switch allegiances away from the German liberal cause, they at first refused even a political switch and, as we have seen, largely retained at least a German cultural link. In the 1880s, for instance, the Viennese-Jewish establishment resisted the blandishments of Count Taaffe to abandon the German cause, even though this led to Taaffe not cracking down on the nascent anti-semitic movement in Austria. Even when what was left of the German liberal coalition accommodated itself to its radical anti-semitic wing, ostracizing the 'Jewish' Viennese liberals in the process, Jews in Austria continued to vote for the German candidates. In the Moravian elections in 1896, for instance, Jews voted for an overtly anti-semitic party list, out of loyalty to the German ('liberal') cause.[41] The emancipatory dream of a German liberal future was strong enough to retain Jewish loyalties despite the ugly realities of German liberalism's presence.

Nevertheless, it was clear by the end of the nineteenth century that the old identification between German and Jewish values and interests, in which emancipated Central European Jewry had been forged, was largely defunct. While Jews might continue to support German liberalism, Germans in the Monarchy increasingly supported one or other form of German anti-liberalism, which also meant anti-semitism. By the 1911 *Reichsrat* elections, 68 per cent of the German vote was cast for parties espousing or tolerating anti-semitism.[42]

If the Germans no longer welcomed Jewish allies, except in special circumstances such as in Prague,[43] Jews were also targets of international rivalries from the other, non-German side, which regarded them as supporters of the hated Germans, which, as we have seen, they often were. This perception, allied with the traditional (and not so traditional) forms of anti-semitism which were also widespread among Czechs, Poles and others, led in the 1890s to virtual pogroms in western Galicia, riots in Bohemia, including Prague, and even the notorious Hilsner Affair, in which, at the dawn of the twentieth century, a Jew was accused of ritual murder of a Christian maiden.[44] Jews thus became the targets of both sides of the nationality conflicts, for the other nationalities as Germans, and for the Germans as Jews. While Jews had prided themselves as being pure Austrians and hence supranational, for the other nationalities their having no nationality made them effectively subnational.

It was in the light of these circumstances that some prominent Jewish individuals led the attempts to rethink the politics of the Habsburg monarchy along more Central European lines. Chief among them was Adolf Fischhof, a leader of the 1848 revolution, who by the early 1880s came to realize that the position of the Germans as the Staatsvolk could not be upheld, and that, in any case, a truly liberal solution to the Habsburg monarchy's nationality problems was the

creation of a system where all nationalities would be equal in status and a federalist system of national-cultural autonomy would provide the basis of national
co-operation.[45] His attempts in 1883 to turn this programme into a political
party were frustrated largely by other Jewish individuals, such as the nationalist-
leaning Heinrich Friedjung, who argued that the Jews should not desert their
German-liberal allies, the defenders of progress: and most in the Viennese-
Jewish establishment at the time agreed.[46]

The 'Austrian idea' of a truly supra- and multinational state, which would
mediate between the national interests, allow each nation full freedom of expression and development, and, incidentally provide 'non-national' groups such
as the Jews a logical place in the supranational structure, was not one which most
integrated Jews, with their German cultural loyalties, were prepared to consider
seriously in 1883. Nevertheless, the worsening position of Jews in the national
maelstrom subsequently led to a growing attraction to this 'Austrian idea',
which was energetically promoted in Vienna by the editor of the *Österreichische
Wochenschrift*, Rabbi Joseph Samuel Bloch.[47] Although it never supplanted the
German loyalties of Jews in the more advanced western parts of the Monarchy,
the 'Austrian' version of Jewish integration into Habsburg society did have some
appeal in Galicia and the Bukovina, where the idea of being treated as a nationality was more and more popular among Jews.

Moreover, among Jews still loyal to German culture and hence national
identity, the 'Austrian' nature of the Monarchy's Jews had already been partially
accepted in 1870, as we have seen, and the two approaches, 'German' and 'Austrian', were often found in combination, with Jews being very prominent both
as German authors and also as cultural mediators. Max Brod in Prague, for instance, did his best to introduce Czech authors to the German-reading public,
and vice versa. The translator of the great Polish writer Mickiewicz into German was Siegfried Lipiner, a friend of Mahler and a leading figure in Wagnerian
and German nationalist circles in his youth.[48] Similarly, the largely Jewish-run
German newspapers of Prague and Budapest served the cultural purpose of
transmitting the latest in modern (German) culture to the other national capitals
and hence into the other national cultures.

Adversely affected as they were by the emergence of nationality and even
worse ethnicity and race as the main ordering concepts of late Habsburg politics,
many Jews did their best to act as mediators in the nationality conflicts. Others
tried to find ways around the national abyss which had blocked their dreams of
a genuinely liberal future. Socialism, which aspired to a human solidarity above
nation or ethnicity, was one option which an increasing number of Jews took,
even though it also fell prey to the centrifugal forces of nationalism before 1914.
The retreat into a purely Jewish identity, whether supranational or national, was
also a way of avoiding or overcoming the minefield of Central Europe, by
not choosing any of the others' identities. Hence the emergence of Jewish
nationalism noted above, and of Zionism, the ultimate escape from Central
Europe's perceived dead-end street. The irony here was that, in Theodor

Herzl's version at least, the Zionist state of the Jews would be a largely German-speaking, but multinational and pluralist society – and hence the fulfilment of at least the Jewish version of a German liberal Central Europe.[49]

The most well-known version of the ethnically neutral space for which Jews searched as somewhere they could once again practise their liberal values and still feel fully integrated, recognized and accepted, was the world of 'Vienna 1900', inclusive of 'Prague 1900' and 'Budapest 1900'. This world of Central European modernism was not a national culture, but a cosmopolitan one, a culture not of the national, but the individual soul. As such it was part of the international world of modernism at the turn of the century, but in certain respects it was very Central European, in its scepticism about ideological claims of absolute effectiveness, in its recognition of the fragility of the individual's position in society and in its pleas for tolerance of the Other. In each of these respects the experience of the problems of, and more importantly the threats to, liberalism and the individual in the ethnic and nationalist mêlée of Central Europe gave the creators of the culture insights which were not so available to their western counterparts before 1914. The Central Europe that emerged from this culture was a Central Europe of the mind, of the spirit, and it is this Central Europe for which many in the region today are nostalgic.

Yet this was not the only or even the dominant culture of Central Europe. The culture of 'Central Europe 1900' – of Freud, Kafka, Lukács, and all the rest – was only one side of cultural life. The other was the culture, political and otherwise, of nationalism and of the conservativism of dynasty, bureaucracy and aristocracy. Sometimes the two sides of culture were difficult to tell apart – modern art was used to support national claims and propaganda, or to encourage allegiance to the state and dynasty. Modernists were not necessarily liberal, nor were they necessarily tolerant of others or intent on mutual understanding. Their individualism was often an individualism aimed against liberalism, not for it, and in some cases was easily enfolded in an extreme, blood-related national-ism.

It is perhaps in the light of such considerations that the remarkable extent to which the 'Central Europe of the mind', the liberal, tolerant side of Central European modernism, was either created, encouraged, paid for or 'consumed' by Central Europe's Jews becomes understandable. Out of all proportion to their numbers in the region, Central European Jewry, provided the bulk of the personnel of 'Central European' culture in Vienna, Prague and Budapest. In this sense the Central Europeans of Central Europe were mostly to be found in the intellectual elites of the Jewish communities of the Central European capitals.

This does not mean that Jews had given up their German loyalties. When the war came in 1914 they too caught the wave of national, chauvinistic enthusi-asm, both in Germany and Austria-Hungary. In the Jewish case this was helped by making Russia the main adversary. The opportunity the war provided for Jews to 'belong' once more in the dionysiac sweep of national or at least state solidarity further strengthened Jewish resolve. By the end of the war, however, this reintegration of Jews into Central European and German society had once more suffered severe setbacks, with anti-semitic accusations of Jewish shirking and Jewish undermining of the home front leading to the fatal concept of 'Jewish-Bolshevism' in the interwar period. The spread of illiberalism in the region during the inter-war era destroyed any chance for the full integration of Central European Jewry into the new nation-states, leaving them largely adrift in a sea of intolerant nationalisms, Czechoslovakia providing the one notable exception. By 1939 the liberal version of Central Europe in which Jews had played such a prominent part was already mortally threatened. The Holocaust eradicated it.

What the lessons of the tragedy that befell Jews and Germans in Central Europe are for modern Europeans is difficult to say. Perhaps there is, however, one aspect that does bear thinking about. At the centre of all the problems of the German presence in Central Europe was the problem that the main force for integration and mediation in the area was also one of the elements to be integrated and mediated. The Germans played a role in Central Europe that was essentially an imperial or colonial, certainly a hegemonic one. In Germany-Prussia this made sense because it was backed up by political and military power. In the Habsburg Monarchy, however, the German hegemonic role became problematic when the ambitions of the other nationalities had to be considered. On the one hand the Germans in Austria continued to regard their role as merely being upholders of the constitution and the state, on a non-national level. German politics developed on largely 'normal' lines, with liberal, conservative, socialist, Christian Social and nationalist parties. In Vienna the art created and consumed was not 'German art' but 'art' *tout court*, with universal validity. To a Czech or a Pole, a Slovene or even a Hungarian, however, this very claim to universal validity on the part of the Germans, their claim that German was 'naturally' the mediating language of the region, was a product of German national arrogance and pretension.

The problem was that German culture, the German language could serve both functions equally well and there was no adequate way of controlling which function it served. In the hands of Georg von Schönerer or Adolf Hitler the German presence in Central Europe could point towards an imperialistic Mitteleuropa. In the hands of someone such as Arthur Schnitzler or Franz Kafka it could produce some of the finer products of modern literature, with a clearly universal validity, of which Central Europeans can be proud. Yet how could the imperial version be separated from the pluralist and liberal, universal one? Because the umpire was also the major player, no such separation was ever really possible. All that this really suggests for solving the future problems of Central Europe is that the inevitable German predominance in the economic or even the cultural life of the region must be mediated not by a German-dominated imperial system, but by the sort of balanced, decentralized network once proposed for the Habsburg Monarchy by Adolf Fischhof, in which the umpire is not suspected of bias. The disintegration of Central Europe because of the German problem, seen in the light of one of its most acute Jewish commentators, is one of the strongest arguments there is for an effective and expanded European Community.

NOTES

1  Oskar Jaszi, *The Dissolution of the Habsburg Monarchy* (Chicago, 1929), pp. 64–71.

2  Istvan Deak, *Beyond Nationalism: A Social and Political History of the Habsburg Officer Corps 1848–1918* (Oxford, 1990), p. 4; Jaszi, *Dissolution*, pp. 90, 142.

3  Sigmund Mayer, *Die Wiener Juden: Kommerz, Kultur, Politik, 1700–1900* (Vienna, 1918), p. 320; Michael John and Albert Lichtblau, *Schmelztiegel Wien – Einst und jetzt: Zur Geschichte und Gegenwart von Zuwanderung und Minderheiten* (Vienna, 1990), *passim*, especially pp. 13–22.

4  Jaszi, *Dissolution*, p. 138.

5  Mayer, *Wiener Juden*, p. 392.

6  Peter Urbanitsch, 'Die Deutschen in Österreich. Statistisch-deskriptiver Überblick', in Adam Wandruszka and Peter Urbanitsch (eds), *Die Habsburgiermonarchie 1848–1918*, Vol. 3, *Die Völker des Reiches* (Vienna, 1980), p. 33.

7  Urbanitsch, 'Die Deutschen in Österreich', pp. 40–1. Largely due to the Jewish switch the 'German' population in Galicia dropped from over 200,000 in 1990 to 90,000 in 1910.

8  Urbanitsch, 'Die Deutschen in Österreich', p. 72.

9  Friedrich Gottas, 'Die deutschen in Ungarn', in Wandruszka and Urbanitsch (eds), *Die Habsburgiermonarchie*, Vol. 3, p. 344.

10  Gottas, 'Die Deutschen in Ungarn', pp. 343–52.

11  Urbanitsch, 'Die Deutschen in Osterreich', pp. 52–4.

12  Gottas, 'Die Deutschen in Ungarn', p. 355.

13  Victor Karady, 'Assimilation and Schooling: National and Denominational Minorities in the Universities of Budapest around 1900', in G. Ranki (ed.), *Hungary and European Civilisation* (Bloomington, 1989), pp. 285–319, especially p. 291.

14  See *Neue Freie Presse* (13 November 1906), p. 1.

15  Urbanitsch, 'Die Deutschen in Osterreich', p. 51.

16  Emil Brix, 'Der Gleichheitsgedanke in der österreichischen Sprachenpolitik um 1900', in Peter Berner, Emil Brix and Wolfgang Mantl (eds), *Wien um 1900: Aufbruch in der Moderne* (Vienna, 1896), p. 183. In the final compromise, German districts received slightly over 45 per cent of the seats in the new, democratic Austrian Parliament.

17  Urbanitsch, 'Die Deutschen in Österreich', p. 133; *Neue Freie Presse* (5 March 1904), p. 1 and (17 September 1906: evening edition), p. 1.

18  In 1857 the Habsburg authorities still counted Jews as a separate nationality. Later censuses regarded them only as a separate religious group. The figure for Cisleithania excludes the Italian universities of Pavia and Padua, which, if included would put Italians as the second largest national group among 'Habsburg' students.

19  Urbanitsch, 'Die Deutschen in Österreich', Tables 9 and 11 (p. 97).

20  Ibid., p. 104.

21  See Harm-Hinrich Brandt, 'The Revolution of 1848 and the Problem of Central European Nationalities' in Hagen Schulze (ed.), *Nation-Building in Central Europe* (Leamington Spa, 1987), pp. 116–23.

22  Mayer, *Wiener Juden*, pp. 391–2.

23  Andrew Whiteside, 'The Germans as an Integrative Force in Imperial Austria: The Dilemma of Dominance', *Austrian History Yearbook*, Vol. 3, Part 1 (1967), p. 178.
24  *Neue Freie Presse* (7 August 1899: morning edition), p. 1.
25  See James Shedel, *Art and Society: The New Art Movement in Vienna, 1897–1914* (Palo Alto, 1981), p.61.
26  *Neue Freie Presse* (7 November 1909: morning edition), p. 1.
27  Deak, *Beyond Nationalism*, pp. 73–4.
28  F. R. Bridge, *The Habsburg Monarchy among the Great Powers 1815–1918* (New York, 1990), pp. 359–700.
29  Milan Kundera, 'The Tragedy of Central Europe', *The New York Review of Books* (26 April 1984), pp. 33–8.
30  Jaszi, *Dissolution*, pp. 173–4.
31  The total Jewish population of the Habsburg monarchy in 1910 was approxiamtely 2,250,000: Woolfdieter Bihl, 'Die Juden', in Wandruszka and Urbanitsch (eds), *Die Habsburgermonarchie* , Vol. 3, pp. 882–3. The total Jewish population of the German Empire was approximately 615,000 in 1910: Peter Pulzer, *The Rise of Anti-Semitism in Germany and Austria* (London, 1988: revised ed), p. 8.
32  Bihl, 'Die Juden', pp. 882–5 and Arthur Ruppin, *Die Soziologie der Juden* (Berlin, 1930), p. 114.
33  On the economic aspect see Werner E. Mosse, *Jews in the German Economy: The German-Jewish Economic Elite 1820–1935* (Oxford, 1987), *passim*, especially pp. 202–10.
34  The figures for Berlin, Budapest and Vienna are taken from Ruppin, *Die Soziologie*, p. 114.
35  For details of the above see Steven Beller, *Vienna and the Jews, 1867–1938: A Cultural History* (Cambridge, 1989), especially pp. 11–70.
36  On this phenomenon and the heated scholarly debate it has caused see Hillel Kieval, *The Making of Czech Jewry: National Conflict and Jewish Society in Bohemia, 1870–1918* (Oxford, 1988), pp. 10–35 and Gary B. Cohen, 'Jews in German Society: Prague 1860–1914' in *Central European History*, Vol. 10 (1977), pp. 37–8.
37  Bihl, 'Die Juden', pp. 905–7. Twenty-four per cent claimed German, whereas 36 per cent claimed Polish and over 31 per cent Magyar. Only 2.5 per cent claimed a Czech (or Slovak) linguistic identity.
38  *Ibid.*, p. 905 and Kieval, *Czech Jewry*, pp. 60–1.
39  On the ideology of emancipation see David Sorkin, *The Transfromation of German Jewry 1780–1840* (Oxford, 1987) and George L. Mosse, *German Jews beyond Judaism* (Bloomington, 1985).
40  *Neuzeit* (3 June 1870), pp. 245–6.
41  *Österreichische Wocchenschrift* (6 November 1896), p. 887.
42  Of the German electorate in Cisleithania, 37 per cent voted for the anti-semitic Christian Socials, 31 per cent voted for the *Nationalverband*, a coalition of German bourgeois parties, liberal and nationalist, which either embraced anti-semitic positions or tolerated them (the Viennese-Jewish deputies were excluded), while 32 per cent voted for the non-anti-semitic Social Democrats. Pulzer, *the Rise of Anti-Semitism*, pp. 205–10.
43  See Gary B. Cohen, *The Politics of Ethnic Survival: Germans in Prague 1861–1914* (Princeton, 1981).
44  Steven Beller, *Vienna and the Jews*, p. 197 and Steven Beller, 'The Hilsner Affair: Nationalism, Anti-Semitism and the Individual at the Turn of the

Century', in R. J. Pynsent (ed.), *T.G. Masaryk, 1850–1937*, Vol. 2 (Macmillan, 1990), pp. 52–75.

45  W. J. Cahnman, 'Adolf Fischhof and his Jewish Followers', in *Leo Baeck Institute Yearbook* (1959), pp. 111–39.

46  Theodor Gomperz, *Theodor Gomperz: Ein Gelehrtenleben im Bürgertum der Franz-Josefzeit* (Vienna, 1974), p. 136.

47  On Bloch see Joseph S. Bloch, *Erinnerungen aus meinem Leben* (Vienna, 1992) and Robert S. Wistrich, *The Jews of Vienna in the Age of Franz Joseph* (Berlin, 1989), pp. 270–309.

48  Paul Natorp, ' Siegfried Lipiner', in Anton Bettelheim (ed.), *Biographisches Jahrbuch und deutscher Nekrolog*, Vol. 18 (1913), p. 285.

49  See S. Beller, *Herzl* (London, 1991), pp. 83–106.

Chapter 3

# Ideas of Economic Integration in Interwar Mitteleuropa

## Peter M. R. Stirk

As in other periods of European history the idea of integration was spawned by the experience of disintegration. The unity, iniquitous though it may have been, which was imposed by the multinational Empires of nineteenth century Europe gave way to a proliferation of new and revived states. From the outset it was clear that the newly won independence of these states posed a threat to the economic prosperity and military security of the region. In recognition of this various forms of integration were espoused, especially from the mid-1920s through to the mid-1930s. Reflection upon these ideas is inevitably marked by the failure to bring about peaceful integration and the subsequent domination of the region by German arms. The unjust borders of the postwar settlement, the indifference of the Western Powers, with the exception of France, and indigenous nationalism have been seen as creating a power vacuum into which a revived Germany stepped, economically at first and then militarily. Economic self-interest and military security of the non-Germanic states appear to have been sacrificed to the demons of nationalism and the ambitions and calculations of the Great Powers. The small states, many of which were to become the first victims of the failure of the Versailles order, have been regarded as scarcely less culpable than their more powerful European neighbours. In the words of one advocate of Danubian federation: 'The crux of the problem was that most of the great and small States regarded the formation of an economic union, or any other co-operation, far too much from the point of view of power politics, and not from that of economic interest.'[1] The presumption that economic self-interest was frustrated by external political intervention and the purblind pursuit of power and nationalistic goals by those who stood to benefit from integration was and is widespread. It has, if anything, been strengthened by the post Second World War history of the region, where external intervention by the Soviet Union and the Cold War division of Europe seemed to have disrupted the natural unity of the region.[2] The common thread running through these views of interwar and post Second World War history is the idea of a natural economic unity which called out for integration but was frustrated in the first place by power politics and then torn apart by the cold war.

The reality of the interwar period was, however, more ambiguous than these judgements suggest. Economic self-interest did not unambiguously point to integration. This was true for both the two major alternative definitions of mitteleuropäisch integration, that is, Mitteleuropa including Germany or excluding Germany. Which of these two definintions one took made a great deal of difference. Industrially, Germany was the most advanced prospective member of Mitteleuropa, even if a heavily indebted one. She was also guided by the overriding goal of regaining the status of a European Great Power, a status denied her by the Versailles Treaty. She was guided, in the second place, by the desire for territorial revision of the postwar order. The alternative, integration without Germany, readily looked like a restoration of the Habsburg Empire, but in fact would have created a much larger unit. The prospective members in this scheme were mostly undeveloped states embarking on a painful process of industrialization and modernization. Their difficulties were compounded by the peculiar impact of the depression upon the region. Strictly speaking they suffered from both the world-wide collapse of production and trade and the collapse of raw material and agricultural prices which paralysed their pre-dominantly agricultural economies. The only two exceptions to this heavy dependence on agriculture were Czechoslovakia, the Czech half of which was industrialized, and Austria.

Danubian integration, excluding Germany, was inevitably associated with the idea of the restoration of lost unity. Its enthusiasts could be quite forthright about this. According to one, 'from the economic point of view, the former Austro-Hungarian Monarchy formed an ideal unit. The restoration of Austria-Hungary not as a political unit but as an economic and industrial unit should be a task of the League of Nations.'[3] For supporters of Danubian federation the creation of a new set of customs borders naturally played a major role in their argument. In advocating economic integration they meant either a customs un-ion or some system of preferences which would restore pre-existing patterns of trade. Although the case for a customs union seemed self-evident to its advo-cates, the rulers of the successor states were not so convinced. Surveying the arguments for and against a Danubian Federation in 1919 the American Archibald Coolidge considered the arguments against a customs union:

> Tariff negotiations are proverbially thorny, and to bring about a commer-cial union between four, five or more equal states is hardly in the range of practical politics. Even if it were brought about, every time any modifica-tion was suggested, there would be fresh trouble. Nothing but universal free trade could obviate this; but if it existed, the chief reason for a con-federation would disappear. And who wants it? Hungary? Yes … but there is little indication that others of the proposed members really desire it. Most of them are brim full of self-confidence in their new found great-ness and believe they are quite able to stand alone.[4]

The restoration of lost unity was not the only argument enthusiasts advanced. The image of a 'balanced economy' also played a major role. According to this argument, what made the old Monarchy so attractive was that it unified industrial regions, roughly parts of postwar Austria and Bohemia, and financial centres, Vienna and Budapest, on the one hand, with agricultural regions and raw-material reserves on the other. Each would provide a market for the other, guaranteeing development and prosperity.

The idea of a balanced economy, however, was a highly elastic one in the sense that it did not of itself set any self-evident limit to the extent of the region. Since the old Monarchy had been losing the race to growth it was natural to look to a larger economic unit, far outstripping the boundaries of the old Monarchy. From this perspective German advocates of a mitteleuropäisch unit could point to the complementarity between an industrialized Germany, incorporating Austria, and the lands to the east. Arguments about the virtues of balanced economies were strengthened and complicated by the widespread belief that the world economy as a whole was dividing up into more or less self-contained economic blocs. All kinds of suppositions and habits encouraged such ideas. Armchair geopoliticians totted up the surface area and populations of these hypothetical blocs, seeking to find some minimum viable size for their own bloc. Not too far removed from these calculations was the supposition that these blocs would engage in warfare and had to be self-sufficient for that purpose. This naturally found much favour in the states of Mitteleuropa which had suffered extensively from the continental blockade of the First World War. Some looked to the United States of America as a model. Economically prosperous, at least in the 1920s, the United States had a much lower dependence upon foreign trade than the industrial states of the Old World. It did not need to rely upon foreign trade because of its large internal market, a market free of restrictive tariffs, and, of course, a market which included the production of raw materials and foodstuffs as well as industrial products. The more economically minded usually sought to bolster their preferred configuration of blocs by pointing to existing patterns of trade – or at least to recent changes in patterns of trade, whichever best suited their preference.

The most cited models of the prospective blocs were, however, even larger than the United States. Not the United States alone but Pan-America, along with the British Empire, seemed to indicate the future trend. This trend was not necessarily reassuring to smaller states, especially to the newly independent East European states which had emerged from the continental Empires. According to one of the most prolific advocates of the integration of Mitteleuropa, the Hungarian economist Elemer Hantos:

> The idea of a customs union in contemporary Mitteleuropa, just like the plan for a Danubian federation, is discredited, because in the past it was always related to imperialism, and even today customs union plans (Greater Britain, PanAmerica, British Commonwealth) appear as near imperialist movements.[5]

The successor states had no desire to be the equivalent of colonies in some greater economy. The suggestion that they ought to fulfil that function was not restricted to the margins of political debate or restricted to ambitious nationalists of neighbouring states. One American financial expert commented in the mid-1920s that: 'The Polish industry is rather overgrown than underdeveloped in relation to agriculture and raw materials. It seems the best future for Poland would be production of agricultural goods and raw materials for the industrial-ized part of Europe.'[6] The idea that in the New World, with its incipient *Grossraum-wirtschaften* (large economic regions), small states would not be viable, that they were not, as German has it, *lebensfähig*, could only compound the con-cern. The response of the elites of the Successor States was to firmly reject their allotted role. They would not be suppliers of foodstufs and raw materials. They would industrialize instead. Military security pointed in the same direction as the desire for economic independence. For in the postwar world it was increasingly evident that warfare depended in large part upon the capacity to sustain modern armies with their mechanized transport and insatiable appetite for munitions.[7]

In many respects the debates around the theme of development and under-development resembled those that were to become common after 1945 in rela-tion to the Third World. The 'economic nationalism' of the interwar successor states contained much that would become commonplace later. Forced industri-alization, often associated with military ambitions, import substitution, failure to rectify or even give serious consideration to inadequate agricultural produc-tivity, along with fears of being held captive within a 'colonial' relationship and appeals for international aid and the international regulation of commodity markets, all found expression. It is true that economic nationalism in East Central Europe often amounted to little more than a collection of slogans loosely bound together by the idea of the national interest.[8] But this charge can equally well be laid against other economic policies and ideas. Alongside the rhetoric and barely cloaked vested intcrests was the sophisticated theory of Mihaïl Manoïlescu which formed part of a long-standing debate in Romania.[9] The broader debate, in public and in the cabinets and ministries of Europe, exhibited many of the insights, as well as the prejudice, hypocrisy and ambition of later times.[10]

For supporters of the idea of integration in interwar Mitteleuropa, the task was to find a persuasive alternative to the allure of economic nationalism. At first glance they could call on some powerful arguments. The experience of disinte-gration induced by the proliferation of customs borders and the dislocation of the immediate postwar phase readily suggested the need for greater cooperation. Further, their ideas seemed to be in harmony with the spirit of the age. If the trend was towards large-scale balanced economies, *Grossraumwirtschaften*, then the small successor states were swimming against the tide. Economic self-inter-est seemed to point in the desired direction. But they also had to face up to some awkward choices. The most pressing of these was the position of Germany in any scheme of integration. Integration with Germany carried with it the threat of subordination. Integration without Germany excluded the most powerful economy, and hence the largest market. Second, Germany's position affected the European, indeed global, distribution of power and economic development and was therefore of great interest to her Western neighbours, above all to France. Third, the relationship between even the non-Germanic states of the region was far from harmonious. The postwar settlement had not created an idyll of peacefully coexisting nation states but a series of multinational states with varying degrees of commitment to the conversion of their minorities alongside more ethnically homogenous states with claims upon their neighbours.

In the immediate postwar phase there was, however, much speculation on the need to salvage something from the decay of the Habsburg Empire. In its place a Danubian Federation was touted as a way of preserving the economic interdependence of the region as well as ensuring its military defence, perpetuating Germanic domination of the region or reviving the dynastic claims of the Habsburgs. The treaty system defining the basic parameters of the postwar order had left some scope for cooperation, but not much. The main principle was the Most Favoured Nation (MFN) principle, according to which concessions in customs made to one state had to be extended to third parties enjoying MFN status. As Hantos pointed out, this was a recipe for high tariffs, at least in the prevailing conditions.[11] Limited exemption was permitted. According to the Treaty of Saint-Germain, the Allies would not invoke the MFN principle:

> to secure the advantages of any arrangements which may be made by the Austrian Government with the Governments of Hungary or of the Czecho-Slovak State for the accord of a special customs regime to certain natural or manufactured products which both originate in and come from those countries … provided that the duration of these arrangements does not exceed a period of five years from the coming into force of the present Treaty.[12]

The limitations were as significant as the concession. Restricted to three countries and of limited duration, there was little prospect that it would be taken up. Moreover, Hungary was soon to be encircled by a system of alliances which came to be known as the Little Entente. Its prime purpose was to safeguard its signatories, Czechoslovakia, Yugoslavia and Romania, all of whom now incorporated substantial ethnic Hungarian minorities, against Hungarian territorial claims. True, before the alliance system was fully formed, in 1920, the Czechoslovak Prime Minister, Edouard Beneš had suggested to the Hungarian Prime Minister Count Paul Teleki an agreement on economic cooperation as a prelude to a settlement of territorial issues and, in the longer run, a 'United States of Central Europe'. It is not quite clear how sincere the offer was. Beneš, however, was more supportive of ideas of economic cooperation in private than in public. In any event Hungary predictably declined the offer.[13] Later in the same year, in October 1920, a conference of the successor states was proposed, to discuss restoring the economic integration of the region. Italy was suspicious of anything that remotely smacked of the restoration of Austria-Hungary, and even seemed to prefer the idea of *Anschluss* between Germany and Austria, much to the surprise of British representatives.[14] The conference was eventually held at Porto Rose in October and November 1921. A protocol agreeing to the suppression of all import restrictions by 1 July 1922 was signed, but never ratified.[15] After the Porto Rose Conference there was little activity until the end of the decade.

Underlying the failure to reach agreement was not only the ethnic antagonisms that dominated the region and the intial self-confidence that Coolidge mentioned, but a more deep-seated motive. This emerges strikingly in a comment by the Czechoslovak leader Beneš:

> The Czechs had fought not for political freedom – for this they had enjoyed to a certain extent even before the war – but for their economic independence, and therefore the scheme for a confederation of the Danubian States, or even of a 'Customs Union', is out of the question for the Czechoslovak Republic.[16]

Beneš' assertion of Czechoslovakian economic independence is all the more emphatic for his elevation of it above political independence. The emphasis upon economic independence among Czech nationalists was probably stronger than among many of the other oppressed nationalities of the Empire. Though the Hungarians, the other major beneficiary of the distribution of political power in the Empire, had long sought to underpin their political position with an industrial base.[17] By the interwar period the supposition that economic independence was at least a condition of full political independence was widespread in the region among the ruling élites and the state bureaucracies.[18] It is true that the more militant nationalists did not gain significant influence over economic policy in East Central Europe during the interwar period. Hence, foreign capital was welcomed in general. Where there was hostility it was often associated with perceived political threats to statehood, rather than being associated with ideas of economic exploitation, though this was far from absent. In Poland, for example, there was considerable hostility to German ownership in key industrial sectors but little concern about American ownership, even though American capital was somewhat larger after 1931.[19] With some exceptions this was not, however, the core of the debate. The real issue was what measures had to be taken in order to industrialize. Often, in fact, protectionist measures would be introduced for other reasons, in order to reduce imports and hence mitigate the strains upon the balance of payments, but would then be perpetuated for the sake of promoting industrial development. It was not so much economic exploitation that was at issue, though this was far from absent, but the need to industrialize to consolidate political independence. It was against this background that the advocates of integration had to make their case.

The mid-1920s saw a surge of debate about European integration of all kinds. the rapprochement between Germany and France embodied in the Locarno Pact of 1925, and related speculations by the statesmen who brought it about,

Gustav Streseman and Aristide Briand, gave heart to the proponents of federation. Subsequent developments, especially the formation of the International Steel Cartel in 1926, seemed to corroborate their hopes. In the political realm and the economic realm the trend seemed to be pointing in the same direction. But what kind of integration was at stake? Equally important, who was to be included in it? Naturally enough, given the cause of this enthusiasm, most looked to a Franco-German axis as the basis of a federal or united Europe. Whether this was to lead to a Pan-European or merely West European federation was a different matter. Further east another question arose within the framework of the most prominent set of organizations involved in the debate on the future of Mitteleuropa; the Mitteleuropäische Wirtschaftstag.

The Mitteleuropäische Wirtschaftstag was launched in Vienna by an industrialist, Meinl, in 1925, to promote free trade within the region. Branches were established in Germany, Czechoslovakia and Hungary. In the same year the first Mitteleuropäische Wirtschaftstagung was held at the initiation of the Hungarian economist, Elemer Hantos. At this meeting a split quickly became apparent between Hantos and German delegates represented by Gothein. Hantos wanted to form a Central European customs union without Germany. His aim was not to exclude Germany in perpetuity. It was to allow the smaller states to gain in strength and confidence before allowing Germany into the union. They would then confront Germany as a bloc, forming an equal pendant to the German collossus. Gothein for the Germans was implacably opposed and succeeded in having the offending passage removed from the resolutions of the first Mitteleuropäische Wirtschaftstagung.[20]

Faced with this kind of dilemma Hantos and others looked for ways of circumventing the hesitation of politicians and the intractability of power politics. They were encouraged in their speculations by doubts about the significance of customs barriers, the main topic of negotiations between states. Although a customs union was the most frequent goal in interwar writing upon integration the significance of customs unions was being increasingly questioned. While tariff barriers had, in the prewar world, been the most important weapon in the hands of states, they were now only one among many. The imposition of quotas, the control of foreign exchange and a myriad of regulations all played a part in the direction of trade. So too did cartels. Although the Americans continued to view cartels with great suspicion, especially European ones, others saw them as the pioneers of integration. The fomer French Premier Edouard Herriot put the case for cartels with great vigour:

> The whole problem to be decided is whether public men will have as much initiative and intelligence as private individuals, or whether in politics, we are going to be content to walk in the old ways, ignoring the great transformation which is silently creating a new world.[21]

The trend Herriot had in mind was the formation of cartels and the private men of whom he wrote were the heads of those organizations.

Elemer Hantos was also a firm follower of the cause of the cartels. The idea was that they would manage the strains and stresses which would inevitably accompany integration, mitigate the threat of bankruptcy and unemployment while managing the rationalization of European industry to take advantage of larger markets. But how plausible was this suggestion? Many of the interwar cartels came into being to manage excess capacity, not to promote competition from new industries in largely agrarian states. They were dominated by the major Western concerns whose behaviour in the less-industrialized states of Mitteleuropa was far from benign. In Poland they suppressed domestic competition, manipulated trade between subsidiaries to export profits and may well have contributed to the overall decapitalization of Poland in the interwar period.[22] According to Hantos, 'The essence of the cartel is indeed to guarantee the weaker concern a rent.'[23] But much depended here upon definitions of weakness. Weaker members of the cartel might be guaranteed a profit at the expense of non-members, financially weak but large members might be guaranteed a profit at the expense of sounder small enterprises. In general, it seems to have been the larger concerns which benefited. Within the International Steel Cartel the Central European Group was headed by the Selling Agency of the United Czechoslovak Iron Works. The agreements it negotiated entailed protection for the Czechoslovak market, a substantial share of the Austrian and Hungarian markets for Czech industry and shares of the Balkan markets for the CEG. In the sphere of chemicals, the other sector with the strongest development of cartels, the German giant IG Farben was, if anything, aided in its attempt to penetrate south eastern markets by international agreements.[24]

Somewhat more plausible was the emphasis upon a kind of functionalist strategy. Again Hantos was a devotee of this road to integration. He made the general point in his *Mitteleuropäischer Postverein*:

> In more reflective circles everywhere the question is now posed: would it not be possible to counter the horrible consequences of the general distraction, of the artificial isolation and narrow mindedness, of the mutual hate and intolerance, through practical [zweckmässige] agreements between states?[25]

The very extent of his list of antipathies cautions against believing that it would. The areas he favoured for these agreements – transport and communications, the free movement of persons, payments and capital – were unlikely to compensate for considerations of industrial development and military security.[26] Hantos himself was often reduced to lamenting the failure to make progress and to recalling the unity that had existed under the old Empire. Where progress was made it was, moreover, frequently on an international level which stretched far beyond Mitteleuropa. Thus, Hantos had to argue for the breakdown of the recently re-etablished International Rail Association into sections, one of which would be a Central European one.[27]

The actual development in East Central Europe during the 1920s was not conducive to cooperation. In the initial postwar period a system of licences and quotas was used to regulate trade. As soon as more normal conditions began to emerge, most of the countries of the region walled themselves behind a series of protective tariffs.[28] The impact of these upon industrialization was a mixed blessing at best. The countries of the region did not manage to keep pace with the development of heavy industry which was leading growth in Western Europe. According to the Hungarian economic historians, Berend and Ránki, whereas per capita consumption of steel increased by between 50 per cent and 100 per cent in Sweden and England in the period 1913 to 1938, it scarcely grew at all in East Central Europe.[29] Industrial growth was concentrated in consumer goods, often to the detriment of the previous division of labour within the region. Thus, whereas spinning had been concentrated in Austria and weaving in Bohemia, the postwar governments set about making their textile industries independent, building up weaving in Austria and spinning in Czechoslovakia.[30]

Equally important was the failure to remedy the low levels of agricultural productivity in the region. This was particularly significant for countries that still had very high levels of agricultural employment. The gap in levels of productivity was substantial. The comparative value of cereal output per hectare in 1939 was estimated at 0.62 for Germany, 0.58 for France but only 0.48 for Hungary and 0.42 for Poland. The gap in the value of livestock production per head of agricultural population was even greater.[31] Low levels of productivity in eastern Europe were widely commented upon. They formed the focus for a debate about the restoration of production in Europe as a whole as well as Eastern Europe. The point was put starkly by one of Europe's most innovative economists, Vladimir Voitinsky: 'The *source of European poverty* and of the waste of its productive resources *is to be found in its fields and pastures.*'[32] As agricultural productivity continued to remain below the international level and as protection of domestic industry forced the prices of industrial products up, the market for consumer goods was restricted. The commitment to industrialization did make sense, at least if coupled with a commitment to raising agricultural productivity. The attempt to create balanced economies, with a full panoply of industrial production and a comparative neglect of agriculture, did not.[33]

The operation of these policies did little to further the prospects of integration in more ways than one. They began to force apart many of the countries of the region. Whereas the old Monarchy had taken some 75.7 per cent of Hungary's trade, the region took 59.3 per cent in 1929.[34] Between 1922 and 1928, the region continued to supply about the same percentage of Austria's imports, but its share of her exports dropped significantly from 51.3 per cent to 40.1 per cent. A similar pattern was evident in Czechoslovakia's trade.[35] It was, moreover, these three countries that were most dependent upon regional trade. The significance of the region for the poorer and smaller economies of the Balkans held up better, or even increased, but was of less significance to them. The adverse effects of the new protectionism were then already evident. It was, however, the impact of the depression and the collapse of the price of raw materials and foodstuffs, aggravated by yet higher customs duties and the revival of other forms of barrier, which was to vastly exaggerate the problem. Whereas in 1928 the region had absorbed some 37.6 per cent of its total exports, the figure had shrunk to 27.3 per cent in 1935.[36]

The vicious circle into which these states became locked is easily illustrated by Hungary. Much reduced by the harsh Trianon Treaty, the industries which Hungary had developed under the Empire suffered from overcapacity. The flour mills that had once served the entire Empire were reduced to working at an estimated average of only 25 per cent of capacity.[37] Other industries did do better, especially before the onset of the agricultural crisis and the depression. Yet industrial development was hindered by a fundamental flaw in the strategy of industrialization. As Hungary imposed tariff barriers and quotas to protect her own industries, her neighbours retaliated in kind, hitting both Hungary's industrial and agricultural exports. The impact on the latter was vital. Although less heavily dependent on rural output than most of her neighbours, Hungary could ill-afford the consequences of enforced industrialization combined with shrinking agricultural markets. The outcome was a suppression of rural purchasing power and a divergence of industrial and agricultural prices. Taking a common base of 100 in 1913, agricultural prices had fallen to 80 in 1937 while industrial prices stood at an index of 125. A substantial part of Hungary's domestic market was being suppressed. This meant, for example, that the shoe industry which had been extensively promoted by the government was working at half its capacity by 1935, with Hungarians purchasing one pair of shoes every two years, compared with two pairs in Germany and five and a half in Britain.[38]

The severity of the crisis for the countries of East Central Europe was evident from the outset. It revived both discussion of regional integration and diplomatic moves to turn them into reality. By the end of 1929, experts from the Danubian countries had already met to discuss some kind of 'export community' to promote the sale of their agricultural products.[39] The pace and level of debate increased the followng year, with a meeting in Bucharest between Romania, Hungary and Yugoslavia. In the following month of August a much larger gathering took place, at Poland's initiative. Among the resolutions that emerged from this meeting were the suggestion of an international convention for the abolition of export premiums for agricultural products, preferential tariffs for European grain and the creation of a financial commission which was to work for agricultural credits for the states.[40] The key idea, which was to dominate the debate for the next three years, was the idea of preferential tariffs. It was also the most contentious, for throughout the interwar period the orthodox response to the problems of stagnating or declining trade was to call for a return to free trade. The favoured device for promoting trade liberalization was the Most Favoured Nation clause. Preferential tariffs flew in the face of the MFN clause.

To add to the difficulties they faced, the question of preferential tariffs also called into play the mutual suspicions of the Great Powers. In July 1930 the German Finance Minister argued in a Cabinet meeting that: 'Agrarian coopera-tion with the French should be rejected. Through such cooperation Germany would become the purchaser for Eastern Europe via French mediation, and she would thereby give up a trump card.' He added, as he warmed to his theme:

> Many of the states created by the peace treaty are economically not viable. They are, for example, partly too small to provide a basis for large-scale industry, like the automobile industry. France wants to help them by means of a European construction which it finds agreeable.[41]

Many German ministers and officials were convinced that their prime weapon, indeed their only weapon, was Germany's economic strength. The fact that it frequently failed to bring them concrete results, leaving them railing against the politically motivated refusal of others to recognize economic reality and economic self-interest, did not dissuade them of its importance. The others, especially in East Central Europe, were well-aware of Germany's economic significance and were worried by it. The problem was reflected in the public debate that surrounded the negotiations for preferential systems and customs unions in these years. One participant, Wilhelm Gürge, sought to counter the supposition that there was a long- term correlation between the wealth of the industrialized nations and the comparative poverty of the agricultural nations. The subsidized industries of the latter, he claimed, were a misuse of capital which actually compounded their fundamental problem: low levels of productivity.[42]

The problems of preferential tariffs and Germany's position within Central Europe exploded on to the international stage in the spring of 1931. In March an Internatational Wheat Conference in Rome failed to reach any agreement in the light of irreconcilable differences between advocates of preferential tariffs and advocates of the MFN clause. In the same month, Austro-German plans for a customs union became public. Interestingly, Hantos was not opposed to the customs union. Looking back at it two years later he wrote that the: 'German-Austrian customs union would have formed a happy pendant for the proposed agrarian bloc, had from the beginning Czechoslovakia been included in the combination as an equal.'[43] In part, Hantos was reiterating his old idea that East Central Europe should unite independently of Germany in order not to become a mere appendage of the latter. He was also reflecting the assumption that salva-tion lay through cooperation between industrial and agricultural Europe.

Others were less charitable. Ever since the success of the German *Zollverein* in the nineteenth century a customs union had been the favoured instrument for the achievement of economic, and indeed ultimately political integration. The Czechoslovak Prime Minister Beneš was well-aware of the analogy, referring explicitly to the 1828 Treaty between Prussia and Hesse-Darmstadt, which he claimed had served as a model of the Austro-German proposal. His point was clear: the 1828 Treaty had led to the *Zollverein* and then political unification; so too would the Austro-German customs union.[44] The prospect of political union, *Anschluss*, between Germany and Austria caused alarm in Paris. German efforts to reassure France and others that the object of the exercise was strictly economic, that Germany and Austria would be equal partners within the union, or even that the union was open to other states, were to little avail. French suspicion was far from unjustified. Some German ministers and officials at least, including Foreign Minister Curtius, did indeed see the customs union as a step on the road to *Anschluss*.[45] For both parties the fate of Austria was the key to the future of the region as a whole. From the German point of view the strategy was stated by State Secretary Bülow in a private letter in April 1931:

> Once the German-Austrian customs union has become a reality, I calcu-late that the pressure of economic necessity will within a few years compel Czechoslovakia to adhere to it in one way or another ... If we should succeed in incorporating Czechoslovakia in our economic bloc, and if in the meanwhile we should also have established closer economic relations with the Baltic States, then Poland with her unstable economic structure would be surrounded and exposed to all kinds of dangers: we should have her in a vice which could perhaps in the short or long run make her willing to consider further the idea of exchanging political concessions for tangible economic advantages.[46]

France was equally convinced of the far-reaching political implications of the move and sought to exert diplomatic pressure and financial pressure to block it. French efforts, bolstered by doubts in Austria, succeeded in September. As part of her initial response France, however, had put forward an alternative scheme, the so-called Plan Constructif, based upon a system of preferences. The French plan was formulated against the background of opposition to the MFN principle which had been mounting in French diplomatic circles since late 1929.[47] The plan, as communicated to Britain on 4 May 1931, consisted of four main points. First, cereal importers were to grant preferential tariffs to East Central European cereal exporters, without receiving any reciprocal preferential treat-ment for their own exports. Second, industrial and agricultural cartels were to be encouraged. Specified contingents of goods regulated by these cartels were to benefit from tariff reductions. Third, credits were to be organized for agricul-ture. Finally, Austria was to benefit from preferences, again for specific quotas of goods. All his was said to be in recognition of 'an exceptional situation and of difficulties of a temporary character.'[48]

The provenance of these ideas is easy to recognize. Preferential tariffs and agricultural credits had been placed on the agenda by the East Central European agricultural conferences. The fact that the plan was put forward immediately after the collapse of the London Wheat Conference was no accident. The idea of using cartels to regulate trade, to mitigate the friction of adjustment, was a common one, vigorously espoused by commentators like Hantos. Equally evident is the absence of any suggestion of a customs union, despite the fact that France herself had held out the prospect of a customs union as part of the Briand

Plan barely a year earlier. In part, the motive for this was straightforward. The French proposal was an alternative to a customs union, an Austro–German one. But France was also less able, and less willing, to expose herself to the financial strains of anything so ambitious as a customs union.

The prospects for the French proposal were not good. It was perceived by the Germans as a counterplan to their own customs-union project, which it was. Moreover, the Germans had their own plans for preferential treaties. They were negotiating these with Romania and Hungary, and were able to proclaim that they were following through France's own idea. The French plan was thus turned against them by Germany. But there were significant differences between the French scheme and the German negotiations. In the first place the French scheme was a multilateral one; the German negotiations were strictly bilateral. The German cabinet was firmly resolved that they should remain so: in the words of the Foreign Minister, 'Preference systems, Germany must unconditionally hold to bilateral preference treaties.'[49] Bilateral treaties would bind the partner states to Germany.

British support for the French scheme was lukewarm at best. Her reply to France reiterated British commitment to the MFN principle. It also pointed to the likely protests of overseas grain exporters, especially Australia, Canada and the Argentine who exported some 60 per cent of their combined output compared with only 16 per cent for the Danubian countries.[50] The point was accurate but slightly disingenuous. The low percentage of exports reflected low levels of productivity and the barriers to trade, not their comparative unimportance for the Danubian states. Moreover, Danubian exports hardly dominated the European market. Even in cereals they accounted for only 9.5 per cent of European imports. Their role in European meat and dairy imports was derisory.[51] The French suggestion for employing cartels was pushed aside; they were 'a matter for the industrialists concerned, and not for Governments.'[52] There was considerable duplicity all round. With some justice the German press cast doubt upon France's ability and inclination to redeem her promises. Theodor Wolff complained that France, a highly protectionist country, largely self-sufficient in grain, was in no position to grant preferences to the South East European states. [53] But German policy was scarcely more constructive. The problems of East Central Europe had been aggravated by Germany's turn towards protective tariffs which helped to cut German wheat imports in half.[54] This indicates a general problem with the preferential systems of these years. Preferences were often offered after tariffs had been raised to near prohibitive levels. As Hantos had argued in the mid-1920s, preferences alone were insufficient. They would work as a stimulant to production only if accompanied by a general lowering of tariffs.[55]

The final collapse of the Austro–German customs-union scheme did noting to solve the broader problems of the region. Germany had managed to conclude bilateral preference treaties with Romania and Hungary in June and July 1931, even if she failed to implement them for some time.[56] Italy came up with its own

version of a preference system in September. According to this version the Great
Powers were to grant preferences to East European cereals and Austrian industrial goods. Unable to resist extracting the maximum benefit for herself Italy
adddded that the Danubian states should grant preferences to any Great Power
with whom they had a positive balance of trade, which was at the time Italy.[57]
The Italian plan came to nothing and the financial and trade position of the
successor states continued to deteriorate, necessitating renewed international
debate.

In this context France launched a new initiative, in fact a revised version of
the Plan Constructif. The proximate cause of the new initiative was a Report of
the League of Nations Finance Committee on 29 January 1932 which warned
of the precarious financial position of Austria and Hungary. Soon after, on 16
February, Chancellor Buresch of Austria issued an appeal to the Ambassadors of
the Great Powers, claiming that Austria stood on the brink of imminent collapse
and calling for economic cooperation with neighbouring countries. The German State Secretary Bülow immediately perceived a threat:

> For France a Danubian confederation would be a great success. It would
> considerably reduce the dangers which France sees in the Anschluss
> idea and in Hungary's revisionist policy. Further it would anchor France's
> desired political hegemony in the Danubian region.[58]

His suspicions were hardly mitigated by subsequent events. For within days,
Tardieu was to present a memorandum to Britain, which envisaged a scheme of
cooperation that, initially at least, purposefully excluded Germany. Tardieu had
already discussed his plan with the British Foreign Minister John Simon. East
Central Europeans also had a hand in the formulation of the plan. Pal Auer,
chairman of the Hungarian Chapter of the Pan-European Union, had convened
a private conference in February 1932, which included Hantos and a host of ex-
ministers. Auer later explained that his motive was fear of *Anschluss* and of Hungary being dragged into Germany's orbit. Alongside the creation of a Comité
pour la Rapprochement de Pays Danubiens, the conference formulated a draft
programme, including the concession of preferences for the Danubian states by
external powers, which was promptly forwarded to Paris by the French Ambassador.[59]

Tardieu's proposal set out from the idea that the formation of a customs
union would encounter 'insuperable difficulties both in the political and in the
economic fields'. His memorandum did not specify what the difficulties were
but Britain had solicited opinions on a customs union of the Danubian states in
January, only to receive a sharp rebuff from Germany. Tardieu suggested as an
alternative that 'the desired result can be obtained by combinations on a preferential basis'. He suggested that the five states in question – Austria, Czechoslovakia, Hungary, Romania and Yugoslavia – should meet and draw up an agreement to which France, in accord with Britain and Italy, would then respond.

The plan then was for a preference system between the five states backed by

financial aid from the Great Powers. But here lay the great difference between
the Plan Constructif of 1931 and the Tardieu Plan of 1932. The former included
the Great Powers within the preferential system, the latter did not. The difference was crucial. The problem, as the ex-Hungarian Premier Count Bethlen
pointed out, was that the markets of the grain importers in the Danubian group,
Austria and Czechoslovakia, were nowhere near large enough to absorb the
surpluses of the grain exporters. He welcomed the abandonment of the MFN
clause but declared quite firmly that 'the Danubian agricultural states cannot do
without the Italian, the German and the Swiss markets'.[60] The same point was
made by the Romanian Finance Minister to the Americans.[61] But this was precisely what France would not allow. The whole point was to prevent Mitteleuropa being reconstructed under German hegemony, hence the deliberate and
unsuccessful neglect of Germany in listing the powers who would respond to
the agreement drawn up by the Danubian states. As they had declared at their
own conference in Bucharest over two years earlier, what the agricultural
exporters needed was preferential access to German markets. This was anathema
to the French and, indeed, to the Americans. When questioned by representatives of the Danubian states, the American response was always that the United
States would look with favour upon a preference system between the Danubian
states but was opposed to including any of the Great Powers. In other words, the
Danubian states could have a preference system only if the most important
potential member was not included!

The dilemma of the Danubian states was clear. Even leaving aside their
substantial mutual antagonisms, they could not bring about their own salvation.
They were dependent on the Western Powers, including and especially
Germany. But agreements with the Western Powers fell foul of their internal
rivalries which meant, rightly or wrongly, that every initiative was seen as an
attempt to exert hegemony over a weakened Eastern Europe. Agreements with
the Western Powers also fell foul of their entwinement in a world economy
whose dominant member, the United States, clung to the doctrine of the MFN
clause. It came as no surpise therefore when the Tardieu Plan failed to get off the
ground at the London Four Power Conference of April 1932.

The plan, and others like it, had to overcome the conflicting and diverging
interests of the East Central European states. These were well brought out by
Hamilton Fish Armstrong, the influential editor of *Foreign Affairs*. In the first
place, there were considerable differences in the importance of countries to each
other. Thus Hungary was heavily reliant on Czechoslovakia and Austria for her
export markets. The two countries took 19 per cent and 34 per cent of her
exports respectively. But Hungary was markedly less important to them, taking
only 7 per cent of Czechoslovak exports and 9 per cent of Austrian exports.
Second, in some cases trade relationships were of minor importance to both
parties. Yugoslavia sent only 8 per cent of her exports to Hungary and took only
6 per cent of Hungary's exports. Moreover, in pursuit of the ideal of a 'balanced
economy', as well as in deference to domestic pressures, the industrialized states,

Austria and Czechoslovakia, protected their own agricultural sectors while the agricultural states sought to protect their infant industries.[62] In brief, it is far from clear that economic self-interest did point to a Danubian federation. Even if we uncouple the idea of self-interest from the economic nationalism of these states and ignore the interests dictated by the distorted pattern of trade which resulted from the associated policies, regional federation was not necessarily the road to salvation. Indeed, as most advocates of integration recognized, Danubian federation, or even leser forms of cooperation, would work only as part of some wider scheme which linked the two parts of Europe. That, however, in turn presumed some coordination of Western European policy and the latter was not forthcoming.[63]

The Stresa Conference of September 1932 took up the problem of Danubian cereal exports once more, but again led to little more than a programme of limited subsidies – and even this was not implemented.[64] An attempt at the beginning of 1933 to give an economic underpinning to the Little Entente was no more successful. Indeed, the Organization Pact in some ways compounded the problem, for it made cooperation with external powers dependent on the agreement of all members of the Entente.[65] There was little room for expansion of trade within the Entente itself. The main problem was that Romania and Yugoslavia had difficulty exporting to Czechoslovakia. Their combined exports to the latter amounted to 7 per cent of their total exports in 1933 and only 10 per cent three years later. Trade between Romania and Yugoslavia remained insignificant throughout the period. Trade was not helped by the emergence of clearing systems in place of payment in foreign exchange. For products which Romania and Yugoslavia could have exported to Czechoslovakia, minerals and oil, they preferred to sell outside the clearing agreements for hard currency.[66]

A slightly more successful bid was made by Italy with the Rome Protocols of March 1934. According to these, Austria and Italy agreed to take high-priced Hungarian wheat while Austria was granted limited preferential treatment for her industrial goods. The real basis of the trade, however, was concealed credit and transport subsidies paid by Italy. The system really worked only in the unusual circumstances of the Abyssinian crisis, though even then it had little impact on Austro-Hungarian trade. By 1937 its underlying weakness was becoming apparent: Italy could not afford it.[67]

During the mid-1930s the Czechsolovak Premier Hodza struggled to link the two competing alliances, the Little Entente and the countries of the Rome Protocols by means of a system of commercial treaties embodying preferences and then to turn this into a defensive alliance against Germany. He made enough progress to worry German diplomats.[68] But the obstacles were too strong and too numerous. Hungary would not sign a non-aggression pact. Bulgaria could not be won over either. After the autumn of 1937 even Romania grew cool.[69]

A final attempt by France in 1937–8 met with no more success. The idea this time was supplied by Richard Schüller of the Austrian Foreign Ministry.

It envisaged the abolition of exchange controls. Britain, France and possibly the United States were to guarantee new exchange rates. The purpose was to liberalize trade, facilitate the region's reintegration within the world economy and counter rising German influence. Once again, considerations of the wider world economy proved to be an obstacle. The British Chancellor of the Exchequer, John Simon, quashed any initial British enthusiasm, arguing that Germany would see it as an attempt to encircle her and that it threatened to wreck the prospects of more general reform of the trading system, currently being prepared by the Belgian statesman van Zeeland. The French continued to press the matter in 1938 but Britain delayed and *Anschluss* in March 1938 finally put an end to it.[70]

If Central Europe could not be organized without, and against Germany, that still left the option of the integration of Mitteleuropa, including Germany. This made more sense for the East Central European states, providing them with a large industrial market. But it also raised fears of subordination to Germany, and for some, fears about their territorial integrity and even very statehood. From the German point of view the idea of integration in Central Europe was encouraged by the supposition that the world was dividing up into economic blocs. It was a trend accepted even by the Deutsche Industrie und Handelstag which wanted to maintain the MFN principle.[71] The real question, however, was: should Germany seek to reorient its trade eastwards, should she turn away from the world market and create an economic empire in the East? The suggestion that German industry could find adequate markets in Eastern Europe was, to say the least, questionable. The suggestion was dubious enough for one commentator to seek to calm Eastern fears of prospective German imperialism by pointing to its evident absurdity:

> Germany's relations to other parts of the world are so varied, her possible markets in the South East still not so significant, that she could set herself against the rest of Europe and the world economy for the sake of a prospective Empire. Above all a mitteleuropäisch solution directed against France, or even against other countries, is not economically viable.[72]

The author, the economic journalist Wilhelm Grottkopp, was right in that it did not make economic sense for Germany to reorient her trade. He was wrong in the sense that she would do precisely this, or at least attempt to do so, for political reasons. The basis for this reorientation was laid under the pre-Nazi Cabinets of Brüning, Papen and Schleicher. The proposed Austro-German customs union would have been a step in this direction. Brüning introduced the control of foreign exchange.[73] Brüning's cabinet had already staked out the clear preference for a system of bilateral preference treaties.[74]

Yet policy continued to lag behind the ambitions of the ideologues of a new Mitteleuropa, whether Nazi or not. A drastic reorientation of policy was hampered by the realities of Germany's entwinement in the world economy. When the United States objected to the implementation of Germany's preference treaties, the Foreign Office drew back. The Foreign Office advised the Ambassador in Bucharest that if the Romanians pressed for implementation he should reply: 'In the negotiations between Germany and the participating Danubian states the starting point for all parties was always that the preferences should only be implemented with the agreement of the most favoured states.'[75] A decisive change came in October 1933 when Hans Posse, who had long been sympathetic to ideas of economic expansion towards the south east, obtained Cabinet approval for an 'active commercial policy based on reciprocity'. This led in turn to the German-Hungarian Treaty of February 1934, which established a clearing system between the two states.[76]

Under the new Economics Minister of the Nazi administration, H. Schacht, the Hungarian Treaty and others were integrated into the so-called New Plan which regulated German trade in the interest of rearmament. The development of raw materials and foodstuffs supplies in South Eastern Europe formed part of this scheme. But this did not yet amount to an attempt to sever Germany's ties with the world market in favour of a German-dominated *Grossraumwirtschaft* in Central Europe. The ties, especially of the larger concerns, to the world market were too important in Schacht's eyes to permit this.[77] She did however take a significant symbolic step in October 1935 when she formally abandoned the MFN principle as the 1923 Treaty with the United States lapsed.[78]

There were other problems, too. Germany, like the other states of the region, was concerned to limit her imports in order to contain her balance-of-payments problem. That meant, for example, that South East European cereal imports did not even reach the levels agreed under the various treaties until after 1937 and even then Nazi restrictions on imports meant they did not attain the level of 1925–8 in constant prices.[79] Moreover, the basic assumptions of the desirability, and viability of regional integration based on complementary economies was flawed. Advocates of Central European integration frequently claimed that there was an 'organic connection' between industrial Germany and the agrarian lands of East Central Europe. The reality turned out to be more complicated. Germany did offer most of the agrarian lands markets for foodstuffs which they had had difficulty finding elsewhere.[80] Access to the German market had, after all, been a prime consideration in the arguments over preference systems in the early 1930s. Not only did they gain access but they probably did so at better prices than they could have obtained elsewhere.

But there was also a substantial conflict of interest. In the first place the East Central European states were not always inclined to lock themselves into an exchange of agricultural products and raw materials for German manufactures. They often wanted to sell their agricultural products for hard currency in order to buy raw materials for their own industries. Furthermore those industries were in competition with certain sectors of German manufacturing.[81] This contributed to a decline in, for example, German textile exports to the region from some RM182.7 million in 1928 to a mere 26.6 million in 1936.82

With the recovery of the cereals market in 1936 to 1937 relieving some of the pressure, the Danubian states were able to exact significant concessions for Germany in a new wave of agreements. The clearing system that tied their imports to their exports to Germany was a constant point of dispute. Thus Romania insisted in 1936 that only 25 per cent of her oil exports to Germany be incorporated in the clearing system.[83] Germany was having difficulty exporting enough to pay for her imports and there were limits to how far the Reichsmark-bloc countries would allow Germany to build up credits to cover her trade deficit in blocked Reichsmark accounts. Germany found a temporary solution in the export of armaments.[84] The underlying problem, however, remained. The basic problem with Germany's trade with the Danubian region was, as an August 1939 memorandum of the Mitteleuropäische Wirtschaftstag noted, that it was based, on an 'import campaign' not an 'export offensive'.[85] The difficulty had been compounded by Germany's expansion. As the memorandum argued:

> Germany now cannot or will not supply a whole range of goods which the southeastern countries depend on, either because she needs them herself or must pay foreign exchange for them. This applies for example to cotton and wool yarns, which the southeastern countries, prior to recent political changes, obtained from Austria, the Sudetenland, and Bohemia-Moravia. To obtain these goods the southeastern countries must attempt to place a certain proportion of their exports in free exchange countries.[86]

The leaders of the Third Reich had only gradually groped their way to a clear conception of a *Grossraumwirtschaft* centred on South East Europe. A decisive turn in crystallizing these ideas in the minds of the Nazi leaders, especially Göring who now directed the Nazi economic programme, was the long-awaited *Anschluss* in 1938.[87] One year later the fallacy of that idea was becoming apparent. Germany had succeeded in obtaining a high profile in the trade of the Danubian states of South East Europe. But these states were not able to supply all the raw materials that Germany was expected to need in the event of war and blockade. By mid-1939 this was all too apparent to Göring and his staff in the Office of the Four Year Plan and to other agencies within the Reich. The Four Year Plan Office and the Army High Command agreed in August 1939 that Northern Europe would have to be incoroporated into the *Grossraumwirtschaft* and that even then access to Russian raw materials would be needed.[88]

Moreover, at the end of the decade Germany had signally failed to fundamentally relocate its trade. As Fritz Eulenburg, an early critic of the idea of relying upon the exchange between industrial and agrarian states, stated: 'Exchange between the industrial states is, on account of the rising demand, stronger than with the pure agrarian states. The latter exhibit a weaker purchasing power and absorptive capacity.'[89] When, under the pressure of preparation for war and an ideological antipathy to the world economy, she sought to reorientate her economy to South East Europe, the limits of this strategy became apparent. If Germany's trading partners are divided into high per capita income countries and low per capita income countries, the outcome, according to the calculations of the historian Alan S. Milward, is that the high-income markets took 54.99 per cent of German exports in the period 1925–34 and 46.59 per cent in 1935–9. The low-income markets of the Reichsmark bloc could absorb only 5.99 per cent in the earlier period and 17.62 per cent in the later period.[90]

Faced with the stagnation of trade with South-Eastern Europe, solutions were sought in two different directions. The first strategy was to cling on to the model of complementary economies and to tell the East European states to restrain their industrial development! This was the response of Emil Wiehl of the Economics Department of the German Foreign Office. The Hungarian delegation which was negotiating the March 1939 German-Hungarian agreement was in no doubt of Nazi intentions to press their country back to the level of a raw material reservoir.[91] A bolder strategy went to the heart of the problem: that is, the limited purchasing power of East Central Europe. The answer, according to Max Ilgner, an adviser drawn from IG Farben, and Reich Finance Minister Shwerin von Krosigk, was not to restrain industrial development but to promote it. Only if Eastern Europe were industrialized could it provide adequate markets for German manufacturing and adequate supplies for the German war machine.[92] Such considerations were, to be subordinated to the exigencies of a war economy and to the racist theories of the Nazi leadership.

In relation to her long-term economic interests, Germany's future could only lie in an orientation to the industrialized economies of Western Europe and North America. From the viewpoint of the other countries of Mitteleuropa, integration with Germany offered some immediate advantages, but it was not difficult to recognize the underlying disadvantages, even if it was difficult to avoid them. The system, as it operated under the exigencies of Germany's pursuit of self-sufficiency and rearmament, did little to improve regional integration. It led to a system of bilateral trade which was in the long-term economic interests of neither Germany nor her partners.[93]

The advocates of integration like Hantos, Woytinsky, Pal Auer and many others, had however been right in insisting that Germany would have to form an integral part of any solution. But they needed Germany as part of a solution that involved the other European powers. They needed capital investment from them, investment which, on the eve of the war, still outstripped German investment. In Romania, for example, Anglo–Dutch capital accounted for some 39.8 per cent of foreign participation, French for 16.6 per cent and American for 12.5 per cent. In Romania as a whole German investment probably accounted for no more than 8 per cent of total foreign investment and in Bulgaria, the most dependent upon trade with Germany, 16 per cent.[94] The East Central European countries were in fact dependent upon the resolution of the conflicts within Western Europe. Western Europe, however, was not dependent upon them for the resumption of growth or even for progress on economic integration, as postwar developments would prove. Yet the states to the east of Germany were not blameless. The purblind pursuit of industrialization, their refusal to accept the costs of adjustment to a regional division of labour, all compounded their problems and hastened their dependence on Germany. Economic self-interest did not point unambiguously to either Danubian integration or to integration incorporating Germany. Nor did it point to protectionism. If anything it pointed to a wider framework of integration.

There were other factors which make such stimple stipulations of economic interest less persuasive. For several of these states, especially in the second half of the period, the threat to statehood posed by Germany was real enough. So too was the prospect of achieving territorial ambitions with German aid, for Hungary at least. Moreover, their mutual antagonism, for ethnic and strategic reasons, was an equally obdurate reality. It is interesting in this context that Hantos offered as one reason for favouring a preference system as opposed to a customs union was that it would not require any kind of common legislation and hence could allow each to retain its own sovereignty.[95] Being in equal measure proud of and fearful for their sovereignty, haunted by memories of the Habsburg Empire, these states were not likely to embark on a road which seemed to lead to political union, as it was assumed a customs union did.

The idea of integration in Mitteleuropa during the interwar years was, in many ways, already obsolete. The region was becoming more and more entwined in a larger economy, albeit one in which interests were radically asymmetric. The interests of East Central Europe in cooperation with the West were much more significant to that region than the interests of the West in East Central Europe. Germany's interest in regional integration was born of a misguided theory about the benefits of a balanced economy and by the military ambitions and racial policies of her leadership. At the end of the day the exigencies of war would reveal the inadequacy of Mitteleuropa for even these malign purposes, unless the idea of Mitteleuropa was expanded to incorporate the whole of Europe.

## NOTES

1 Frederick Hertz, *The Economic Problem of the Danubian States* (London, 1947), p. 68.
2 See, for example, Richard Davy, 'The Central European Dimension', in William Wallace (ed.), *The Dynamics of European Integration* (London, 1990), who writes of the position in the 1980s: 'The underlying identity of Central Europe was beginning to re-emerge. To an increasing extent, Europe's customary traffic was penned behind political barriers and waiting to be released' (p. 141).
3 Quoted by Johannes C. Barolin in Barolin and Kurt Schechner, *Für und Wider Donauföderation* (Vienna, 1926), p. 9.
4 *Papers Relating to the Foreign Relations of the United States. The Paris Peace Conference 1919*, Vol. 12, p. 243.
5 *Die Handelspolitik in Mitteleuropa* (Jena, 1925), p. 92.
6 Quoted by Zbigniew Landau and Jerzy Tomaszewski, *The Polish Economy in the Twentieth Century* (New York, 1985), p. 60.
7 The states of the region, apart from Czechoslovakia, made little progress in this direction, though Poland and Hungary had ambitious plans at the end of the 1930s. Neverthless, H. Schacht observed, 'In a similar way the

agrarian states are forced, out of military considerations, to support certain industries which they believe are necessary for their military armament. It is clear from this, how far the disarmament problem is not only a political problem, but, in the highest degree, an economic problem as well.' *Das Ende der Reparationen* (Oldenbourg, 1931), p. 226.

8  Jan Koffman, 'How to Define Economic Nationalism?', in Henryk Szljfer (ed.), *Economic Nationalism in East-Central Europe and South America* (Geneva, 1990), p. 49.

9  See Mihaïl Manoïlescu, *The Theory of Protection and International Trade* (London, 1931) and Kenneth Jowitt, *Social Change in Romania 1860–1940. A Debate on Development in a European Nation* (Berkeley, 1978).

10  A link between the two sets of debates is provided by P. N. Rodenstein-Rodan, 'Problems of Industrialisation of Eastern and South-Eastern Europe', *The Economic Journal*, Vol. 53 (1943), pp. 203–11.

11  Hantos, *Die Handelspolitik in Mitteleuropa*, p. 77.

12  *The Treaty of Versailles and After*, p. 816.

13  The offer was made at a meeting in March 1921. Stephen Barsody, *The Tragedy of Central Europe* (New Haven, Yale Concilium on International and Area Studies, 1980), p. 19.

14  *Documents on British Foreign Policy*, First Series, Vol. 22, Doc. 20, pp. 37–8.

15  On the Porto Rose Conference see A. Orde, *British Policy and European Reconstruction after the First World War* (Cambridge, 1990), League of Nations, *Commercial Policy in the Interwar Period: International Proposals and National Policies* (Geneva, 1942)

16  Hertz, *The Economic Problem of the Danubian States*, p. 65.

17  On Hungary see Andrew C. Janos, *Politics of Backwardness in Hungary 1825-1945* (Princeton, 1982).

18  Jan Kofman, 'Economic Nationalism in East-Central Europe in the Interwar Period', in Szlajfer (ed.), *Economic Nationalism in East-Central Europe and South America*, p. 205.

19  Henryk Szlajfer, 'Economic Nationalism of the Peripheries as a Research Problem', in Szlajfer (ed.), *Economic Nationalism in East-Central Europe and South America*, p. 107.

20  'Protokoll einer Besprechung zum Zwecke der Gründung eines Mitteleuropa-Instituts in Dresden 3 Dezember 1927', in Reinhard Opitz (ed.), *Europastratagien des deutschen Kapitals 1900–1945* (Cologne, 197), p. 535.

21  Edouard Herriot, *The United States of Europe* (London, 1930), p. 152.

22  Zbigniew Landau and Jerzy Tomaszewski, 'Foreign Policy and International Business in Poland: 1918-39', in Alice Teichova *et.al.* (eds), *Multinational Enterprise in Historical Perspective*, p. 283.

23  Hantos, *Die Handelspolitik in Mitteleuropa*, p. 87.

24  Alice Teichova, 'Industry', in M. C. Kaiser and E. A. Radice (eds), *The Economic History of Eastern Europe*, Vol. 1 (Oxford, 1985), pp. 320–2.

25  Hantos, *Mitteleuropäische Postverein*, (Vienna, 1929), p. 76.

26  Hantos, 'Der Europäische Zollverein', p. 238.

27  Elemer Hantos, 'Das mitteleuropäische Verkehrsraum', in Wilhelm Gürge and Wilhelm Grotkopp (eds), *Grossraumwirtschaft. Der Weg zur europäischen Einheit* (Berlin, 1931), pp. 125–6.

28  A clear and concise summary is given by Frederick Hertz, *The Economic Problem of the Danubian States*, pp. 69–72. More detail can be found in Z. Drabek, 'Foreign Trade Performance and Policy', in Kaiser and Radice

(eds), *The Economic History of Eastern Europe*, Vol. 1, pp., though the general trends are often obscured.

29  Iván T. Berend and György Ránki, 'The Economic Problem of the Danube Region after the Breakup of the Austro-Hungarian Monarchy', in Bela K. Kiraly, Peter Pastor and Ivan Sanders (eds), *War and Society in East Central Europe*, Vol. 6 (New York, 1982), p. 101. See also Teichova, 'Industry', according to whom the share of producer goods in 1938 in the structure of industry was, for Germany 61.5 per cent, and for Hungary 39.5 per cent and for Bulgaria 20.2 per cent (p. 243).

30  Berend and Ránki, 'The Economic Problem of the Danube Region', pp. 98–9.

31  The figures are ooo zlotys. They are quoted by Henryk Tennenbaum, *Central and Eastern Europe in World Economy* (London, 1944), p. 18.

32  Quoted by Hilde Monte, *The Unity of Europe*, p. 43.

33  The policies of import substitution, industrialization and the comparative neglect of agriculture and opposition to free trade were all repeated in the Third World after 1945. For a survey see Richard Pomfret, *Diverse Paths of Economic Development* (Hemel Hempstead, 1992).

34  Drabek, 'Foreign Trade Performance and Policy', p. 421.

35  Hertz, *The Economic Problem of the Danubian States*, p. 82. Hertz's figures here relate to trade between Austria, Czechoslovakia, Hungary, Yugoslavia, Romania, and Poland.

36  Ibid., p. 82.

37  Ibid., p. 192. For other factors behind the 'scissors crisis' see Roland Schönfeld, 'Die Balkanländer in der Weltwirtschaftskrise', *Vierteljahrsschrift für Sozial – und Wirtschaftsgeschichte*, Vol. 62 (1975), pp. 193–6.

38  Hertz, *The Economic Problem of the Danubian States*, pp. 194–5.

39  Jacques Bariety, 'Der Tardieu-Plan zur Sanierung des Donauraums', in Josef Becker and Klaus Hildebrand (eds), *Internationale Beziehungen in der Weltwirtschaftskrise 1929–1933* (Munich, 1980), p. 366.

40  *Akten der Reichskanzlei. Weimarer Republik. Die Kabinette Brüning 1 u. II*, Vol. 1 (Boppard, 1982) Doc. 111, p. 423.

41  Ibid., Doc 68, p. 282. The 'European construction' was Briand's plan for a European federal union.

42  Wilhelm Gürge, 'Der Aufbau Mittel-und Südosteuropas als wirtschaftliche Forderung', in Gürge and Grotkopp (eds), *Grossraumwirtschaft*, pp. 24–5.

43  *Memorandum on the Economic Problems of the Danube States* (Budapest, 1933), p. 11.

44  In a discussion with Wilhelm Regendanz, a former director of the Austrian bank, Kreditanstalt. *Akten zur Deutschen Auswärtigen Politik 1918–1945*, Serie B, Vol. 17, Doc. 66, p. 174.

45  For a convincing assertion of this see F. G. Stambrook, 'The German-Austrian Customs Union Project of 1931: A Study of German Methods and Motives', *Journal of Central European Affairs*, Vol. 21 (1961), pp. 15–44.

46  Quoted in ibid., p. 43. German Foreign Office confidence in the potential significance of German economic power was high. See also Doc. 81 *Akten zur Deutschen Auswärtigen Politik 1918–1945*, Serie B, Band 17.

47  See Bariety, 'Der Tardieu-Plan', pp. 364–5. Bariety suggests that Hantos' work may well have influenced French judgement.

48  Doc. 31, *Documents on British Foreign Policy 1919–1939*, Second Series, Vol. 2.

49  *Akten der Reichskanzlei. Weimarer Republik. Die Kabinette Brüning 1 u. II*, Vol. 2, Doc. 293, p. 1076.

50 *Documents on British Foreign Policy 1919–1939*, Second Series, Vol. 2, Doc. 37, p. 54. The reply was communicated to France on 4 May 1931.

51 A. Basch, *The Danube Basin and the German Economic Sphere* (New York, 1943), pp. 40–3.

52 *Documents on British Foreign Policy 1919–1939*, Second Series, Vol. 2, Doc. 37, p. 54. This was also the German view. See *Akten der Reichskanzlei. Weimarer Republik. Die Kabinette Brüning 1 u. II*, Vol. 2, Doc. 293, p. 1076.

53 Oswald Hauser, 'Der Plan einer Deutsch-Österreichischen Zollunion von 1931 und die europäische Föderation', *Historische Zeitschrift*, Vol. 179 (1955), pp. 76–7.

54 Basch, *The Danube Basin and the German Economic Sphere*, p. 45.

55 Hantos, *Die Handelspolitik in Mitteleuropa*, pp. 93–5. See also Wilhelm Grotkopp, 'Handelspolitische Möglichkeiten und Notwendigkeiten', in Gürge and Grotkopp (eds), *Grossraumwirtschaft*, pp. 34–5, who argued that British imperial preferences had done nothing to reduce tariffs and drew the conclusion that only a customs union would help.

56 David E. Kaiser, *Economic Diplomacy and the Origins of the Second World War* (Princeton Uninversity Press, 1980), pp. 20ff.

57 Ibid., pp. 67, 72.

58 Bülow to the Embassy in Vienna, 2 March 1932 *Akten zur Deutschen Auswärtigen Politik 1918–1945*, Serie B, Vol. 20, Doc. 4, p. 11.

59 Pal Auer, 'Initiatives toward Cooperation in the Danube Basin in the 19th and 20th Centuries', in Francis S. Wagner (ed.) *Toward a New Central Europe* (Astor Park, Florida, 1970), pp. 190–1. Auer claimed the programme was the basis for Tardieu's plan. This seems exaggerated. The ideas were widespread and had already been put forward earlier by the French.

60 I. Bethleñ, 'The Danube States and the Tardieu Plan', *Political Science Quarterly*, Vol. 47 (1932), p. 360.

61 *Foreign Relations of the United States*, 1932, Vol. 1, pp. 851–2.

62 Hamilton Fish Armstrong, 'Danubia: Relief or Ruin', *Foreign Affairs*, Vol. 10 (1932), pp. 607–8.

63 For all its faults the contemporary European Community has, through its Association Agreements, provided a template which has facilitated cooperation between the East Central European states of the Vísegrád group. On this see the Introduction to this volume.

64 *Memorandum on the Economic problems of the Danube States* , p. 12.

65 Ibid., p. 10.

66 Basch, *The Danube Basin and the German Economic Sphere*, pp. 154–7.

67 Ibid., pp. 161–4.

68 See the report from von Papen of 12 January 1937. *Documents on German Foreign Policy* Series D, Vol. 1, Doc. 196.

69 Milan Hodza, *Federation in Central Europe* (London, 1942), pp. 127–39.

70 Kaiser, *Economic Diplomacy and the Origins of the Second World War*, pp. 205–7.

71 In a submission to the government of 9 October 1930. *Akten der Reichskanzlei. Weimarer Republik. Die Kabinette Brüning 1 u. II*, Vol. 1, Doc. 136.

72 Wilhelm Grottkop, 'Handelspolitische Möglichkeiten und Notwendigkeiten', p. 47.

73 On the complex of motives and implications see Gilbert Ziebura, *Weltwirtschaft und Weltpolitik 1922/24–1931* (Frankfurt am Main, 1984), pp. 157–67 and 217–18.

74 But the German delegation to the 1932 Lausanne Conference did concede that a collective system was more effective. See *Akten zur Deutschen Auswärtigen Politik 1918–1945*, Serie B, Vol. 20, Doc. 254, p. 543.
75 Ibid., Doc. 116, p. 254. This forced the Foregin Office to consider implementing the treaties within the wider context of a plan of European reconstruction (Doc. 203, p. 446).
76 Kaiser, *Economic Diplomacy and the Origins of the Second World War*, pp. 73–6. On Hans Posse see Eckart Teichert, *Autarkie und Grosraumwirtschaft in Deutschland 1930–1939* (Munich, 1984).
77 Ibid., pp. 114–15.
78 The Embassy in Washington had advised that this was not really necessary since exchange controls allowed Germany to discriminate without formally renouncing the principle. Hans-Jürgen Schröder, *Deutschland und die Vereinigten Staaten 1933–1939* (Wiesbaden, 1970), pp. 161–2.
79 Kaiser, *Economic Diplomacy and the Origins of the Second World War*, p. 134 and Alan. S. Milward, 'The Reichsmark Bloc and the International Economy', in Gerhard Hirschfeld and Lothar Kettenacker (eds), *The 'Führer State': Myth and Reality* (Stuttgart, 1981), p. 393.
80 Poland was not included in the Reichsmark bloc of countries linked to Germany through clearing agreements, nor was Czechoslovakia. On the other hand Turkey and Greece were.
81 Kaiser, *Economic Diplomacy and the Origins of the Second World War*, p. 142.
82 Ibid., p. 141.
83 Ibid., p. 45.
84 Ibid., pp. 162–5.
85 Ibid., p. 271.
86 Quoted in ibid., p. 272.
87 Alfred Kube, 'Aussenpolitk und "Grossraumwirtschaft". Die Deutsche Politik zur Wirtschaftlichen Integration Südosteuropas 1933 bis 1939', in Helmut Berding (ed.), *Wirtschaftliche und politische integration in Europa im 19. und 20. Jahrhundert* (Göttingen, 1984), pp. 188–200.
88 Hans-Erich Volkmann, 'Die NS-Wirtschaft in Vorbereitung des Krieges', in Wilhelem Deist *et. al.* (eds), *Das Deutsche Reich und der Zweite Weltkrieg*, Vol. 1 (Stuttgart, 1979), pp. 355–6.
89 F. Eulenburg, 'Gegen die Idee einer europäischen Zollunion', in Hans Heiman (ed.), *Europäische Zollunion* (Berlin, 1926), p. 116.
90 Alan. S. Milward, 'The Reichsmark Bloc and the International Economy', p. 403.
91 Kaiser *Economic Diplomacy and the Origins of the Second World War*, p. 268 and Volkmann, 'Die NS-Wirtschaft in Vorbereitung des Krieges', p. 343.
92 Hans-Erich Volkmann, 'NS-Aussenhandel im "geschlossenen" Kriegswirtschaftsraum (1939–1941)' in Friedrich Forstmeier and Hans-Erich Volkmann (eds), *Kriegswirtschaft und Rüstung 1939–1945* (Düsseldorf, 1977), p. 109.
93 Alan. S. Milward, 'The Reichsmark Bloc and the International Economy' takes issue with claims that the Reichsmark bloc entailed exploitation of the South East European states and that it impaired their industrialization. But see also the reply by Bernd-Jürgen Wendt, 'Südosteuropa in der nationalsozialistischen Grossraumwirtschaft', in Hirschfeld and Kettenacker (eds) *The 'Führer State'*, pp. 414–28.
94 Alan. S. Milward, 'The Reichsmark Bloc and the International Economy', pp. 386–8.

95 Hantos, *Die handelspolitik in Mitteleuropa*, p. 90. His assumption that a customs union would require a common legislature probably arose from the existence of the *Zollparlament* in the German *Zollverein*.

Chapter 4

# Britain and East Central Europe 1918–48

## *Alan J. Foster*

The greatest single consequence of the Versailles peace settlement was the emergence, or the re-emergence, of an independent East Central Europe, an independent East Central Europe with a resurrected Poland at its heart.[1] This political outcome had in no sense been among Britain's declared or undeclared war aims upon her initial entry into the war in August 1914. At that stage her objectives had been of a much more generalized character consistent with the traditions of her foreign policy, though the precise *casus belli* had been provided by German infringement of Belgian neutrality.

The essence of that foreign-policy tradition lay in Britain's commitment to the preservation of the balance of power on the European continent. It was therefore an axiom of British policy that she must resist at all costs the predominance on that continent of any single power, whether it be the Spain of Philip ll, the France of Louis XIV or Napoleon, or indeed the Germany of Kaiser William ll. In doing this Britain acted out of self-interest but it was part of her self-image to see herself as acting out of something more than simply that. She alone of the Great Powers had no territorial ambitions on the European continent. As the greatest trading nation in the world she had a vested interest in peace. Alone of the great European powers she dispensed with military conscription – even in wartime. In maintaining the balance of power she was helping to preserve the liberties of the peoples and states of Europe as well as her own. Of course there had always been some European observers unconvinced that this was quite the whole story. They had detected elements of disingenuity, if not hypocrisy in those foreign-policy traditions regarding the balance of power so freely invoked by British foreign secretaries. While the British might insist on a military land balance of power on the European continent, they had never had the slightest intention of allowing an equivalent naval balance of power at sea and therefore in the wider world beyond Europe. Indeed, they had traditionally insisted on an imbalance of power at sea and when occasion demanded it ruthlessly asserted their own naval predominance as vital to their strategic security, their imperial responsibilities and their commercial activities. It had been Germany's apparent challenge to this insistence on absolute naval mastery, after all, that had, more than any other single factor, set Britain and

Germany on a collision course long before August 1914. This in turn meant that in the supreme crisis of August 1914 Britain could not stand aside and watch France be defeated.

In this sense therefore the emergence of an independent Eastern Europe had been originally neither planned nor intended. It would come about under the natural dynamics of war itself, as Britain and her allies came in time to see in the doctrine of national self-determination a potentially powerful weapon available for employment against the Central powers. Moreover, that doctrine had the added attraction that it exercised an especially strong appeal to the American mind. In the event, the simultaneous collapse at the end of the war of the three Empires of East Central Europe removed at a stroke those powers which, in concert and in competition, had historically suppressed the national aspirations of the peoples of that region. This was not a scenario that anybody could have confidently predicted in 1914.

An independent East Central Europe became therefore a cardinal feature of the Versailles peace settlement of 1919. Unfortunately for the states and peoples of that region no international peace settlement in history would suffer such a rapid erosion of support among the powers that had fashioned it. This would be particularly true of Britain. In a remarkably short space of time, substantial and influential sections of British public opinion would grow increasingly disenchanted with what had been done in its name in Versailles, both on grounds of natural justice and on grounds of political realism. As the popular indictment of Versailles lengthened, so revisionist sentiment in this country strengthened. That indictment rested on a number of counts. In the first place, once the immediate passions of war cooled, doubts grew about the wisdom of the 'war guilt' clause of the Versailles treaty in circumstances where Germany was no longer seen as solely and uniquely responsible for the coming of the war. Moreover, to echo Edmund Burke, how did one draw up the indictment of a whole nation? Second, and more substantially, many of the territorial and colonial adjustments brought about by the treaty were now seen as punitive and manifestly unfair to Germany. Third, the financial provisions of the treaty, particularly those relative to reparations, came increasingly to be perceived as obstacles not only to the economic recovery of Germany but to the economic reconstruction of Europe more widely. Finally, though the disarmament provisions of the treaty in regard to Germany in themselves caused little unease, they nonetheless, in the circumstances in which they operated, contributed to the general disenchantment with the settlement, as the victors of 1919, France in particular, showed little inclination to follow where Germany had been forced to lead.

However, the general indictment of the Versailles settlement is not the direct concern of this chapter. Its direct concerns are the implications of that indictment for British policy and attitudes towards interwar East Central Europe; and it is to these that we now turn.

The Versailles settlement had originally been constructed on the understanding that it would be underpinned by a global framework of collective security to be provided by the League of Nations. This understanding was itself demolished when the United States Senate repudiated the handiwork of its own President, the chief architect of the settlement, and returned America to isolationism. The absence from the League of others among the Great Powers further undermined the credibility of the League. As the inadequacies of the League as a security system became only too readily apparent throughout the 1920s, the policy-makers of the various states, including Great Britain, began to take independent action to satisfy their security requirements. In the British case this action culminated in the Locarno accords of 1925. These accords symbolized both the extent and the limitations of Britain's commitment both to the Versailles settlement and to European security more generally. They also set the pattern for all interwar British governments until the eve of the Second World War itself. In essence they were a declaration of a policy of limited liability on the European continent. Interwar British governments were prepared, acting in concert with others, to guarantee the West European frontiers established at Versailles. What no British government was prepared to do was to guarantee those East European frontiers similarly established. Locarno symbolized therefore the ambivalence of the British attitude towards the Versailles settlement and signalled to the rest of the world that His Majesty's Government would not necessarily oppose the revision of the Versailles settlement in Eastern Europe, provided that this were done, if it were to be done at all, by peaceful means and with the free agreement of all interested parties. The Locarno accords effectively created two classes of frontiers in Europe: those that were recognized by all concerned as fully legitimate, and those that were seen as, if not the bastard children of Versailles, at least as being of doubtful parentage.

British reservations about the Versailles settlement in East Central Europe tended to be reinforced rather than relaxed as the years passed. At Versailles an attempt had been made to reconstruct East Central Europe on the basis of the twin principles of national self-determination and representative government, reflecting in large part the belief, in particular the American belief, that in these two democratic doctrines lay the keys to a permanent peace in Europe. In practice however this attempt had been deeply flawed in its application. Most conspicuously the doctrine of national self-determination in particular had been constrained and modified when its full logical application was perceived to be damaging to the security interests of the Western powers and their new Eastern European friends and allies and advantageous to the German nation. In this matter we touch upon one of the great dilemmas that faced the victorious allies at Versailles: that any scrupulous application of the doctrine of national self-determination in East Central Europe inevitably confirms German predominance in that region, given the realities of demography and geography. As the immediate passions inflamed by the war cooled, interwar British governments steadily grew to accept those realities of power and influence in East Central Europe that the Versailles settlement had originally sought to disguise and frustrate.

British unease about the wisdom of the Versailles settlement in that region, however, extended well beyond simply this example of the discriminatory treatment of a defeated Germany and was altogether more systematic in character.

In British eyes the Versailles settlement had been based on a whole series of illusions. The first was that tranquillity in Europe could be secured by the general extension of representative democracy. In fact postwar experience had confirmed the wisdom of Mill's conclusion of a century earlier that a high level of cultural and economic development was an essential prerequisite for the successful operation of representative institutions. Of nowhere had this proved more true than Eastern Europe. Events had demonstrated that one could not transplant parliamentary institutions native to Western Europe and confidently expect them to flourish in the thin, stony soil of Eastern Europe. Here we should recollect that, long before Hitler's rise to power in Germany, representative government had largely disappeared throughout Eastern Europe, Czechoslovakia apart, to be replaced by varied forms of political authoritarianism.

As for the doctrine of national self-determination, far from proving to be a formula for peace in East Central Europe, it had proved instead to be a recipe for permanent turmoil, given the racial confusion of the region. At Versailles, in part becaue of this ethnic complexity, and in part because of the need to balance ethnic considerations against strategic and economic considerations, all kinds of compromises had had to be made by the map-makers in their construction of the new Europe. Whatever the intentions of the architects of the newly independent states of East Central Europe, the results were, from a British perspective, clear to see. The whole region was torn by irredentist conflicts and separatist and autonomist movements. The chief consequence of this was that, far from a newly emancipated East Central Europe making a contribution towards a wider European stability, as had been hoped in 1919, East Central Europe had become in itself a new fault-zone. Relations between the successor states of that area were, if anything, even more poisonous than those that had obtained between the old empires of the region: relations that in the end had resulted in the catastrophe of 1914. Indeed, it would be Hitler's skill in exploiting these rivalries that would lead to many of his diplomatic triumphs after 1933.

This last reflection brings us in turn to a further consideration that would prove to be a factor in shaping British disenchantment with the Versailles settlement. That settlement had been fashioned without the participation, for differing reasons, of either of the 'natural' great powers of East Central Europe, Germany and Russia, and consequently had largely ignored their interests, including their legitimate interests, as Great Powers. As these two powers stabilized and then gradually recovered their natural strengths, could a settlement that had ignored the interests of both be reasonably expected to endure? If not, this would raise for British policy-makers one simple question. Whose predominance in Eastern Europe, Germany's or Russia's, could be deemed as least threatening to Britain's own interests? There could only be one answer to this question for interwar Conservative governments. As Germany revived so the expansion of German influence in Eastern Europe must be accepted. Indeed, in so far as it provided a natural barrier to the growth of Soviet influence, it should be welcomed, as long that is as German penetration of the region confined itself to the use of diplomatic, political and economic leverage.

Given intelligent restraint and patience on the part of Germany, there were therefore no reasons why Britain and Germany should find themselves on a collision course in Eastern Europe. In her security arrangements Britain had made the sharpest of distinctions between Western and Eastern Europe. It became axiomatic to her foreign policy between the wars that all British governments must avoid any security commitments in Eastern Europe in peacetime. It was also axiomatic that she would not allow France to commit her by proxy in that region. There would be much talk in the late 1920s and early 1930s of an 'Eastern Locarno', none of which received any support from London. For British policy-makers, Locarno had been the last step in this country's acceptance of a continental commitment, not the first step in a grander design, as some continental observers had hoped. Moreover even after signing the Locarno accords, Britain had not entered into any staff talks with the French nor had her defence planners altered their assessment of her strategic responsibilities. 'Never again' remained basic to British thinking on Europe. Accordingly, no plans were laid down for the dispatch of a major land army to fight a continental war.[2] That being so, it was doubly the case that Britain had no intention at all of getting involved in any entanglements in Eastern Europe that might eventually lead her into war. Her defence priorities were first, the defence of India and the empire, second came home defence, and third the defence of Western Europe. This order reflected her assessment of her vital interests. Eastern European security did not figure amongst them. In addition, British policy-makers saw many of the problems of Eastern Europe, particularly those raised by the doctrine of national self-determination, as intractable to the point of insolubility. Given the fact that Eastern Europe was not seen as vital to Britain's own security; the fact that there was no significant pressure from British public opinion to extend our obligations into that region; and the fact that any solution to its complex and numerous problems was seen to lie beyond our political wisdom to remedy, and beyond our material and military resources to influence decisively, Britain's policy of limited liability on the European continent made obvious sense to the foreign-policy community.

Indeed the support for that policy extended far beyond that narrow élite to tap a virtual consensus of national opinion. A mere handful of MPs had voted in the Commons against the Locarno accords and rarely can a British Foreign Secretary have enjoyed such a flattering press as that accorded to Austen Chamberlain after his Locarno triumph. It is instructive to register where the few notes of criticism came from. Much the loudest emanated from the Beaverbrook press, faithful as ever to that press peer's commitment to complete isolationism. Their indictment of Chamberlain therefore was not that he had made too few security commitments in Europe but that he had already made too many. In its sustained though abortive campaign against Locarno the Beaverbrook press found itself in a position of virtual isolation in Fleet Street. The sole exception to this generalization was provided by the *Workers Weekly* – the predecessor of the *Daily Worker.*[3] This newspaper's objections to Locarno were somewhat different from those entertained by the *Express* group. The newspaper saw in Chamberlain's diplomacy little more than an attempt to divert Germany's revisionist and expansionist energies to the east in a Machiavellian ploy intended to embroil her with the Soviet Union.

All that has been said hitherto in this chapter about the way in which Britain came to reserve her position on the Versailles settlement in Eastern Europe and to signal to the rest of Europe that she at least did not regard that settlement as in all circumstances sacrosanct has been predicated on one condition – the condition that German policy-makers were intelligent and patient enough not to resort to force or to the threat of force. At one stroke Hitler's accession to the German Chancellorship in 1933 nullified this presumption that Germany could be relied upon to continue to act 'reasonably' in international affairs, either in Eastern Europe or indeed in Western Europe. What was likely to be the British reaction should the new Germany decide to act unilaterally in repudiation of the Versailles settlement? What would be the reaction of Britain if Hitler used, or threatened the use of, force? Europe did not have to wait long to receive an answer to these questions. According to *The Times,* the rise of Hitler placed Europe in the dilemma of having to yield to extremism what had been denied to moderation. That Europe must do the right thing, albeit for the wrong reason, and yield, that newspaper had no doubt.[4] The history of the next few years could be seen as a melancholy commentary on *The Times'* prescription as the Western powers responded to each of Hitler's sudden initiatives with impotence. This humiliating retreat under the impact of a whole series of unilateral moves by Germany would only come to an end in March 1939 when German troops occupied the rump Czech state in clear breach of the Munich Agreement. Hitherto, the principle of national self-determination had provided some modest cover for the German dictator's arbitrary conduct. The incorporation effectively on 15 March 1939 within the *Reich* of manifestly non-German territory and people removed this cover.

These events produced a revolution in British foreign policy, a revolution that found expression in Neville Chamberlain's declaration of the British guarantee to Poland on 31 March. Hitler's brutal suppression of Czech independence caused the British government to do what all previous interwar British governments had been adamant in opposing, when it extended a security commitment to Warsaw, the first in a series to be offered throughout Eastern Europe. For the first time a British government accepted, what had traditionally been the position of France and her Eastern allies: that West European and East European security were intimately linked.

In many ways Poland was an unlikely candidate as Britain's first ally in Eastern Europe. Militarist and authoritarian in political character, Catholic in

religious persuasion, strongly nationalist in character despite her many and substantial minorities, Poland had rarely previously been, from a British perspective,
the most helpful of partners in international affairs. Indeed, practically from the
first moments of her resurrection as a state she had alienated important sections
of British opinion. At the time of the destruction of that state Molotov would
refer to Poland as that 'monstrous bastard of Versailles' and Stalin would call it
'pardon the expression, a state' but, as Norman Davies has pointed out, these
ugly attitudes were to some degree prefigured in London twenty years earlier.
At that time it was Keynes who would dismiss the new Poland as 'an economic
impossibility whose only industry is Jew-baiting', E. H. Carr who described that
state's resurrection as 'a farce', Lloyd George who discounted Poland as 'an
historic failure' and Lewis Namier who characterized Poland's condition as
'pathological', whilst at the same time warning British policy-makers that Polish
imperialism was a greater threat to European recovery than Bolshevism.[5] This
unforgiving and uncharitable attitude towards a state which, whatever its short-
comings, might surely more fairly be seen as, historically, more sinned against
than sinning, set the pattern for the future. The myth that TUC industrial action
frustrated British government plans to offer military aid to Poland when the
fortunes of war turned against Poland in her struggle against Bolshevik Russia
has proved obstinate. The truth is that as far as Lloyd George was concerned
the trade unionists were pushing against an open door. And according to newspapers like Beaverbrook's *Sunday Express,* Poland was 'the mad dog of Europe
and she must be chained up'.[6]

   A few years later, when the Locarno accords were receiving a rapturous reception in the House of Commons, Poland was perceived in some quarters as
having conducted an unsuccessful wrecking operation against this major triumph of European appeasement despite Austen Chamberlain's perfunctory
tribute to the constructive role played by Polish diplomacy at Geneva and elsewhere. Lloyd George spoke for others as well as himself when, brushing aside
these normal hypocrisies of diplomacy, he roundly denounced the obstructive
role played by Poland, 'that possessor of five Alsace Lorraines'.[7] As for the Poles
themselves they drew their own conclusions about the implications of Locarno
in regard to the signals that London was sending to Berlin. They also drew their
own conclusions about the reliability of their French allies when those allies
were forced to choose between London and France's Eastern European allies,
particularly the most faithful of them. Poland would have to look to her own
salvation in future in a dangerous world.

   In the meantime she found herself in the late 1920s and early 1930s, after
German admission to the League, repeatedly in the dock at Geneva because of
her treatment of her German minority. In this matter she found that she
received little sympathy or understanding from London in the face of a
skilful propaganda campaign conducted from Berlin and even less support from
the London press. Poland compounded these difficulties with London by her
campaign for a seat on the Council of the League as a balance for accepting

Germany's admission. However, Poland's German minority was only one of her many minorities and by no means the most substantial. In 1930 serious disturbances broke out in the Polish Ukraine in reaction against Polish policies of assimilation. Polish counter measures of police and military pacification of the disaffected areas attracted widespread Western comment, little of which was sympathetic to Warsaw. The local correspondent of the *Manchester Guardian* denounced the 'Polish terror in the Ukraine' as 'worse than anything that is happening anywhere else in Europe' while in London *TheTimes* more soberly referred to 'a sharp and unpleasant reminder of one of the few latent wars that continue to be waged by a wholly submerged nationality. The conflict is between the Poles who are sovereign and the Ukrainians or Ruthenians who are subject'.[8] To add to the irritable condition of Anglo-Polish relations, largely owing to the pressure of British public opinion on the issue, the case of Eastern Galicia was brought before the Council of the League in January 1931, under the minorities' provisions of the League Charter. However, so weak was the resolution adopted on the matter by the Council and so ill-equipped was the League for decisive intervention in such matters, that this initiative proved on the whole counter-productive. The Poles were alienated, the Ukrainians were not effectively helped and Anglo-Polish relations cooled further.

This expression of League impotence was not lost on the Poles. More seriously, the wider impotence of the Western powers was not lost upon the Poles when Hitler's accession to the German Chancellorship in 1933 was met with inaction from London and Paris. Clearly, if Poland were to save herself, it would only be by independent action. Moreover, dangerous times called for dangerous remedies. Thus an astonished Europe came to witness the strange spectacle of the Poles, the single greatest beneficiary of the Versailles settlement, becoming the first European state to seek successfully, by the Treaty of Non-Aggression of January 1934, a diplomatic accommodation with the new Germany, whose Chancellor had built his whole political career on a pledge to undo the Versailles settlement. From the British perspective the Poles were acting with reckless opportunism that might well prove suicidal. As for the Poles themselves, they then proceeded to compound their sins by denouncing in September 1934 the Minorities Treaties of the Versailles settlement. According to the Polish delegate at Geneva, these constituted an intolerable limitation on Poland's sovereignty and independence, providing an unacceptable pretext for all kinds of outside interventions.

This cynical behaviour on Poland's part won her few friends in Paris or London but it did mean that for the next five years any differences that Poland traditionally had had with Germany disappeared from the international agenda and from the headlines of the world's press. Yet in a number of ways the Poles would continue to damage their standing in London and reinforce Britain's tendency to detach herself from the affairs of Eastern Europe.

In Poland there resided the biggest Jewish settlement in Europe. Certain sections of Polish society and Polish life had long been disfigured by anti-semitism. However, with the passing of Pilsudski, Polish Jews lost a Polish leader many of them regarded as a protector. His successors introduced measures of official discrimination against the Jews in the professions and in education, thus further alienating liberal opinion in England. These measures also served to cool further official relations between the British and Polish governments because of their wider international implications.

In the 1920s the major single source of Jewish immigration into Palestine had been Poland. Most of the early Zionist leaders were from those lands now incorporated in Poland. Perhaps surprisingly, this pattern would remain the same in the early years of the Nazi revolution. In the period 1932–5 total Jewish immigrants into Palestine numbered 134,000. Exiles and refugees from Germany (where Nazi policy encouraged the process) made up less than one eighth of this total whilst 43 per cent of the new settlers came from Poland.[9] Most of this Jewish immigration into Palestine from Poland was economic in inspiration as the already miserable conditions for the Jewish masses in Poland further deteriorated under the impact of the great depression. Yet whatever its source, the scale of this immigration (which the Polish authorities encouraged) served only to excite Arab fears of being reduced to minority status in their native land. These fears exploded in the Arab rising of 1936. Having put down the rising the British quickly moved to introduce stringent new immigration controls. As general war in Europe threatened, so the negotiating hand of the Zionists weakened, as considerations of realpolitik increasingly dictated British policy. Jewish support against Hitler's Germany could be taken for granted given the character of the regime. Arab support had to be won and kept. The 1939 White Paper on Palestine which so outraged Zionist opinion was the result of this unsentimental calculation of the realities of power.

In these fevered circumstances it was only too natural that British policy-makers should look with disfavour on any regime that added to Britain's own problems, like that of the Polish colonels, by introducing anti-semitic regulations.[10] Nor was it surprising that committed pro-Zionist newspapers like the *Manchester Guardian* and the *News Chronicle* should be deeply critical of Poland's conduct.

However, Poland's standing with British opinion would probably reach its nadir over Czechoslovakia in 1938. When, in an exercise in jackal diplomacy, after Hitler's dismemberment of the Czech state, the Poles seized the bone of the Teschen that the German leader had contemptuously thrown them, Poland seemed to have lost its soul. Of this episode Churchill would later write that it had been a painful reminder to Poland's friends that there had in fact always been two Polands, that she had been 'Glorious, in revolt and ruin : squalid and shameful in triumph. The bravest of the brave, too often led by the vilest of the vile … one (Poland) struggling to preach the truth, the other grovelling in villainy'.[11] During Czechoslovakia's hour of trial the Foreign Minister, Colonel Jozef Beck, had organized a propaganda campaign in the Polish press about the sufferings of the Polish minority in the Teschen and then followed this up by concentrating Polish troops on the Czech frontier. At the Council of the League the Polish delegate had ostentatiously read a newspaper while Halifax and Litvinov were speaking on the Czech crisis. In March 1938 Beck had already demonstrated his conversion to the new diplomacy by issuing an ultimatum to Lithuania compelling that state to resume full diplomatic relations with Poland under the threat of military action. In the words of the historian of the League of Nations, Poland had 'made its full contribution to the deterioration of the general situation of Europe' and in doing so, the regime of the colonels had 'vied with Hitler and Mussolini in its contempt for the League'.[12]

Yet, to repeat, this would be the state that only a few months later would be the improbable beneficiary of a diplomatic revolution in Britain's position on Eastern Europe, following a British reassessment of Germany's ultimate foreign-policy intentions. This new reading suggested that what Hitler sought extended beyond a legitimate German predominance in Eastern Europe to continental mastery and, perhaps, to world power, aims that could only be achieved by methods of force and the threat of force. Such aims Britain was bound to oppose.

That the Polish Guarantee represented a revolution in British foreign policy there can be no doubt. When the then new Polish Ambassador, Raczynski, had first arrived in London (for his second spell) in 1934 he had found Anglo-Polish relations 'correct but cool' but despite great personal efforts had experienced no success at all in trying to convince British ministers that the security of Western Europe was intimately and inextricably bound up with the security of Eastern Europe.[13] Overnight this fundamental principle had now been conceded. Nevertheless, this fundamental revolution in British foreign policy should not blind us to the fact that this revolution was far from being total. Important elements of continuity remained and would continue to remain in British policy towards East Central Europe, as *The Times* would point out in a provocative leader on the morrow of Chamberlain's sensational statement.[14] What Britain was guaranteeing was the 'independence' of Poland not, by implication, that country's territorial integrity. The same tacit qualification would subsequently apply to the guarantees that Britain would extend to Romania and Greece. And in due course the same qualification would find its way into the formal Anglo-Polish Treaty of Mutual Security of 25 August 1939. Unusually, among treaties of mutual security, this treaty's varied clauses, open and secret, would make no reference at all to the territorial integrity of either contracting party. These qualifications are eloquent in what they tell us about the continuities that persisted in Britain's European policy: namely, that she had no intention of guaranteeing in all its particulars the Versailles settlement in Eastern Europe. In a word, in the immediate crisis of March 1939, Chamberlain was signalling that he still looked forward to a time when more reasonable men prevailed in Berlin and less obstinate ones ruled in Warsaw. As *The Times* had put it in its controversial leader of 1 April 1939, on the Prime Minister's statement:

> The Prime Minister's statement ... was one in which every word
> counted. It should be read and re-read if its exact implications are to be
> appreciated correctly ... The new obligation which this country yesterday
> assumed does not bind Great Britain to defend every inch of the present
> frontiers of Poland. The key word in the statement is not 'integrity'
> but 'independence' ... Mr. Chamberlain's statement involves no blind
> acceptance of the status quo, his repeated references to free negotiation
> imply there are problems in which adjustments are still necessary ... The
> relative strength of nations will always and rightly be an important con-
> sideration in diplomacy ... This country has never been an advocate of the
> encirclement of Germany, and is not now opposed to the extension of
> Germany's economic activities and influence, nor to the constructive
> work she may do for Europe. Germany is admittedly bound to be the
> most powerful continental state.

Though Chamberlain deftly distanced himself from the storm of protest that this
leader produced in the anti-appeasement press and in Parliament, he contrived,
by clever footwork, to do so without actually repudiating the substance of what
*The Times* was actually saying about the new course of British foreign policy.
This was just as well because *The Times'* gloss on his statement had in fact been
inspired from the very highest quarters.[15] *The Times* had in fact got the matter
exactly right.

In any analysis of the evolution of British policy towards East Central Europe
this point merits emphasis, for careless talk of Britain having guaranteed in 1939
Polish independence *and* Polish territorial integrity would tend to recur later in
circumstances where the Polish authorities themselves might not, for very understandable reasons, see it as their most pressing responsibility to educate public
opinion in this matter. Yet what is important in this context to stress remains this
central point: that Britain did not go to war in 1939 simply to restore the *status
quo ante bellum* in Eastern Europe for the very good reason that, even after she
had lost patience with Hitler, she continued to view the Versailles settlement as
inherently unstable. As Chamberlain himself would constantly remind his listen-
ers, Britain would go to war to maintain a very different principle: the principle
that any changes that might come about in East Central Europe must come
about only on the basis of freely negotiated changes between all interested parties. As for Britain herself her spokesmen would repeat, once battle was joined
with Germany, that she had no intention of recognizing any frontier changes in
Europe that were the result of war or the threat of force. These were the
grounds on which Chamberlain's Cabinet brushed aside Hitler's peace offensive
of November 1939.

This would remain in essence Britain's position on Eastern European changes
in the first phase of the war. However, Russia's entry into the war in June 1941
introduced an entirely new dimension into affairs and it is to this we now turn.
British policy towards East Central Europe in the interwar period had been

based, as we have seen, on a number of principles. In the first place she accepted that some at least of Germany's grievances over Versailles were legitimate. Second, she accepted Germany's right to seek redress for these grievances, so long as this was done peacefully. Third, she committed herself to the preservation of the Versailles territorial settlement in Western Europe. Fourth, she opposed any attempts to encircle Germany in the east by a system of alliances as favoured by her close ally France. Fifth, she accepted that ultimately, Germany – preferably a democratic Germany but if needs be an authoritarian Germany, would necessarily play the leading role in East Central Europe as German power revived. All this was, however, based upon one, usually unspoken, further assumption: the exclusion, or self-exclusion of the Soviet Union from European affairs, an assumption, that is, that the Soviet Union as a pariah state could never be converted into a constructive force in the management of European affairs. It remains of interest that interwar British governments in contrast never quite lost hope that Hitler's Germany, with a little sympathy and some indulgence, might be rehabilitated so as to become such a force.

Within weeks of Russian entry into the war the Soviet Union was pressing Britain to recognize her 1941 frontiers, frontiers that is which reflected Stalin's gains under the secret protocol of the Molotov-Ribbentrop Pact, and incorporated in the Soviet Union the former eastern provinces of Britain's ally, Poland. Initially this pressure was resisted but by the spring of 1942 Churchill, desperate to keep a beleaguered Russia in the war, was tempted to concede recognition and was saved from doing so only by the clear American policy of reserving all such matters for decision at the envisaged postwar peace conference.

Nonetheless these events set the pattern for the future. As the Red Army first contained the German onslaught and then began the long and painful process of rolling back the *Wehrmacht*, so, with every step the Russian forces took towards Poland, Soviet pressure on London to concede the frontiers of 1941 mounted. Ultimately, this pressure was to succeed though the real 'betrayal' of Poland would actually come at Teheran not at Yalta as mythology still suggests.[16] This pressure raised for the British government the whole question of the nature of its obligations to Poland, together with the wider issue of the proper role that it saw Russia as playing in a postwar Europe where, once victory was achieved, there could be no question of simply excluding her as before.

When Chamberlain had made his dramatic declaration of the Polish Guarantee in March 1939 all eyes had been on Germany for it was from that direction that all immediate danger to the Polish state came. In the following months it had been a main objective of British policy to bring the Soviet Union itself into an association with both Britain and Poland in the construction of a system of collective security against Germany. Despite, therefore, the fact that Chamberlain's words appeared to indicate that Britain was extending a comprehensive and unilateral guarantee of Poland against all comers, no alert mind on the Commons backbenches, nor any sharp pen in Fleet Street, had thought to ask the question as to whether the guarantee also applied in the case of Russian aggression against Poland – not a purely academic question as history might suggest.

One reason why Chamberlain had not named Germany as the potential aggressor in March 1939 – and one reason why the published clauses of the Anglo-Polish Treaty of Mutual Security of 25 August 1939 maintained the same discretion – was out of deference to German sensibilities. However, at all times it was made clear to the Poles in negotiations that the British Guarantee applied to the case of German aggression against Poland and German aggression alone. In the spring and summer of 1939 nobody saw the Soviet Union as a potential threat to Poland in any immediate sense, as all eyes were on Berlin. Indeed, the Soviet Union was being courted as a potential ally by the Western powers. When the Anglo-Polish Treaty was eventually ready for signature in late August, the international situation had indeed been transformed by the sensational news of the Molotov-Ribbentrop Pact and Russia was no longer seen as a potential ally. This in no way changed the British position. They had no intention of guaranteeing Polish independence against both German and Russian aggression and so the fact that the British Guarantee applied only in the case of German aggression was written into the secret protocol of the treaty. However, it was written into the secret protocol in circumstances where nobody in London appears to have anticipated that the whole matter might soon become a public issue. For, however deplorable Stalin's conduct had become from the British perspective, nobody suspected that he would actually join Hitler in aggression against Poland.

In the spring and summer of 1939 some of Chamberlain's critics had condemned the Prime Minister for his 'recklessness' in guaranteeing Poland against Germany. Reckless Chamberlain may or may not have been on this occasion. Yet no British Prime Minister would have been so reckless as to guarantee Polish independence against both Germany and Russia, the two natural Great Powers of Eastern Europe. Moreover, Britain had long harboured doubts about Poland's title deeds to her eastern provinces. These, it will be recollected, lacked even the flawed legitimacy bestowed by the Versailles settlement, being the result of the Russo-Polish war and the subsequent Treaty of Riga.

On 17 September 1939 Soviet troops crossed the Polish frontier. The general public had no knowledge of the secret protocol of the Anglo-Polish Treaty. As Britain had to all outward appearances given a general guarantee of Polish independence, did this new situation mean that Britain was contractually bound to declare war on Russia? The Foreign Office was circumspect. A statement issued on 19 September from there condemned the Soviet attack upon Poland and promised that Britain was pledged to fulfil all her obligations to Poland but no mention was made of what these obligations might or might not be with specific reference to Russia. This remarkably moderate statement was shorn of any threat to take any kind of action in retaliation against the Soviet Union, whether military, diplomatic or economic. More significantly there was no obvious public pressure by Polish officials on her Western allies to retaliate. All this might have suggested to the attentive student of international affairs that there was more, or rather less, to the British Guarantee to Poland than met the eye. In the face of this confusion the Foreign Office acted to clarify the position. A question was 'planted' in the Commons which allowed the Minister of State, R. A. But- ler, to tell the House on 20 October that 'During the negotiations which led to the Treaty between the Polish Government and H.M.G. it was agreed that aggression should only cover the case of aggression by Germany; and the Polish Government would confirm this.'[17] The truth of the matter was now in the open for all to read – including the Soviet Ambassador, Maisky. Whatever the moral position might be, Britain had no contractual obligations of any kind in strict international law to defend Polish independence, still less Polish territorial integrity, against Russia. When, some few years later, Britain, after Yalta, would release the secret protocol of the Anglo-Polish Treaty to the public, in defence against charges then widely circulating in London that Churchill had 'betrayed' Poland, this reading would be confirmed. Except, that is, in one particular. The Poles had very good grounds for arguing that Churchill had infringed the Treaty's provisions by entering into discussions and arrangements as to a revision of Poland's frontiers with any third party.

The exact nature and limitations of Britain's obligations to Poland have been dwelt upon at some little length in this chapter for a wider purpose. For, as the years passed, and as ultimate Allied victory became more assured, British policy- makers had to turn their minds to the question of the likely shape of a postwar Eastern Europe and to a reading of the Soviet Union's ultimate intentions in that region. As the Red Army steadily pushed back the German forces, the evidence of unilateral Soviet political moves in liberated areas would grow ever more alarming. Here the Polish example was particularly significant, for whatever Britain's contractual obligations to Poland Churchill always accepted that she had an overriding moral obligation to do all that she could for Poland. One problem in realizing this objective was the position of the Americans, so acutely sensitive was Roosevelt to the supposed danger of the Western powers even appearing to 'gang up' on the Soviet Union. Another problem was raised by the simple realities of power in military terms in Eastern Europe. There could be no disguising the fact, as the war years passed, that with the coming of the peace the Red Army would in effect be left in control of Eastern Europe. Given these realities of power in the region, what did British policy-makers hope to achieve for the region?

In the first place, as we have seen, at all times it was accepted that there could be no simple return to the Versailles settlement. It had never been a declared British war aim to restore the *status quo ante bellum* in East Central Europe. In British eyes that settlement had been inherently unstable. It had already been responsible for a second European war; if restored it would breed other wars. Second, what might be called the 'German option' was no longer acceptable. Germany had now demonstrated for a second time that her ambitions extended beyond a legitimate regional predominance in East Central

Europe to continental mastery and world power. There would be no third chance for her to show her maturity.

All this added up to one conclusion: Soviet leadership in postwar Eastern Europe must be freely accepted, if not welcomed. Yet what was meant by Soviet leadership? What was not meant by this term was what *The Times* meant by the term in those wartime leaders, the handiwork of E. H. Carr, that so frequently irritated the Foreign Office. In a private memorandum Carr would put these views forward even more ruthlessly. The key, according to this, to postwar tranquillity in Europe, was for Britain to concede to the Soviet Union immediately 'a free hand in Eastern Europe'.[18] For all kinds of reasons, not the least moral reasons, such an option was closed to any British government as an exercise in realpolitik.

What British policy-makers would try to achieve in the last years of war and the first years of peace was something very different in Eastern Europe. In the first place they sought to maintain the wartime harmony of the Allies and go further by putting an end to unilateral Soviet political moves. Second, they accepted the special sensitivity of Soviet security needs in the region as fully legitimate though they were unconvinced by the Soviet stipulation that what it had the right to require throughout Eastern Europe was a set of 'friendly' governments which excluded all 'fascist' elements, largely on the grounds that these terms were far too flexibly and arbitrarily employed by the Soviets as the Polish experience only too amply showed. To reassure the Russians in matters of security the British government exercised what influence it possessed to encourage the states of Eastern Europe to be 'realistic' about the necessity for accommodating Soviet security concerns in the postwar world. Thus the British hoped that what might be achieved might be something akin to a classical, if enlightened, 'sphere of influence' for Russia in Eastern Europe, though no such rude phrase could ever be used in the American presence. According to this model, in return for demonstrating their fundamental goodwill by aligning their defence and foreign policies with the perceived security needs of the Soviet Union, Russia, in return, might be prevailed upon to respect the right of the states of Eastern Europe to order their internal political arrangements as they themselves thought fit. In a word, what would obtain in postwar Eastern Europe would be a system of 'semi-sovereign', 'semi-independent' states, 'friendly' to Russia, as required, but not 'unfriendly' to the Western powers. The London Poles never believed that such a goal was ever attainable, not at least by those methods of appeasement that they judged Britain to be following. They took a much blacker view of Stalin's ultimate purposes in Eastern Europe and translated all the Russian talk about 'friendly governments' and 'fascist elements' as so much cover for the real Soviet agenda, that is, the communization of the whole region. The tendency of the Foreign Office and much outside British opinion was to put much of this down to the atavistic reflexes of the Poles, that most Russophobe of the slavic nations. In contrast, much more was expected of the Czechs, that most Russophile of slavic nations, the Bulgarians perhaps excepted. As the war moved to a close, and through into the first years of the peace, we find much praise of the 'realism' of Beneš and the Czechs in the Foreign Office documents and in the press. As often as not this is contrasted with the self-destructive 'romanticism' of the London Poles. It certainly helped the situation that Stalin harboured no sizeable territorial claims on Czech territory. Indeed, so accommodating to Soviet sensibilities would be Beneš and the Czechs in wartime London that, ironically, an element of irritation with the Czechs sometimes appears in the Foreign Office documentation. If the London Poles could be too obstinate and unbending where Russia was concerned, then the London Czechs on occasion could be too flexible and appeasing!

It is in this overall context that the Prague coup of February 1948 marks a turning point. In British eyes Beneš had done all that could possibly be reasonably required of him to reassure the Soviet Union that his government was a 'friendly' government towards the Soviet Union, and he had done more. Yet the Czech reward for this was to receive in the slightly longer run precisely the same treatment as the Poles. Beneš' only sin, but it clearly was deemed by the Russians to be a sin, was his attempt to maintain friendly, civilized relations with the Western powers. It was clearly going to be Stalin's policy henceforth not merely to circumscribe the freedom of movement enjoyed by the states of Eastern Europe in foreign affairs but also to dictate their form of internal political organization. The Cold War had begun.

## NOTES

1 Both 'East Central Europe' and 'Eastern Europe' are used in this chapter. The latter has been used where there was an implied contrast with the 'West'. Elsewhere 'East Central Europe' has been preferred.

2 On this see, inter alia, Brian Bond, *British Military Policy Between The Two World Wars* (Oxford, 1980), and Michael Howard, *The Continental Commitment* (London, 1972).

3 This would not be the first or indeed the last time that the Beaverbrook press would take a foreign policy line consistent with the security interests of the Soviet Union. For a more systematic treatment of this theme see my article, 'The Beaverbrook Press and Appeasement: The Second Phase', *European History Quarterly*, Vol. 21 (1991), pp. 5–38.

4 *The Times* (28 June 1933).

5 Norman Davies, 'Lloyd George and Poland', *Journal of Contemporary History*, Vol. 6 (1971).

6 *Sunday Express* (25 May 1920).

7 *The Times* (26 March 1925).

8 *Manchester Guardian* (14 October 1930); *The Times* (12 December 1930).

9 Alan Bullock, *Ernest Bevin, Foreign Secretary* (New York, 1983), p. 45.

10 The 'Government of the Colonels' was the name given to the regime after Pilsudski's death in 1935. As the name suggests, military figures, initially promoted under Pilsudski, played a prominent role in the regime. On the various factions see Jerzy Holzer, 'The Political Right in Poland', *Journal of Contemporary History*, Vol. 12 (1977), pp. 395–412.

11 W. S. Churchill, *The Gathering Storm* (Boston, 1948), p. 323.

12 F. P. Walters, *A History of the League of Nations* (London, 1960), p. 793.

13  Edward Raczinski, *In Allied London* (London, 1962), p. 1.

14  *The Times* (1 April 1939).

15  A. J. Foster, 'An Unequivocal Guarantee? Fleet Street and the British Guar-
    antee to Poland 31 March 1939', *Journal of Contemporary History*, Vol. 26
    (1991), pp. 33–47.

16  Keith Sainsbury, *The Turning Point* (London, 1985).

17  *Parliamentary Debates, The Commons*, Vol. 352, Col. 1082, 20 October.
    1939.

18  D. McLachlan, *In The Chair* (London, 1971), p. 222.

Chapter 5

# Reforging Mitteleuropa in the Crucible of War
## *The Economic Impact of Integration under German Hegemony*

## *Anthony McElligott*

I'm the last hope for Europe! The new Europe will not be created through parliamentary decisions, nor through discussions and resolutions, but solely through force.

(Adolf Hitler)[1]

INTRODUCTION

Surveying the European continent in 1945 after six years of Nazi domination, contemporaries concluded that it had been the 'costliest and most destructive war in history', leaving behind an audit of mass human and material destruction not seen in Europe since the Thirty Years' War.[2] The Germans, under Nazi leadership, had ravaged Europe. They had plundered, exploited and absorbed private business and enterprise and even whole economies.

In 1945 damage to European capital stock was extensive, production had fallen to around two-thirds of that of 1938, already a relatively sluggish level. Imbalances had appeared in the economic structures of most economies. The continental monetary systems were in chaos with rampant inflation, trade and investment had been severely distorted and national and intra–European transport and communications were severely disrupted as a result of destruction and stock depreciation, notably in Central Europe and in the Balkans.[3]

If the task of material reconstruction was a daunting one, as US Secretary of State Edward Stettinius acknowledged at the time,[4] the task of social reconstruction appeared even more awesome. The death toll stood at over fifty million with millions more wounded; civilian populations were displaced and millions on the move; all were considerably weakened through hunger and disease. Social discontent was high, while the likes of Harry Lime, the black marketeer and petty gangster in Carol Reed's film, *The Third Man*, set in post-war Vienna, was a real, commonplace figure in Europe's towns and cities.[5]

But little more than ten years later, the bleak assessment of Europe in 1945 was substantially modified. Arnold Toynbee, in the introduction to the volume of *Survey of International Affairs*, published in 1955 and dealing with post-war Europe, described the Nazi New Order as the 'Sole, but signal, constructive achievement' of the regime.

> Hitler's forcible military, political, and economic unification of Europe had been a practical answer to Europe's most pressing need; and, though Hitler's brutal way of solving Europe's problem had been made odious to the reluctant beneficiaries by the acts of aggression through which it had been achieved, the methods of barbarism by which it had been enforced, and the selfish German national purposes for which it had been exploited, it was nevertheless, a grave misfortune for Europe that part of the price for her release from German tyranny should have been the loss of the one great benefit that this tyranny had brought with it.[6]

Toynbee was writing in the context of a divided Cold War Europe. It is striking, nonetheless, that he should have implied that somehow an economically integrated Europe under the Germans had been both a feasible and positive aim, if not in the means employed.

This acceptance of a Germanocentric economic Mitteleuropa, was not unusual, indeed, it was widely shared both during and after the war. Doreen Warriner, in a pamphlet published for the Fabian Society in 1940, wrote of the 'inevitablity' of Germany's economic pull upon the economies of Eastern Europe. She called for a federation of industrial and agrarian Europe under Anglo-German leadership.[7] This was a view held even by erstwhile collaborators in occupied Europe, who saw in economic integration, the possibility of a national rebirth, in spite of their recent experience.[8] At the end of the war, Robert Machray, an expert on Central and Eastern Europe wrote in a similar vein.[9] And one anonymous author went so far as to replicate Nazi dreams of German-dominated Mitteleuropa in an article published in the influential journal *International Affairs*. [10]

These writers, and subsequently a considerable number of authors on the subject, start from the premise that between the incorporation of Austria in March 1938 and the fall of Berlin in the spring of 1945, the Nazis embarked on a coherent policy of integration of the European economies based on the idea of Mitteleuropa in what has been called the New Order; that they were deflected from their path of pursuing a mitteleuropäisch New Order by the strains imposed by war, especially after the failure of Blitzkrieg in the Russian campaign and the German débâcle at Stalingrad.[11] However, a radically different argument is that the Nazi attempt to reforge Mitteleuropa was doomed to fail on its own terms. Not least because it was a mass of contradictions as well as a smokescreen for nationalist aggressive exploitation, which would inevitably meet with resistance.[12] Taking the two positions outlined here as a framework for discussion, this chapter will explore the Nazi attempt to reforge Mitteleuropa in the crucible of war.

REFORGING MITTELEUROPA IN THE CRUCIBLE OF WAR

After the defeat of France in June 1940 the path towards a Nazi-German hegemony in Europe through military triumph appeared assured. Within a year of the armistice at Compiègne, Hitler's generals and political administrators controlled most of continental Europe, extending from the western provinces of Poland in the east to the French coast of the English Channel in the west, from Denmark, Norway and Finland in the north to Yugoslavia and Greece in South Eastern Europe (though strictly speaking, the latter together with Albania came under the Italian occupation authorities). Elsewhere in the Balkans, Hungary, Romania and Bulgaria, later joined by the new client states of Croatia and Slovakia, provided willing partners in the Nazi project of recasting Europe.

Prior to the attack on Russia in June 1941, Hitler controlled a compact area of Europe comprising 3,277 square kilometres, containing a population of around 250 million people, mostly with a high consumption and production capacity.[13] The pinnacle of Nazi military domination in Europe, achieved during the second half of 1942, also represented the phase of the war when its economic mastery of the continent appeared at its height before coming to a halt at Stalingrad in the winter of 1942–3.[14] Thereafter the extent of German domination of the continent contracted as the Allies took the initiative with increasing success. Nevertheless, Germany's control over large parts of the continent remained until 1944, during which time its leaders continued in their attempts to rescusitate Mitteleuropa 'from Scandinavia to Turkey' (see Map 5).

A key element of reshaping Europe was its racial reordering: cleansing the heart of Europe of 'non-Aryans'. In Europe the concept of *Lebensraum* (living space) predicated on racial doctrine was exclusive to Nazism. A causal nexus was postulated by Nazi ideologues between climate, race, technical development and efficiency of the population. Accordingly each race carried out economic tasks suited to its level of biological development in its allotted natural geographical space.[15]

Traditional ideas of a Germanic Mitteleuropa can be found in economic and geo-political discussions since the mid-nineteenth century.[16] These gained a wider currency as German industrialization and the expansion of its market for raw materials and primary goods proceeded at a rapid pace. By the beginning of the twentieth century Europe's economic gravity appeared to have shifted to the *Reich*. Germany's defeat in 1918, leading to the loss of some of its industrial capacity through territorial adjustments, coupled with the break-up of the Hapsburg Monarchy and the emergence of smaller competing units, and followed by domestic and international economic uncertainty in the 1920s, led to Germany's economic dislocation and the fragmentation of markets and production at the heart of Europe.

Although we can differentiate in broad terms between Nazi aims and traditional German geo-political objectives, an element of congruence between the two can be discerned. During the 1930s policy formulations concerning the reordering of Europe according to Nazi racial doctrine had become almost indistinguishable from traditional ideas of Mitteleuropa.[17] Here it is best typified in the writings of the publicist Werner Daitz, who promoted the restructuring of the European economy along racial-biological lines in order for it to compete better in a future international division of labour based on *Grossraumwirtschaften* (large economic spaces).[18]

The economic depression at the beginning of the 1930s, coinciding as it did with Hitler's accession to power, provided the critical impetus for re-establishing Mitteleuropa as an economic, though not yet political or racial, reality.[19] The political dimension emerged in a radical manner at the end of the 1930s, brought about by the three major political events in Europe before the outbreak of war: namely, the incorporation of Austria in March 1938, followed by the Munich Agreement that September, which ceded the Sudeten to Germany, and by the occupation of the rest of Czechoslovakia little more than six months later. These events established the core of a re-emerging Mitteleuropa dominated economically and politically by Germany.[20] They also marked the end of achieving this without war.

In German eyes the European order to emerge from the Great War, and codified in the Versailles Treaty, had been guided by selfish interests, notably those of France and Britain, jealous and afraid of German economic and political ascendancy in Europe. Many parts of the Treaty had been revised by Hitler by the late 1930s, when the power of the German market was undisputed. Nevertheless, the war-time Allies were alleged to be still endeavouring to hinder German progress in the peaceful restoration of a mitteleuropäisch trading bloc in Central and South Eastern Europe.[21] Some of the countries concerned were also growing apprehensive of German economic might and its political uses, as well as of the consequences for their own industrial development. There were thus limits to peaceful economic expansion, and, by extension, to the primacy of German political influence on the continent. Ultimately, war provided a means to removing this constraint to European economic integration under German hegemony when bullying and threats failed.[22]

In two New Year speeches in 1940, Hitler told the nation that war had been a necessary device in revising the past injustices of the Versailles treaty, and in seeking to restore to the 'eighty million Germans in middle Europe' what was rightfully theirs.[23] A month later, the Führer told an eager audience that Germany's war aims were directed towards:

> The securing of our own living space, and by this I mean everything that has been cultivated, civilised and economically tapped by the Germans and not by the English. There are a few such areas. In Mitteleuropa at least, the invigorating British influence from the past to the present has yet to make itself noticeable. This Mitteleuropa has been built up through

Germany and we want to live in this German living space. We will not let ourselves be threatened here.[24]

Here we find the kernel of Nazi policy, later to be echoed by Economics Minister Walther Funk in his 'New Order' speech of 25 July 1940.[25]

However, in the early days of war and occupation, few, least of all the German leadership, had a clear idea of what the final shape of a transformed Europe would be.[26] Government and business agencies produced a plethora of schemes for reconstructing European production and trade under German hegemony in the wake of the French defeat. The war, while creating its own requirements, also provided an opportunity for Germany's capitalists to extend and cement their control over European production and markets and to integrate these fully into their own homebase operations. In this respect, the aims of the Nazi military machine and the profit goals of Germany's capitalists converged.[27]

The consequence of this broad alliance of convenience was reflected in the many plans for reconstructing and exploiting Europe. At the practical level of everyday administration, the various agencies' practices of implementing policy was very often contradictory mirroring economic and institutional rivalries.

However, the most coherent exposition of what an integrated 'New Europe' would resemble is to be found in a memorandum written by Karl Ritter and Carl Clodius, who were, respectively, the Head and Deputy of the Economics Section at the Foreign Office. This memorandum served as the blueprint for Funk's July speech outlining economic plans for Europe, and reiterated in a further memorandum sent to Göring in August 1940.[28] This set out the basic objectives of European economic integration centred on the Germanic core. It lists six goals necessary for the creation of a 'New Order'. These were: (1) securing European production for German (war) needs; (2) extending European production beyond its present level; (3) the creation of a European payments system (based on clearing agreements); (4) control of intra-European and extra-European trade policy; (5) integrating the European economies in terms of (a) organizational form, (b) cartels, (c) control of investment, (d) securing control of management positions; and (6) the creation of a European free trade area.

Achieving these six goals would require a 'careful adjustment of the economic policies of the European countries to one another',[29] thereby creating complementarity, union and harmony. The 'abolition of the atomistic economic structure of Europe', together with the regulation of trade and the removal of barriers, Funk claimed, would insure against the vagaries of the trade cycle, end unemployment and bring a higher standard of living to Europe.[30]

But experts at the Royal Institute of International Affairs, in a prescient report published in August 1940, warned against relying too much on Funk's blueprint for Europe:

> To assume that any announced plan will be adopted would be extremely dangerous, and to imagine that any closely defined pattern will be

followed everywhere and in every circumstance would be even more unsafe. The German plan is taking shape on paper. The shape that can at present be discerned may be quite unrecognizable in what is actually done.[31]

They correctly understood that the war would keep fluid both the plans for and the geographical boundaries of Mitteleuropa. War opened and closed opportunities and not even Hitler could control its course.

The discussion in this chapter will be limited to Central and South Eastern Europe, incorporating the territories of Hungary, Romania, Bulgaria, Greece and partly that of Czechoslovakia and Yugoslavia. The choice of these countries might be construed as arbitrary, especially if we accept that Mitteleuropa in the period we are dealing with had no fixed boundaries.[32] Nonetheless, these were the countries of Europe which had been fixed for a long time in the sights of German economic and political strategists and which, together with the smaller nations to the west of Germany, were central to the idea of mitteleuropäisch economic integration as well as serving more immediate strategic war aims.[33]

Their place in Mitteleuropa was to be that of an ancillary economic bloc complementing a German-led industrially advanced core, determined by three structural primary characteristics: they were endowed with extensive existing and potential mineral ores; they possessed a vast reservoir of cheap unskilled and semi-skilled labour; and they provided an outlet for German capital investment. The supply of the first two, coupled with demand for the third, would result in 'organic industrialization' based on natural resources and German investment/ trade receipts, but only 'as far as this accords with the concept of a Greater Economic Sphere'. There was to be little or no place for advanced industrial activity, contrary to their interwar attempts to promote industrialization.

These countries, therefore, figured in German ideas for reconstructing Mitteleuropa in two respects. First, they provided a 'natural' larder of foodstuffs and other primary agricultural products: for instance, cereals, livestock and certain dairy products, vegetable and olive oil, certain fruit, such as currants and so forth, hemp, rape-seed, and tobacco and timber.[34] Second, they represented a hitherto under-exploited mass reserve of mineral ore and non-ferrous metals, principally bauxite (Hungary; regional production of this accounted for 28 per cent of world output), petroleum (Romania), zinc and copper (Yugoslavia), chrome ore and nickel (Greece; South Eastern Europe produced 8 per cent of world output) as well as lignite, antimony, silver and iron pyrites (sulphur).

The rest of this chapter will deal in turn with the impact of Nazi attempts to reforge the European economy along the principle of a German-centred Mitteleuropa according to the six aims of the New Order outlined above. Thus the first section will look at the effects upon production in Central and South Eastern Europe, the second section will analyse the impact upon trade, the third section will deal with the question of a payments system and the final section will look at investment and control of management positions.

THE ECONOMIC IMPACT: PROGRESS OR RETARDATION?

What were the economic consequences of Nazi attempts to reforge Mitteleuropa? There is little doubt that the impact varied from country to country (this, incidently, partly explains the differences in the national rates of postwar recovery), and between economic sectors within a country. Clearly, it mattered if a country was or was not allied to Germany and what future role had been assigned to it in the new Europe.[35] But there were two further factors which operated independently of the plans for future restructuring. First, the unfolding events of war determined the extent to which certain types of industrial activity would be allowed, and this might or might not accord with Nazi plans for a national economy within the framework of reforging Mitteleuropa, as we shall see below. Second, a significant factor was the relative strength or weakness of a national economy before Nazi attempts to orchestrate its activity to the mitteleuropäisch tune.

From the mid-1930s all countries of Central and South Eastern Europe had been experiencing some degree of accelerated industrial activity, encouraged by government policies. While Western European production struggled to regain pre-1929 levels, indices of industrial production in Greece, Bulgaria, Hungary, Romania and Czechoslovakia show impressive growth rates, notably in primary, textile and food-processing industries.[36] Nonetheless, with the exception of Czechoslovakia, these economies were starting from a low base and all countries of the region, again with the exceptions of Czechoslovakia and partly that of Hungary, were dominated by overwhelmingly backward agrarian sectors.

Contrary to Nazi intentions to divert South Eastern Europe from the path of industrialization, the immediate impact of being drawn into a German-led Mitteleuropa under war conditions, was, in some cases, to advance pre-war trends. The reason for this lies in the strategic importance of primary and secondary industrial production for the German war effort. The mining of coal and lignite, together with iron and steel manufacture and other existing industrial operations, for instance the exploitation of various ores and non-ferrous metals such as bauxite, chrome, copper, nickel, lead and zinc, petroleum, chemicals and synthetic oils, to name some of the more essential items, made these economies of Central and South Eastern Europe indispensable to Germany.

To illustrate the point briefly: Germany received 56 per cent of its iron ore requirement from occupied Europe; nearly 42 per cent of coal production came from the annexed territories, as did 40 per cent of crude steel.[37] It depended on South Eastern Europe for its chrome. The *Reich* consumed an annual average of 40,000 tons of chrome between 1939 and 1944, of which probably around half was accounted for by the countries of South Eastern Europe, notably Greece, Bulgaria and Yugolsavia.[38]

In general terms, industrial production grew at a strong though variable pace in the first years of the war, levelled off in 1942–3, and was followed thereafter by stagnation and decline, mostly as a consequence of disruptions in transport, shortages in raw material and in the supply and reliability of labour. According to data published by Brian Mitchell, the production of hard and brown coal, steel and iron expanded until 1943, thereafter falling into rapid decline.[39]

The success of coal output and iron and steel production in Central and South Eastern Europe lies in the fact that since the beginning of the war a large part of new industrial capacity under German control had been encouraged here.[40] Even after taking into account the differences between Nazi policy towards its allies, where political considerations had to be borne in mind, and the occupied countries, German policy, almost from the outset (Poland excepting) aimed less at dismantling than at building up industrial operations. What did tend to suffer were manufacturing industries such as cotton and woollen textiles.

An earlier policy of crude plunder was replaced by a more 'refined' one of seeking collaboration. Some in the administration, such as Gustav Schlotterer, an Under Secretary in the Economics Department of the Foreign Ministry, recognized that future cooperation in Mitteleuropa depended in part on how Germans behaved during the war. He called upon German businessmen to act with more caution and foresight in their dealings with foreign enterprises.[41] Others, such as Hitler's Munitions Minister, Albert Speer, argued on economic grounds for a more rational, cost-effective local utilization of labour and industry in the occupied countries, rather than to dismantle plant or ship labour to the greater *Reich*.[42] This reconsideration of how best to exploit resources had become necessary as the course of hostilities, and the struggle on several fronts, made ever greater demands on Nazi Germany's own war economy.

*The Economist* observed a halt to outright dismantling and acquisition of foreign industries in parts of occupied Europe in the second half of 1941. In its place a policy of 'economic collaboration' was substituted whereby contracts were distributed among local firms.[43] This led both to a partial reconstruction and revitalization of industry and production in some countries as investment followed, often representing transfers either from occupation levies or from blocked clearing account credits or from local bank credits. This 'economic collaboration' became typical of the situation in Western Europe and was also widespread in parts of Central and South Eastern Europe.[44]

Germany's Central European allies were the first to reap the benefits of war. Hungary's role as an axis partner and its strategic geographical position at the fulcrum between east, west and south East, opened a 'new era in its economic history'.[45] The Hungarian economic historians, Ivan Berend and Grygor Ranki, note how German contracts valued at 'hundreds of millions' of *pengös* were now directed to industrial production, although a large German investment already existed, notably in oil and mineral exploration. The opportunities of war production meant that its industrial operations expanded vigorously, especially in mining and metallurgy and particularly in aluminium production. Hungary became the main continental supplier of bauxite, overtaking France, as its production doubled between 1939 and 1943. This in turn enabled aluminium production to quintuple, thus allowing Hungary to give a much stronger performance than that of other producers. Understandably, industrial manufacturing workshops increased between 1939 and 1941 from 3,910 to 5,379.[46] Overall, industrial production increased by 37 per cent, while the value of industrial output in current prices rose nearly threefold between 1938 and 1943. A German Balkans expert even concluded that after the war Hungary would acquire partner status on almost equal terms to the *Reich*.

Another ally, Bulgaria, also benefited from German contracts. Its manufacturing output rose considerably in the early part of the war (17 per cent by 1941), though this was later to fall back to prewar levels. Much of the expansion came in agriculture, but chemicals and mining played an important role too, while machinery imports for the mushrooming manufacturing enterprises in and around Sofia were estimated to have been twice the 1938 tonnage in 1943.[47]

However, any positive economic developments were not necessarily incumbent on political-military status. According to Lampe and Jackson, the 1940s were bleak years for industrial development in Romania, an ally, and in Greece, an occupied enemy. Nonetheless, the shift in the fortunes of war against the Nazis allowed Romania to continue in its limited prewar development, mostly in crude oil and other extractive sectors of the economy.[48] This was in spite of Hitler's desire that this country should give up its pretensions to becoming an industrial economy and remain, instead, primarily a supplier of raw materials to Germany. Romanian soybean and sunflower oilseed production prospered under German direction. This crop was almost exclusively cultivated with success in Bessarabia under the technical and financial aegis of the IG Farben through a subsidiary, Solagra. Similarly, flax production was run by another German controlled subsidiary, the Südostropa.[49] But in general, serious imbalances were created in the country's economic structure, while output of its most important commodity, oil, stagnated.[50]

Although Greece was nominally a part of the Italian *Lebensraum*, its economy was in fact subordinated to German needs.[51] Economic planners intended that Greece, like its neighbours, should reform its agriculture in order to serve the German and European market, primarily with livestock, cereals, fruit, olives, olive oil, tobacco and industrial crops. However, as the European theatre of war took on a new direction in the course of 1941 and 1942, Greece's hitherto under-exploited mineral ore reserves began to loom more prominently in the Nazi war effort. It was already one of the most important European sources of magnesite, it had ample deposits of chrome and useful reserves of nickel. In spite of a dispute with the Italian authorities over conquerer's rights (restored to German interests in September 1943), measures were taken to secure and improve production in the mines, initially with mixed results, until output fell in the final stages of the occupation as labour productivity ground to a halt as a consequence of partisan activity, heightened German repression and economic collapse. All

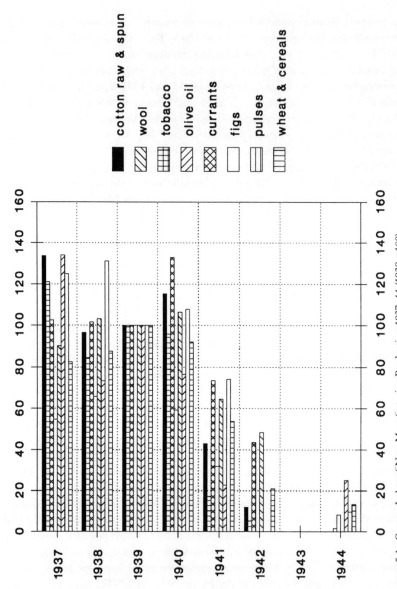

GRAPH 5.1: Greece: Index of Non-Manufacturing Production 1937–44 (1938 = 100).
Source: BAK 127/11 Bl.4-13 (Aktenvermerk betr. Griechenland, 1 August 1942); 1944 based on Athanasios Sbarounis, *Meletai kai anamniseis ek tou 2. Pankosmiou Polemou* (Athens 1950), p. 258. Cf. A. F. Freris, *The Greek Economy* (London 1987), p. 119.

attempts to integrate Greece into a mitteleuropäisch New Order failed abysmally. For during the occupation, the Greek economy, already in a weak position, was devastated and totally fragmented to the point of causing severe retardation.

In both Romania and Greece, unlike in Hungary and Bulgaria, underlying structural weaknesses in the economy remained uncorrected. Indeed, the policies of occupation dictated in the short-term by military needs, exacerbated weaknesses. E. A. Radice in his work on Central and Eastern Europe has already noted how over-exploitation, especially in the closing stages of the war, was very often uneconomic, leading to the exhaustion of industrial plant, disinvestment and loss of productive capacity by 1944–5.[52] Hungary's experience in the closing stages of the war underscores this observation. Its relative advantage before 1943 turned from that year into a negative development as the burden of military occupation (from March 1944) 'increased the pace of deterioration'.[53] Meanwhile, policies in Yugoslavia and Czechoslovakia as in other parts of Eastern Europe, had a deleterious effect upon the native economies. The territorial alterations, accompanied by racial policy leading to the cleansing of areas of non-German populations, proved economically counter-productive.[54] Where industrial production was maintained, as in certain key areas such as in the Protectorate, it was kept under tight German control with little real benefit percolating down.[55]

The retardation of particular sectors of the economies of Central and South Eastern Europe could be seen in the impact of war upon agricultural production, distribution and markets, which proved disastrous, and, in the case of Greece, accounts for its famine in the winter of 1941–2.[56] For instance, Greece's stock of 270,000 draught animals was reduced by more than a third between 1940 and 1944; the country had had a small number of tractors, which were then requisitioned for military use. Barely 150 survived service (about 15 per cent) and would have been useless anyway because of lack of petrol. The tripartite partition of the country between Italy, Germany and Bulgaria, had left it economically fragmented, with dire implications for food provisioning. The country's most important crops, produced for both domestic consumption and export, suffered a continuous decline, shrinking to negligible proportions (Graph 5. 1). One contemporary observer estimated that agricultural output had fallen to around 24 per cent of its prewar level by 1944.[57]

In the Danubian states, where cereal harvests were said to have been indifferent, the drain exercised by German exploitation on all sectors of economic life had been increased by dislocation, due to territorial changes and, subsequently, active participation in the war.[58] This compounded an already difficult situation because of poor harvests. Thus whereas 1939 had seen bumper crops, the 1940 harvest was poor: down by between 20 and 30 per cent of the previous year's level in Bulgaria, 40 per cent in Yugoslavia, and even as much as 70 per cent in Romania. Output continued to fall in grain production, though with intensive production of sugar beet and some root crops the opposite held true.[59]

TABLE 5.1: Index of agricultural output for selected crops, 1944.
(1938=100)

| Country | Wheat | Rye | Barley | Oats | Maize | P'toes | Sugar Beet |
|---|---|---|---|---|---|---|---|
| Bulgaria | 74 | 82 | 48 | 102 | 142 | 284 | 252 |
| Czech | 69 | 65 | 52 | 55 | 47 | 93 | 117 |
| Hungary | 86 | 80 | 94 | 103 | 86 | 123 | 75 |
| Romania | 68 | 32 | 54 | 103 | 81 | 106 | 98 |
| Yugoslavia | 62 | 93 | 88 | 88 | 92 | 112 | 141 |

Source: Brian Mitchell, *European Historical Statistics,* Table C2.

Although the above data compiled by Brian Mitchell can be treated with some caution, they nonetheless provide us with a convenient picture of the approximate situation towards the end of the war.

The foregoing evidence shows that any German intentions of creating an efficient regional supplier of agricultural products remained unfulfilled.

One of the chief means by which a mitteleuropäisch New Order would be reforged was that of a multilateral – albeit regulated – trading and clearing system centred on Berlin with the Reichsmark as chief currency. Germany itself was highly dependent upon Europe, both as a source of supply and for its manufactured goods. Throughout the 1930s it drew around 57 per cent of its imports from its continental neighbours, both nearby and further afield, and these in return took over 70 per cent of its exports.[60] A large part of this trade was governed by long-term preferential bilateral agreements, initiated by Hjalmar Schacht with the New Plan in 1934. The intention under this scheme was to guarantee to Germany a supply of essential raw materials and foodstuffs, as well as semi-finished articles, in return for price stability, guaranteed markets and technical aid.[61] The plan, however, was never fully successful in achieving an autarchic continental trade bloc under Germany's lead.[62]

Mitteleuropa protagonists, including Funk, argued for a continental trade system based on multilateralism rather than bilateralism. They believed the war provided the opportunity for the transition because it inevitably forced the economies of Europe closer together. From 1940 Germany's superior position allowed it to manipulate the flow of trade and exchange. Thus in the course of that year the Nazis were able to bring more countries into clearing arrangements rigidly controlled by Berlin, in the expectation of getting the full benefit of this, including that of reducing its huge clearing debt.[63]

In December 1940 trade between countries either occupied by or tied to Germany, were being cleared through Berlin.[64] Operating via the clearing house in Berlin, ten countries settled payments with Belgium, eight with Holland, seven with Norway and five with the General-Government. Between eleven and sixteen countries were involved in the above arrangements.[65] By the end of

1941 this system applied to all the continental economies; British observers concluded that between 50 and 85 per cent of continental trade with Germany was conducted in this manner by 1942.[66]

The war certainly seemed to have brought European economies closer. In a memorandum circulating in March 1942 on trade between the Scandinavian 'economic space' and the Balkans, the author, probably Franz Neuschank, wrote how the:

> possibilities for cooperation between the various countries go well beyond the opportunities of earlier bilateral agreements. Instead of individual planning, total planning within the framework of the greater economic sphere will take place, ... to be further integrated within European economic planning.[67]

However, such 'possibilities' were never fully realized. Rather, the pattern of continental trade during the war years resembled a spider's web with Germany at the centre. However, even this picture, primarily of German trade domination, especially in Central and South Eastern Europe, needs some qualification.

Bulgaria, Romania, Hungary and Greece were already heavily involved with Germany before the war. Of the first three, Bulgaria was the most committed, with nearly 59 per cent of its exports and nearly 52 per cent of its imports going to and coming from Germany in 1938. Hungary followed with respective figures of 46 and nearly 42 per cent. Romania's reliance on Germany as a market was less marked: it sent only 26.5 per cent of its exports to the *Reich*, while German goods accounted for nearly 37 per cent of total imports. German exports to Greece formed 30 per cent of total imports, while Greek exports to Germany accounted for 40 per cent of its total exports. A number of long-term trade agreements in 1939 stiffened these countries dependence on Germany (excluding Greece). The war cemented the relationship. Germany's share of the value of trade with Bulgaria, Romania and Hungary increased dramatically, notably from 1941.

At a superficial level, the increased trade with Germany indicates some success in getting these economies to respond to German needs. And in some respects this is indeed what happened. For instance, both Bulgaria and Romania exported mainly agricultural items and raw materials and imported machinery, metals and iron products, as they were meant to under the New Order. But there is also evidence to suggest that neither country allowed Germany to control fully the structure and level of trade in spite of fixed-quota agreements. Although the data dwindles for the mid-years of the war, it is still possible to observe how Bulgaria failed to export either wheat or maize at the required needs of the *Reich*, in spite of agreements to supply its surplus to Germany and Italy,[68] nor was it inclined to oblige with eggs before it had satisfied its own requirements. It was not so much a case of 'cannot deliver' but of 'will not' deliver. Only where the Germans had control of production were deliveries either maintained or even increased.

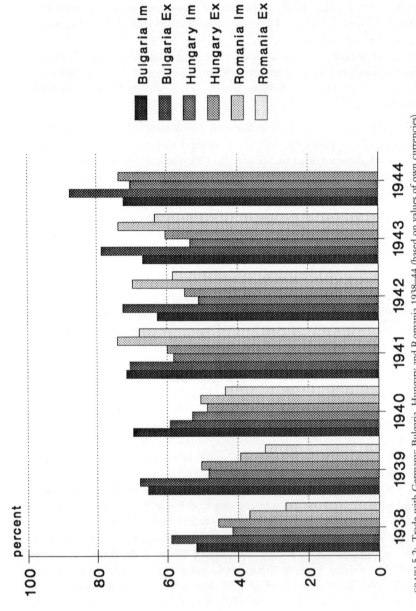

GRAPH 5.2: Trade with Germany: Bulgaria, Hungary and Romania 1938–44 (based on values of own currencies).
Source: League of Nations, *Monthly Bulletin of Statistics*, Volume 26, Nr.10 (October 1945); *ibid.*, Vol. 27 Nr.11 (November 1946).

Limits to trade exploitation were also experienced in the case of Romanian petroleum, vital to Germany. Here too, exports stagnated after 1940, possibly satisfying little more than a third of German needs by the later years of the war.[69] The Nazis were unable to secure deliveries of a greater share of Romania's stagnating production, clearly a blow to its war-effort, given that around two-thirds of its oil consumption (as that of wheat) came from Romania.

The economic historians, Berend and Ranki, argue that as the war progressed, there is incontrovertible evidence showing that Hungary's economy was pressed further and further into the service of Germany, so that production 'became more firmly oriented ... [to] ... the needs of the German market'.[70] This is illustrated in the case of bauxite extraction, essential for producing aluminium, and over which Nazi Germany had long exercised a controlling hand. However, it is by no means self-evident that Hungary developed into a trade satellite of the *Reich*.[71] Exports to Germany were much more evenly spread than in the case of the other two economies. In 1943 its exports to Germany divided almost equally between agricultural products and raw materials. As well as bauxite, mineral oils, livestock, vegetable oils, hemp and hemp tow, dried vegetables and wheat all appear to have been the principal items exported. A similar picture pertains to its imports. Chief among these were coal, coke, lignite, paper, machines and semi-finished and finished iron manufactures, with no single item dominating.[72]

Overall, Greek exports had only a minor share of total imports into the *Reich* (barely 2 per cent). But individual items played a much more important role in sustaining both the military and home fronts. In the context of a shaky food supply, the calorific and nutritional importance for Germany of currants, raisins and figs loomed large. In 1942 Greece supplied nearly 90 per cent of Germany's import needs of these items, the following year, however, it delivered barely 56 per cent. Of even greater importance to Germany were Greek minerals, notably chrome and nickel, especially when deliveries from elsewhere looked less assured. Delivery of these important mineral ores declined dramatically. Altogether they covered 42 per cent of German requirements in 1942, but fell to just 12 per cent in 1943; a similar reduction can be seen in the supply of lavat and sulphurous oil.[73] During the same period, Greek supplies of these items accounted for over 50 per cent of German imports, but this was halved in 1943. A slight decline was also noted in magnesite. By 1943 few of the chief mines were working because of partisan activity.[74] The significance of this is clear once we understand that part of the Nazi war effort depended on these supplies.

The foregoing discussion suggests that in addition to economic dysfunctioning a political reluctance to adhere slavishly to German demands existed, and is demonstrated by the expansion of trade elsewhere, principally with Italy, even if the lion's share still went to the *Reich*.[75] The point has relevance when one considers Germany's military predicament at that stage of the war, and that the rate at which alternative trade spheres developed, such as those with Italy or

Turkey, was either the same or in some cases, much stronger than with Germany. Moreover, while the aggregate value of trade with Greater Germany increased during the war, it was not matched by an increase in the volume of trade, which, in 1941, was already 20 per cent below the level of 1938.[76]

By 1943 deliveries of essential raw materials from South Eastern Europe had become a critical economic factor in Nazi Germany's struggle for survival, but less and less was coming through. Deliveries from the occupied areas during the later stages of the war were increasingly hindered by partisan activity. But economic factors, principally monetary ones, also played a critical role in curtailing production and disrupting deliveries to the *Reich*. The conclusion to be drawn from this is that in addition to the conditions arising from war, the satellite and occupied countries were able to place limitations on German demands, as Roland Schönfelder has recently demonstrated in the case of Croatian and Serbian deliveries of raw materials, notably copper (from the Mines de Bor in Serbia) and bauxite, to the *Reich*.[77] The wartime division of labour and trade, where it emerged, was a forced one and bore no relation to natural development consistent with older ideas of Mitteleuropa. Instead fragmentation of both the European and national markets rather than integration took place.

Germany's reliance on supplies of essential items led to it becoming an import economy, especially since its military position after France's defeat relieved it from the laws of exchange and thus the need to export to occupied countries. It thus rapidly became a debtor country. For instance, its clearing debt with France, Belgium, Holland, Denmark, Hungary, Romania, Bulgaria and the Protectorate increased over a thousand per cent from 1,665 million to 18,045 million Reichsmark between December 1940 and September 1943.[78] By September 1944 the sum of Germany's total clearing debt is estimated to have stood at 31.5 milliard Reichsmark.[79] This increase in Germany's clearing debt was not consistent with the vision of a financially-integrated Mitteleuropa with Berlin at its centre. Indeed, Germany's trade debt greatly weakened the position of the Reichsmark as the currency unit for the settlement of payments.[80]

At the Vienna Fair in September 1940, Walther Funk had announced his intention to stabilize exchange rates – within a burgeoning European Economic Union well inside the framework of Mitteleuropa (to include a European Bank of Settlement located in Vienna) – by realigning currencies against the Reichsmark, thereby introducing arithmetic consistency and thus eliminating fluctuations in value. On the one hand, western countries, such as The Netherlands, Belgium and Luxemburg, followed the Austrian example after their occupation, in having their currencies revalued upwards in order to bring them into line with Germany. On the other hand, during the months following Funk's announcement, the Yugoslav dinar, Romanian lei, Greek drachma and Hungarian pengö were all revalued against the Reichsmark, leading to an effective devaluation of those currencies of between 20 and 25 per cent.[81] And further downward, revaluations followed in the course of the war. When new currencies were introduced in the client states of Slovenia, Croatia and Slovakia, they too were aligned to the Reichsmark at a low parity. There were no immediate plans for a currency union.[82]

Germany thus reaped an immediate benefit because of its ability to expand its purchasing power in these countries. However, artificially fixed exchange rates, based on political expedience together with occupation monetary policy, soon neutralized any advantage by unleashing inflation which was then exported to Germany in the form of fewer over-priced commodities, especially from 1942.[83] The only single attempt in Europe to overcome this, in the late autumn of 1942 in Greece, failed abysmally.

Rather than promote the harmonious integration of the European market through stable exchange rates, the result of the above policy of realigning currencies, imposing unrealistic occupation levies and forcing loans from the national banks, was to fuel monetary and price inflation throughout Europe as the authorities on the ground were called upon to increase their note issues in order to subsidize exports to Germany in the absence of earned foreign exchange.[84] Monetary chaos played a major part in disrupting trade to Germany and elsewhere and had a profound effect upon the future development of some of the occupied economies, notably that of Greece.

Conquest allowed German businessmen to speed up the process, begun in 1938, of neutralizing their rivals in Europe in order to assert their own predominance.[85] However, whereas military authorities were able to confiscate or directly administer industrial and business undertakings, 'in the interests of the Reich', private industry could not act with such commissarial impunity. Instead, they had to follow mundane legal processes in order to obtain their booty. They achieved their goals by intensifying capital penetration, the acquisition of shares, joint-finance planning committees, long-term production and delivery agreements and so forth. While a cloak of legality covered German actions in Western Europe, in Central and South Eastern Europe a mixture of both legal and semi-legal expropriation was practised.[86] Direct confiscation, carried out mostly by Göring's Office for the Four Year Plan, tended to be reserved for Eastern Europe, the Baltic States, occupied Russia, and those countries incorporated into the *Reich*, in accordance with Nazi plans to obtain in economic terms the 'full Germanization of ... space and the population'.[87] But in spite of the different methods reserved for different parts of Europe, the result amounted to the same thing. A correspondent for the *Economist* observed in early 1942:

> A glance at the economic map of the continent, ... shows that the administration of the most important industrial areas of occupied Europe has been profoundly changed. Some areas are now under direct German administration; others are controlled by German cartels or continental companies; German state companies, such as the H. Goering Works, and semi-state organizations, such as the numerous firms owned by the German Labour Front, are leading in the control of foreign industries.[88]

The process of establishing a foothold had already been greatly enhanced after

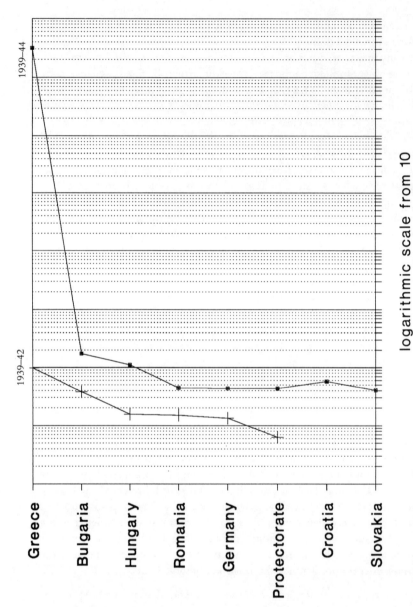

logarithmic scale from 10

GRAPH 5.3: Central and South Eastern Europe: Percentage Increase in Note Circulation 1939–42, 1939–44.

Note:     From July 1939 to latest month in 1942 and 1944: i.e. Greece and Bulgaria: September; Croatia: December; Germany: December;
          Hungary: November; Protectorate: December; Romania: June; Slovakia: December; Greece: June 1934–November 1944.

Source: League of Nations, *Economic Survey 1941/42*, (Geneva 1942) p. 126, *ibid., 1942/44*, p. 202.

the *Anschluss* of Austria in 1938, the occupation of Prague a year later, and then by the occupation of Western Europe and the virtual takeover of their firms and banks leading to greater opportunities in Central Europe and the Balkans. The range of German industrial, financial and business control was said to be 'far reaching' by the end of the war. And it was mostly big business that benefited.

The state-owned holding company, Reichswerke Hermann Göring, had been established in 1937 with a capital of 5 million Reichsmark; as a consequence of the *Anschluss*, astute business manoeuvres and a fair degree of bullying, this concern grew eight-fold within a year. Its major growth, however, came as a result of its predatory role in wartime. It consolidated its pre-eminence in Central and South-Eastern Europe by extending its control over mines, iron-works and steel-rolling plants and various manufacturers. For example, in the dismembered Czechoslovakian state, it acquired the Handlova coal mines, the Aussiger Chemische copper works in Slovakia (by taking over the shares of the Zivnostenska Bank) and rented the iron plants of Podbrezova from the client Slovakian government.[89] Elsewhere, this Nazi-Combine came to control heavy industry formerly owned by foreign capital. It took over the largest copper works in Europe, the formerly French-owned Société des Mines de Bor in Yugoslavia. It also gained control of four fifth's of Romanian iron and steel production through a series of contracts. By 1943/44 its capital stood at 4,000 million Reichsmark.[90]

The other industrial giant closely associated with Nazi expansion, the chemical concern IG Farben, had an original capital base in 1926 of 646 million Reichsmark; it underwent steady expansion in the 1930s, securing markets for its products rather than expanding investment. Like the Göring Works, the opportunity for achieving control over production and markets via majority investment at the expense of its European rivals came with military success. IG Farben took control of the largest chemical works in the region, based at Usti, and extended its influence through its shares in the former Czechoslovak Dynamit Nobel.[91] It also finally acquired the Austrian-owned explosives works, Pulverfabrik Skodawerke Wetzler AG, which it had long coveted, and the Donau-Chemie AG. In 1939 the Czechoslovakian Aussiger-Verein was forced to sell its operations in Aussig and Falkenau.[92] As a result of acquiring the Prague-based Aussiger Verein, the chemical firm of Hungaria Kunstdünger-Schwefelsäure- und Chemische Industrie A. G. (Budapest), fell into IG Farben's hands, and this in turn led to further acquisitions.[93] By 1942 IG Farben had expanded its capital base to 1,400 million Reichsmark, with a tentacle-style 'network spread all over Europe'.

The British historian Richard Overy's assertion that the economic map of Mitteleuropa was largely determined by the interests of the Hermann Göring Works and other state-owned monopoly corporations, such as the Kontinentale Öl A.G., rather than private business interests, while to some extent justified, does not do full justice to the complexity, diversity and competition of interests.[94] To be sure, the Hermann Göring Works in particular had extensive interests spread throughout German and European industry in the form of subsidiaries and shares, but there were other major beneficiaries. Germany's large private corporations and firms also derived the full benefit of conquest, for instance, the heavy industrial, mining, manufacturing and electrical concerns of Krupp, Mannesmann, Otto-Wolff, Schering and Siemens, or the Hamburg-based tobacco corporation Reemstma, and the two north German shipyards, Howaldt (Hamburg) and Deutsche Werft (Kiel), to name but a few.[95] The following case offers a good illustration of the way the war helped to promote German private interests as well as opening new opportunities within the framework of a reforged Mitteleuropa.

Immediately on occupying Greece in May 1940, the German military authorities, together with state corporate and private business interests set about 'securing' Greek production 'for the *Reich*'. For instance, during the first days of occupation, the Hansa-Leichtmetall AG attempted to secure the ownership of all bauxite firms; the Norddeutsche Aluminium AG, similarly laid claim to a share of Greek bauxite; and Rheinmetall-Börsig and the Mitteldeutsche Montanwerke both revealed their interest in the Greek armaments industry, centred mostly in and around Athens. Pickings proved to be very lucrative to both state and private interests. Thus the occupation authorities in Athens estimated that the tobacco harvests from 1939 and 1940, amounting to over 80 million tons, had a value of 175 million Reichsmark, would produce around 80 thousand million cigarettes and would provide the Nazi government with a revenue from taxation of 1.4 milliard Reichsmark. A representative of the tobacco firm, Reemstma AG was brought in to advise. However, the firm to stake a primary claim in Greek industry *per se* was the private company of Friedrich Krupp of Essen.

Within the first ten days of occupation in May, Krupp either gained outright ownership or majorities, or twenty-five year leaseholds, or exclusive rights to production and deliveries of at least 26 mines in order to 'secure long-term for Germany the entire mining production of iron pyrites, iron ore, chrome, nickel, magnesium, lignite and gold'. This was achieved through a mixture of lobbying the authorities in Berlin, or by exerting pressure and issuing threats to Greek owners. The company's expert in Greece, a mines engineer called Sohl, believed that the capacity of these important undertakings could be expanded with the 'correct technical investment'. Nickel, emery, chrome and magnesium were important to the company and the German war-effort, and for their uses in various chemical and metal processes, construction and armaments production. Germany's, and specifically Krupp's, acquisition of Greek ore deposits closed any possible gaps in a future European market under its domination.

The same pattern of penetration and concentration of control held for finance. Indeed, without the active participation of German banks, 'control' and 'leadership' of industrial production would not have been possible. Before the war German capital occupied a weak position in Central and South Eastern Europe. Financial control traditionally lay in English, French, Belgian, Swiss and

Czech hands.[96] This was radically altered as a consequence of the war. Territorial conquest opened the way to pre-eminence for German financiers. In September 1940 an assurance to Germany's bankers came from Funk's ministry that he would do everything possible to create favourable conditions for the acquisition of foreign shares.[97] And acquire they did. Throughout Europe, and particularly in Central and South Eastern Europe, German bankers accumulated major interests in central and private banks, usually as a result of expropriating Western banks. For instance, the acquisition of the two Belgian banks, Continental and Société Générale, or the French Union Parisienne, or the Dutch Handels Trust, led to extensive control of finance and industry in the Balkans.[98] The Dresdner Bank, for instance, took over 75 per cent of the capital of the Romanian Banca Commerciale. It took over the former Yugoslav Bank in Croatia upon obtaining a former Czechoslovakian bank. After procuring English and French shares, it gained control of the Merkur Bank in Hungary. Together with the Commerz Bank and Reichskredit AG, the Dresdner acquired majority interests in other Romanian banks. And together with the Deutsche Bank it was very active in Bulgaria, Greece and Yugoslavia.[99] The creation of subsidiaries and joint agreements also facilitated German control. Between 1937 and 1942 the Dresdner managed an eightfold increase in the number of its foreign branches, while its representatives came to sit on directorates throughout Europe's banking world. A typical example is that of Hans Pilder, who sat on the boards of banks in Belgrade, Vienna, Bucharest and Athens.[100] The Commerzbank founded the Hansa Bank in Riga and Tallinin, consolidating thereby the bridgehead for the capital penetration of the Baltic states.[101] And like the Deutsche and Dresdner banks, it also concluded a number of agreements with Greek banks.[102]

Not surprisingly, the five main German banks became the chief beneficiaries of such expansion.[103] Together they controlled and administered directly or indirectly at least seventy different banks and branches across the continent.[104] Their total assets rose from 10,143 million Reichsmark to 15,927 million Reichsmark between 1939 and 1941. In 1941 alone, their assets had increased by 22.5 per cent. By 1944, the largest of them all, the Deutsche Bank, through its extensive holdings in Germany and throughout Europe, had assets worth 11 milliard Reichsmark, twice the level of 1940 and three times that of 1933 and was thus the most powerful bank in Europe.[105]

Its closest rival, the Dresdner Bank, underwent a similar growth pattern, though it remained about one-third smaller than the Deutsche. In 1945 it had assets totalling 6,176 million Reichsmark compared to 2,034 million Reichsmark in 1938.[106]

By extending industrial and financial control throughout Europe, the owners and managers of private and state-run corporations placed themselves in key positions for the German domination of the European market. From this position they attempted to regulate the price of raw materials, the process of production and the final marketing of finished goods. A close investigation of the archive sources shows that, with few exceptions, little consideration was given to the consequences of this policy for the victim economies. Thus while the Nazi New Order did succeed in integrating European economies by means of cartels, control of investment and managerial positions, the economic reality of Mitteleuropa was that it was little more than a synonym for German economic hegemony.

CONCLUSION

In 1915 Friedrich Naumann argued that a Mitteleuropa based on Germany and Austria-Hungary would not be large enough to survive in the new world order of the twentieth century.[107] However, the attempt to forge a larger entity in the 1930s and finally in the crucible of war in the early 1940s, did not survive the forces of the new world order either. Because our concern in this chapter has been limited to a brief overview of the economic impact of German hegemony, a full discussion as to whether or not this failure was due exclusively to the pressures of war, or whether the project was doomed from the start, has been left undeveloped. In conclusion, therefore, some brief observations in this respect will be made.

Those who have argued the former case accept the feasibility of Mitteleuropa but emphasize its war-time limits, ending in a 'lost opportunity'.[108] That is to say, they argue the case of the practicality of the *Großraum* blueprints, especially those of 1940. Thus Funk's scheme for an economic expression of Mitteleuropa in the form of the New Order could have, in essence, materialized, had the outcome of the war gone in favour of the Germans.[109]

Those who reject the viability of Mitteleuropa as conceived of by the Germans, such as Paul Einzig, and argue instead that its forging was but a thin disguise for German national aggression, come, perhaps, closer to the truth.[110] After all, it was precisely the war which allowed in the first place the attempt to put such a design into action. In the words of Robert Krötz, the war 're-established Germany at the heart of Europe'.[111] Hitler's racial and political goals in Europe provided both further means and wider opportunities for the attempt to reforge a traditional understanding of Mitteleuropa based on economic imperatives.[112] But in keeping with the nature of the regime by which they prospered, rival business leaders embarked on a wild scramble for personal and corporate gain. As the former East German economic historian, Dietrich Eichholtz, put it, German business leaders resembled little more than a pack of hyenas fighting over the spoils of war.[113]

We conclude where we began, in 1945. Chaos, anarchy and partial retardation characterized the economic terrain of Central and South Eastern Europe at the end of the war, in spite of some war-specific expansion of domestic industrial capacity. In terms of regional economic integration, Hitler's desire to do away with what he alluded to as the post-Versailles *kleinstaatengerümpel*, the 'rag-bag' of small, competing national entities in the middle of Europe, and impose instead a mitteleuropäisch New Order, ended unrequited. Talk of – though little real preparation for – integrating Europe around a Germanic hub continued nonetheless into 1943. Ribbentrop's Foreign Ministry even established a Europe Committee in April that year to discuss arrangements for a federal European Union.[114] And in May 1943 Hitler told his lieutenants that 'the creation of a united Europe must remain the goal of our struggle'.[115]

The historical irony is that some semblance of a Mitteleuropa (only by another name) occupying Central and Eastern Europe was to emerge after the war, not under German leadership, and precisely at the moment Toynbee was writing wistfully of economic integration under the Nazis. But historians today need not join with Toynbee or those who appear to accept the inherent viability of the German forgemaster's blueprint and thus equally 'overrate the power of economics to cement a Germanocentric Mitteleuropa'.[116] For, in the crucible of war, the economies of Europe were melted down and poured into different casts, all of which were too brittle and none of which could give a lasting shape.

## NOTES

Note: This chapter is partly based on a longer and ongoing study of the relationship between Germany and the smaller economies of Eastern and Central/South Eastern Europe within the framework of *Mitteleuropa*, that the author is carrying out together with Dr Tim Kirk of the University of Northumbria at Newcastle. Footnotes have been kept to a minimum, usually referring to secondary sources. The discussion of industry and agriculure and of Greek trade is largely based on unpublished archive material held in the Bundesarchiv Koblenz, the Bundesarchiv-Militärarchiv Freiburg, and the National Archives Washington (Captured German Documents), the latter kindly supplied by Dr Tim Kirk.

1 Hitler to Martin Bormann, February 1945, cited in Andreas Hillgruber, 'Das Problem "Nation und Europa" seit dem 19.Jahrhundert', in Michael Salewski (ed.), *Nationale Identität und Europäische Einigung* (Göttingen/Zürich 1991), p.8.

2 *The World Almanac and Book of Facts for 1946* (New York, 1946), p. 35, citing a report by the economist James H. Brady. See A. S. Milward, *War, Economy and Society 1939–1945* (London, 1977), pp. 60f., 329f.

3 Angus Maddison, 'Economic Policy and Performance in Europe 1913–1970' in Carlo M. Cipolla (ed.), *The Fontana Economic History of Europe*, Vol. 5, Part 2, (London 1976) p. 471; Milward, *War, Economy, Society*, Chapter 10; *The Economist*, 7 April 1945, 'Commercial History and Review of 1944'; Imre Bencze and Erzsebet v. Tajti, *Budapest: an Industrial-Geographical Approach*, (Budapest, 1972), p. 25; Fred Singleton, *A Short History of the Yugoslav Peoples*, (Cambridge, 1985), p. 206; Alice Teichova, *The Czechoslovak Economy 1918–1980* (London and New York, 1988), p. 84; A. F. Freris, *The Greek Economy in the Twentieth Century*, (London 1986), p. 120f.

4 In an address to the Council of Foreign Relations in Chicago, 4 April 1945, *Documents of American Foreign Relations*, Vol. 7, 1944–5 (Princeton, 1945), p. 31.

5 Neville M. Goodman, 'Health in Europe' in *International Affairs*, Vol. 20 (1944), pp. 473–80; Anna C. Bramwell (ed.), *Refugees in the Age of Total War* (London, 1988); Michael R. Marrus, *The Unwanted: European Refugees in the Twentieth Century* (Oxford, 1985), Chapter 5; Alan Kramer, '"Law-abiding Germans"? Social Disintegration, Crime and the Reimposition of

Order in Post-war Western Germany, 1945–9', in Richard J. Evans (ed.), *The German Underworld: Deviants and Outcasts in German History* (London, 1988), pp. 238–62. *Idem, The West German Economy 1945–1955* (New York, Oxford,1991), Chapter 3. Jörg Roesler, 'The Black Market in Post-war Berlin', *German History*, Vol. 7 (1989), pp. 92–107. Rainer Schulze, 'Growing Discontent: Relations between Native and Refuge Populations in a Rural District in Western Germany after the Second World War',*German History*, Vol. 7 (1989), pp. 332–49; Paul Ginsborg, *A History of Contemporary Italy. Society and Politics 1943–1988* (Harmondsworth 1990), pp. 17–38.

6  Royal Institute of International Affairs, *Survey of International Affairs 1939–1946: 'The Realignment of Europe* (Oxford 1955), p. 19.

7  Doreen Warriner, *Eastern Europe After Hitler.* Fabian Society Research Series No. 50, (London, 1940), pp. 33ff.

8  See former Greek minister, Sotiros Gotzamanis, on this subject in a memorandum from 1943 on the 'New Europe', in Mark Mazower, 'Inside Hitler's Greece', mss. pp. 121–5. I am grateful to Dr Mazower for allowing me access to his work before publication.

9  Robert Machray, *The Problem of Upper Silesia* (London 1945).

10 'A Canadian Economist', 'Economic Reconstruction in Europe', *International Affairs,* Vol. 20 (1944), p. 539. For a British view of post-war regional planning with echoes of a *mitteleuropäische* New Order, *The Economist* 28 October 1944, pp. 568–9.

11 *The Economist*, 26 August 1944, pp. 292–3; Arnold Toynbee and Veronica Toynbee (eds), *Hitler's Europe*, (London, New York, Toronto, 1954), Part II, Patricia Harvey, 'The Economic Structure of Hitler's Europe', pp. 189–91. Milward, *War, Economy, Society,* pp. 162–3.

12 P. Einzig, 'Hitler's "New Order" in Theory and Practice', *Economic Journal,* Vol. 51 (April 1941), pp. 1–18.

13 J. Noakes and G. Pridham (eds), *Nazism 1919–1945: A Documentary Reader* Vol. 3, 'Foreign Policy, War and Racial Extermination', (Exeter, 1988), Doc. 622, p. 886. C. W. Guillebeaud, 'Hitler's New Economic Order For Europe', *Economic Journal,* Vol. 50 (December, 1940), p. 455; *Hitler's Europe,* p. 201.

14 *The Economist*, 14 March 1942, 18 March 1944 and 7 April 1945; League of Nations, Economic, Financial and Transit Department, *World Economic Survey 1942/44* (Geneva, 1945), pp. 267ff.

15 *Kölner Zeitung*, 2 July 1940. J. F. Freymond, 'Aspects of the Reich's Ministry of Economics Concept of An Economic Reorganization of Europe (1940)', *Studia Historiae Oeconomicae*, Vol. 14 (1980), pp. 5–14. See also H. R. Trevor-Roper (ed.), *Hitler's Table Talk*, (London 1953), Doc.11, (27 July 1941), pp. 15–6, 23 (23 September 1941), pp. 37–8 and 24 (25 September 1941), p. 40. For a recent and concise discussion, Peter Stirk, 'Authoritarian and National Socialist Conceptions of Nation, State and Europe', in *idem* (ed.), *European Unity in Context. The Interwar Period* (London, 1989).

16 Friedrich Naumann, *Mitteleuropa* (Berlin, 1915). Henry Cord Meyer, *Mitteleuropa in German Thought and Action 1815–1945* (The Hague 1955). Hans-Dietrich Schultz, 'Deutschlands "natürliche" Grenzen. "Mittellage" und "Mitteleuropa" in der Diskussion der Geographen seit dem Beginn des 19. Jahrhunderts', in *Geschichte und Gesellschaft*, Vol. 15 (1989), pp. 248–81. Fritz Fischer, *War of Illusions. German Policies from 1911 to 1914* (London,

1975), Chap. 21. Peter Theiner, '"Mitteleuropas"–Pläne im Wilhelm-inischen Deutschland', in Helmut Berding (ed.), *Wirtschaftliche und politische Integration in Europa im 19. und 20. Jahrhundert* (Göttingen, 1984). Wolfgang J. Mommsen, *Max Weber and German Politics 1890–1920* (Chicago 1984), Chapter 7 and 217ff., in particular, Robin Okey, 'Central Europe/Eastern Europe: Behind the Definitions', *Past and Present*, N. 137 (November, 1992), pp. 102–33.

17  Royal Institute for International Affairs, *Occupied Europe: German Exploita-tion and its Post-war Consequences* (London,1944), p. 7; *Hitler's Europe*, pp. 48, 52, 61, 166, 171; *Hitler's Table Talk*, Doc. 53, (26–27 October 1941), p. 93. Timothy Garton Ash, 'Mitteleuropa?', in Stephen R. Graubard (ed.), *Eastern Europe ... Central Europe ... Europe* (Boulder Colorado, 1991), p. 2.

18  Werner Daitz, *Der Weg zur Volkswirtschaft, Grossraumwirtschaft und Gross-raumpolitik* (Dresden 1945), in particular Chapter 4; Dirk Stegmann, '"Mitteleuropas" 1925–1934. Zum Problem der Kontinuität deutscher Außenhandelspolitik von Stresemann bis Hitler', in Dirk Stegmann, Bern-Jürgen Wendt, Peter-Christian Witt (eds), *Industrielle Gesellschaft und Politisches System. Beiträge zur politischen Sozialgeschichte. Festschrift für Fritz Fischer* (Bonn, 1978); *Hitler's Table Talk*, Doc. 45 (18 October 1941), p.73.

19  Roland Schönfeld, 'Die Balkanländer in der Weltwirtschaftskrise' in *Vierteljahreschrift für Sozial- und Wirtschaftsgeschichte*, Vol. 62 (1975), pp. 179–213. Hans-Jürgen Schröder, 'Der Aufbau der deutschen Hegemon-ialstellung in Südosteuropa 1933–1936', in Manfred Funke (ed.), *Hitler, Deutschland und die Mächte. Materialien zur Außenpolitik des Dritten Reiches* (Düsseldorf, 1976), pp. 757–73. Alan S. Milward, 'The Reichsmark Bloc and the International Economy', in Gerhard Hirschfeld and Lothar Kettenacker (eds.), *Der "Führerstaat": Mythos und Realität* (Stuttgart 1981). Bernd-Jürgen Wendt, *Großdeutschland. Außenpolitik und Kriegsvorbereitung des Hitler-Regimes*, (Munich 1987).

20  George Hallgarten and Joachim Radkau, *Deutsche Industrie und Politik. Von Bismarck bis in die Gegenwart* (Reinbek, 1981), p. 363. Okey, 'Central Eu-rope/Eastern Europe', p. 114.

21  Günter Schmölders, 'Die Bedeutung der Warenkreditabkommen im Handel Großdeutschlands mit Südosteuropa', *Zeitschrift für National-ökonomie*, Vol. 9 (1939), p. 567.

22  Dietrich Eichholtz, *Geschichte der deutschen Kriegswirtschaft 1939–1945*, Vol-ume 1, 1939–1941 (East Berlin, 1971), p. 145. For the First World War, Guillebaud, 'Hitler's New Economic Order', pp. 452–3.

23  Speeches of 1 and 30 January, in Max Domarus (ed.), *Hitler Reden und Proklamationen*, Vol. 2, Part 2 (Munich, 1965), pp. 1443, 1453, 1455–6.

24  Speech 19 February 1940, commemorating the 20th anniversary of the Party Programme. Reprinted in *ibid.*, p. 1465. Wolfgang Michalka (ed.), *Das Dritte Reich*, Band 2, Weltmachtanspruch und nationaler Zusammenbruch 1939–1945, (Munich 1985), Doc. 60, p.136.

25  A copy of Funk's speech is printed in Royal Institute of International Affairs, *Documents on International Affairs 1939–1946*, Vol. 2, Hitler's Europe, (London, 1954), pp. 29–35.

26  Royal Institute of International Affairs, *Review of the Foreign Press*, Series A, No. 48, 26 August 1940, Supplement: Foreign Research and Press Service: 'Interim Survey of Germany's Plan for Europe and the World'. *Hitler's Europe*, p. 48. See also Klaus Olshausen, 'Die deutsche Balkanpolitik 1940–1941', in Funke (ed.), *Hitler, Deutschland und die Mächte*, p. 713.

27  Dietmar Petzina, *Autarkiepolitik im Dritten Reich. Der nationalsozialistische Vierjahresplan* (Stuttgart 1968), p. 143. Franz Neumann, *Behemoth. The Structure and Practice of National Socialism 1933–1944* (London, 1944: 2nd edition),

28  Reprinted in Noakes and Pridham, *Nazism*, Vol. 3, Doc. 625, 889ff.

29  Walther Funk, quoted in *Deutsche Volkswirt*, 26 July 1940.

30  At the opening of the Trade Fair in Vienna on 1 September, quoted in *Völkischer Beobachter*, 3 September 1940.

31  'Interim Survey'.

32  Okey, 'Central Europe/Eastern Europe', pp. 103–4. Kube, 'Außenpolitik und "Großraumwirtschaft". Die deutsche Politik zur wirtschaftlichen Integration Südosteuropas 1933 bis 1939', in Berding (ed.), *Wirtschaftliche*, p. 186. Trevor-Roper, *Hitler's Table Talk*, Document 35, 13 (October 1941), pp. 52–3, on the ever-changing prospects.

33  *Frankfurter Zeitung*, 9 December 1938. In general, Konstantin Loulos, *Die deutsche Griechenlandpolitik von der Jahrhundertwende bis zum Ausbruch des Ersten Weltkrieges* (Frankfurt am Main, 1986). Hans Paul Höpfner, *Deutsche Südosteuropapolitik in der Weimarer Republik*, (Frankfurt am Main, 1983). Given the constraints on space, my discussion will not focus on Western Europe or Scandinavia or Eastern Europe and the Soviet Union. Important country studies for these regions already exist and little would be added to their wartime economic and social history here. Alan S. Milward, *The New Order and the French Economy* (Oxford, 1970) and *The Fascist Economy in Norway* (Oxford 1972); Alfred Sauvy, *La Vie Économique des Français de 1939 à 1945* (Paris, 1978); The Polish Research Centre London (ed.), *Upper Silesia* (London October 1941). For Eastern Europe as an area for colonization, see the memorandum by Otto Felix Brautigam, General Consul in the Reich Ministry for Occupied Eastern Territories, dated 25 October 1942, in Herbert Michaelis and Ernst Schraepler (eds), *Ursachen und Folgen. Vom deutschen Zusammenbruch 1918 und 1945 bis zur staatlichen Neuordnung Deutschlands in der Gegenwart,* Vol. 18. 'Das Dritte Reich. Die Wende des Krieges'. (Berlin, n.d.), Doc. 3291f, p. 581; *Hitler's Europe*, Parts II-VI, in particular; J. M. Winiewicz, *Aims and Failures of the German New Order* (Polish Research Centre, London, 1943); M. C. Kaser and E. A. Radice (eds), *The Economic History of Eastern Europe,* Vol. 2, 'Interwar Policy, the War and Reconstruction', (Oxford, 1986); Alexander Dallin, *German Rule in Russia* (London, 1981: 2nd edn).

34  The Royal Institute of International Affairs, *South-Eastern Europe. A Brief Survey*, (London, 1940), pp. 121–2.

35  *Occupied Europe*, p. 28; *Hitler's Europe*, pp. 180ff., 194ff., and 201; Hans Umbreit, 'Die deutsche Besatzungsverwaltung: Konzept und Typisierung' in Wolfgang Michalka (ed.), *Der Zweite Weltkrieg. Analysen, Grundzüge, Forschungsbilanz* (Munich, 1989).

36  The Royal Institute of International Affairs, *The Balkan States*, Vol. 1 (London 1936), pp. 14ff. 114–124; *South-Eastern Europe*, Chapter 6; John R. Lampe and Marvin R. Jackson, *Balkan Economic History, 1550–1950* (Boomington, Indiana 1982).

37  *Occupied Europe*, pp. 492–3.

38  Anke Wappler, 'Grundzüge der Okkupationspolitik des faschistischen deutschen Imperialismus gegenüber Griechenland vom März 1943 bis Oktober 1944' (Diss. Akademie der Wissenschaften, Berlin, 1986), p. 51, emphasizes Bulgarian and Greek deliveries, whereas Eichholtz, *Geschichte*

*der deutschen Kriegswirtschaft,* Vol. 2, 1941–1943, (East Berlin, 1985), p. 496, lays stress on Yugoslavian and Greek supplies.

39  B. R. Mitchell, *European Historical Statistics 1750–1970* (London, 1978: abridged edition), Tables D2, D7 and D8.

40  *The Economist,* 28 March 1942, p. 432. *Großraum* planners are said to have recognized that 'the economic future of Upper Silesia … (was) … closely linked up with its hinterland in the east and south-east of Europe'. Machray, *The Problem of Upper Silesia,* pp. 32–5, 57, 61ff., 105f.; Walter Greiff, 'Raumordnung und Wirtschaftsplanung', in *Deutsche Monatshefte,* April-June 1942, p. 429; 'Hitler's Europe', p. 195f.

41  Michalka, *Das Dritte Reich,* Vol. 2, Doc. 60, p. 137; Gustav Schlotterer to the Foreign Trade Committee of the Reichsgruppe Industrie on the 'New Order in Europe', 19 June 1940; Petzina, *Autarkiepolitik,* pp. 141–2; Eichholtz, *Kriegswirtschaft,* Vol. 1, pp. 179, 182; Hallgarten and Radkau, *Deutsche Industrie,* p. 413.

42  *Hitler's Europe,* p. 233. Milward, *War, Economy, Society,* p. 150. Petzina, *Autarkiepolitik,* p. 148f.

43  *The Economist,* 7 March 1942.

44  'Aufzeichnung über die wirtschaftlichen Leistungen Frankreichs zugunsten Deutschlands und die deutschen Lieferungen an Frankreich', 19 March 1942, printed in *Ursachen und Folgen,* Vol. 18, as Doc. 3271. Even Polish armaments, originally dismantled, were revived, though on a smaller scale. Radice (ed.), *Eastern Europe,* Vol. 2, pp. 405, 428f., 450.

45  As a reward for Axis membership, the two Vienna Awards (March 1939 and August 1940) provided Hungary with the southern parts of Slovakia, the Carpatho-Ukraine, parts of Transylvania and the Bacska region, thereby doubling its territory (settled by the Trianon Treaty 1920) and greatly adding to its economy. I. T Berend and G. Ranki, *Hungary: A Century of Economic Development* (London, 1974), pp. 168–76. League of Nations, *World Economic Survey 1942/44,* pp. 73–4. Rolf Wagenführ, *Die Deutsche Industrie im Kriege 1939–1945* (Berlin, 1963: 2nd edn), p. 29; Mitchell, *European Historical Statistics,* Tables D4 and D9; C. J. Schmitz, *World Non-Ferrous Production,* (London, 1979), pp. 50–1, 203.

46  Radice, (ed.), *Eastern Europe,* Vol. 2, pp. 402, 407–8, 438, 448.

47  Lampe and Jackson, *Balkan Economic History,* pp. 527, 562–3 (Table 13.12), 560.

48  Radice, (ed.), *Eastern Europe,* Vol. 2, pp. 439–43. Romania was Germany's largest supplier of crude oil.

49  Acreage of soybean and sunflower seed tripled and output rose by two-thirds until 1943; Südostropa was under the direction of Franz Neuhausen. See Lampe and Jackson, *Balkan Economic History,* pp. 527–30.

50  Output stagnated throughout the war in spite of German control, Radice, *Eastern Europe,* Vol. 2, p. 441 and Table 17.3 p. 402.

51  Private industry had taken a keen interest in Greek ores since the 1930s, recognizing their importance for German and European economic development. For the inter-war period see Mark Mazower, *Greece and the International Economic Crisis* (Oxford, 1991).

52  Radice (ed.), *Eastern Europe,* Vol.2, pp. 400, 410, 450.

53  Berend and Ranki, *Hungary,* p. 179.

54  T. Kirk, 'Limits of Germandom: Resistance to the Nazi Annexation of Slovenia', in *The Slavonic and East European Review,* Vol. 69 (1991), pp. 646–67.

55  Alice Teichova, *The Czechoslovak Economy 1918–1980* (London, 1988), pp. 83–4.
56  Greek agriculture was already the poorest in the region. Kathleen Gibberd, *Greece*, (British Survey Handbooks III, Cambridge, 1944), p. 72. On the general point, *Occupied Europe*, p. 22. The League of Nations calculated that a daily intake of 2,400 calories was necessary for the well-being of an average adult. In 1942 the calorific distribution in Greece was one-tenth of that, the lowest in occupied Europe. Inter-Allied Information Committee, *Conditions in Occupied Territories Nr.2: Rationing under Axis Rule* (London, 1942), pp. 1–9.
57  Athanasios Sbarounís, *Meletai kai anamníseis ek tou 2. Pankosmiou Polemou* (Athens, 1950), p. 258.
58  *The Economist*, 14 March 1942.
59  *The Economist*, 30 November 1940, p. 668, and 7 March 1942, pp.327–8, and 14 March 1942. League of Nations, *Monthly Bulletin of Statistics*, Vol. 27 (April, 1946), pp. 132, 142.
60  *South-Eastern Europe*, pp. 109–10; League of Nations, *Europe's Trade* (Geneva, 1941), p. 78f.; *Statisches Jahrbuch des deutschen Reiches*, Vol. 59 (Berlin, 1942), pp. 322–3.
61  Larry Neal, 'The Economics and Finance of Bilateral Clearing Agreements: Germany 1934–38', *Economic History Review*, 2nd series, Vol. 32 (1979), pp. 391–404.
62  Hans-Joachim Braun, *The German Economy in the Twentieth Century* (London, 1990), p. 101f.
63  *Hitler's Europe*, pp. 199–200, see the next section. This was not the only benefit. Germany had entered the war without substantial assets and was now in a position to utilize the clearing system and blocked Mark arrangements to draw on the resources of other countries in order to prosecute the war (in addition to claiming reparations and imposing occupation levies), ibid., p. 268, and Christoph Buchheim, 'Die besetzten Länder im Dienste der deutschen Kriegswirtschaft während des Zweiten Weltkriegs', in *Vierteljahreshefte für Zeitgeschichte*, Vol. 34 (1986), pp. 117–145.
64  The system worked according to the following principle: (1) Romania has an active balance of payments with Holland; (2) Holland cannot clear its debts with Romania by exporting; (3) Holland has an active balance of payments with Germany; (4) Germany can offer commodities to Romania; (5) Holland transfers blocked credit balances in Germany to Romania and thereby clears its debts to Romania; (6) Romania uses these to purchase from Germany. *The Economist* (28 February 1942), p. 293.
65  Review of Foreign Press, Series A, No. 71, 3 February 1941, 'Further Survey of Germany's Plans for Europe and the World', p. 3. Braun, *German Economy*, pp. 117–19, gives the slightly higher number of 16.
66  *The Economist*, 28 February 1942. *Hitler's Europe*, p. 275.
67  This was prepared for publication in the *Deutsche-Westfälische Zeitung*, 3 March 1942. The original text can be found in BAK R63/250a. Cf. Dietrich Orlow, *The Nazis in the Balkans*, (Pittsburgh, 1967), p. 105, fn. 30.
68  *South-Eastern Europe*, pp. 109–110. Lampe and Jackson, *Balkan Economic History*, p. 530.
69  *World Economic Survey 1942/44*, p. 30. League of Nations, *Monthly Bulletin* (April 1946), p. 145.
70  Berend and Ranki, *Hungary*, p. 173. Gyorgy Ranki, 'The Hungarian

Economy', in Peter F. Sugar *et.al.*, (eds), *A History of Hungary* (London, 1990), p. 367.
71 Ibid., p. 365.
72 League of Nations, *Monthly Bulletin* (April 1946), pp. 479–480.
73 Wappler, 'Grundzüge', p. 11.
74 Christos Hadziiossif, 'Griechen in der deutschen Kriegsproduktion', in Ulrich Herbert (ed.), *Europa und der "Reichseinsatzs". Ausländische Zivilarbeiter, Kriegsgefangene und KZ-Häftlinge in Deutschland 1938–1945* (Essen, 1991), pp. 213, 217, fn. 26 for list of mines affected by partisan activity. Wappler, 'Grundzüge', pp. 9, 52, 76–7.
75 Lorand Tilkovsky, 'The Late Interwar Years and World War II', in Sugar, *A History of Hungary*, p. 350.
76 *The Economist*, 28 February 1942.
77 Roland Schönfelder, 'Deutsche Rohstoffsicherungspolitik in Jugoslawien 1934–1944', in *Vierteljahreshefte für Zeitgeschichte*, Vol. 24 (1976), pp. 244, 247.
78 *World Economic Survey 1942/44*, p. 269.
79 M. Lanter, *Die Finanzierung des Krieges, Quellen, Methoden und Lösungen seit dem Mittelalter bis Ende des Zweiten Weltkrieges von 1939 bis 1945* (Lusanne, 1950), pp. 104–5, quoted in Fritz Blaich, *Wirtschaft und Rüstung im "Dritten Reich"* (Düsseldorf, 1987) p. 120. Braun, *German Economy*, p. 119, gives the following sums: end of 1940: 953 million Reichsmark, mid-1942: 3,251 milliard Reichsmark; mid-1944: 28 milliard Reichsmark.
80 'Further Survey', p. 4.
81 *Ibid.*, p. 3. Meanwhile the currencies of those countries incorporated into the Greater Reich were revalued upwards, thus bringing them into line with the Reichsmark, *World Economic Survey 1939/41*, p. 158. The Director of Naval Intelligence Division, *Luxembourg*, (Geographical Handbook series BR528, London, 1944), pp. 220f.f, 308–9, and *idem.*, *Holland*, (BR549, London 1944), p. 610ff.
82 *World Economic Survey 1939/41*, p. 158 and Chapter VIII. David Marsh, *The Bundesbank. The Bank that Rules Europe*, (London 1992), p. 133.
83 *World Economic Survey 1942/44*, Chapter VI. Janovsky, 'Bericht', pp. 12–3. *The Economist*, 14 March 1942, p. 359, and ibid., 'Commercial History and Review of 1941', p. 16. 'Commercial History and Review of 1943', *The Economist*, 18 March 1944, p. 9.
84 For government expenditures, debts and note circulation see, World Economic Survey 1942/44, pp. 154–9, 174, 202.
85 *The Economist*, 30 November 1940. Eichholtz, *Kriegswirtschaft* Vol. 1, p. 177, and Vol. 2, p. 490 stresses the planned nature of economic integration and subordination through military conquest. Cf. Milward, *War, Economy, Society*, p. 161. Hallgarten and Radkau, *Deutsche Industrie*, pp. 364, 369.
86 *Occupied Europe*, p. 28. Petzina *Autarkiepolitik*, p. 140. Milward, *War, Economy, Society*, p. 158f.
87 Vaclav Prucha, 'Integration of Czechoslovakia in the Economic System of Nazi Germany', (Paper presented to the Second International Conference, Leverhulme Trust/University of Hull, 'European Unity in Context: "Making the New Europe?" The problem of European Unity and the Second World War', Hull University, Summer 1988), p. 4, for quote. *Hitler's Europe*, pp. 180–4. Radice, (ed.), *Eastern Europe*, p. 305. Dallin, *German Rule*, pp. 383ff., 393. Eichholtz, *Kriegswirtschaft*, Vol. 1, p. 154. Petzina, *Autarkiepolitik*, p. 143.
88 *The Economist*, 7 March 1942, p. 432.

89  *The Economist*, 14 March 1942, 'Commercial History and Review for 1941'.
90  *Occupied Europe*, p. 37. In general see, Overy, *Goering*.
91  This passage and the following is based on, Inter-Allied Information Committee, *Conditions in Occupied Territories*, No. 5: 'The Penetration of German Capital into Europe' (London, 1942).
92  Hallgarten and Radkau, *Deutsche Industrie*, p. 360.
93  Eichholtz, *Kriegswirtschaft*, Vol. 2, p. 399. Peter Hayes, *Industry and Ideology. IG Farben in the Nazi Era*, (Cambridge, 1987), p. 273, ascribes a 'defensive' role to IG Farben's actions. On the interwar period see, Verena Schröter, 'The IG Farbenindustrie AG in Central and South-East Europe 1926–1938', in Alice Teichova and P. L. Cottrell (eds), *International Business and Central Europe, 1918–1939* (Leicester and New York, 1983).
94  Overy, *Goering*, p. 111 and 'German Multinationals and the Nazi State in Occupied Europe', in A. Teichova et al. (eds), *Multinational Enterprise in Historical Perspective* (Cambridge, 1986). Neumann, *Behemoth*, pp. 298–305. Eichholtz, *Kriegswirtschaft*, Vol. 2, p. 480. Radice (ed.), *Eastern Europe*, Vol. 2, p. 440.
95  The Bundesarchiv Koblenz holds a rich vein of material on individual firms in the context of this subject. In general, Eichholtz, *Kriegswirtschaft* Vol. 2, pp. 460–77, 480, and Table 110 for a further list of subsidiary firms and holdings. Neumann, *Behemoth, op.cit.* Hallgarten and Radkau, *Deutsche Industrie,* p. 364.
96  Mirko Lamer, 'Die Wandlungen der ausländischen Kapitalanlagen auf dem Balkan', in *Weltwirtschaftliches Archiv,* Vol. 48, Part 3 1938, pp. 501ff.
97  Memorandum of 20 September 1940, cited in Office of Military Government for Germany, United States Finance Division, *Ermittlungen gegen die Deutsche Bank* (ed.) Hans Magnus Enzensberger, (Nördlingen 1985), p. 190. See Chapter XII, 'Auslandstätigkeit der Deutschen Bank', in general. See also, *Hitler's Europe*, p. 205f.
98  *Ermittlungen gegen die Deutsche Bank*, pp. 229f., 235. Inter-Allied Information Committee, 'Penetration', pp. 6–8, and the following country sections.
99  *The Economist*, 7 February 1942, p. 190 and 23 May 1940, p. 719.
100  *Ermittlungen gegen die Dresdner Bank*, pp. 251–5. Pilder sat on a total of forty boards of financial and industrial concerns, all of them in Germany, Central and South-Eastern Europe.
101  *Ermittlungen gegen die Dresdner Bank*, pp. 17, 167.
102  Inter-Allied Information Committee, 'Penetration', p. 15.
103  These were: Deutsche Bank, Dresdner Bank, Commerzbank, Reichskredit AG and the Handels-Gesellschaft (Berlin). *The Economist*, 14 March 1942, p. 359 and 23 May 1942.
104  Inter-Allied Information Committee, 'Penetration', pp. 6–7, for a list of these.
105  *Ermittlungen gegen die Deutsche Bank*, pp. 27, 354, Table 1. The Bank owned 21 per cent of total investment and 18.5 per cent of total wealth of the 653 banks in Greater Germany; it also had 490 branches and deposit banks, and acquired two of the most important central banks: the Creditanstalt Vienna and Société Générale de Belgique. Inter-Allied Information Committee, 'Penetration', p. 6.
106  *Ermittlungen gegen die Dresdner Bank*, pp. 9, 17.
107  *Mitteleuropa*, p. 165.

108   This is the conclusion of Patricia Harvey in, *Hitler's Europe*, pp. 194, 279;
      Hans Umbreit, 'Die deutsche Besatzungsverwaltung', pp. 719, 725–6;
      idem., 'The Battle for Hegemony in Western Europe', in Militär-
      geschichtliches Forschungsamt (ed.), *Germany and the Second World War*,
      Vol. II, 'Germany's Initial Conquests in Europe', (Oxford 1991), p. 316; E.
      A. Radice, *Eastern Europe*, pp. 306–7, among others.
109   Kube, 'Außenpolitik', pp. 187, 210. Vögel, 'Deutschland und Südost-
      europa', pp. 542–6. Petzina dates the 'eclipse' of the Greater Economic
      Sphere centred upon *Mitteleuropa* and under the auspices of the Office for
      the Four Year Plan, to 1942, *Autarkiepolitik*, p. 148. Milward, *War,
      Economy, Society*, p. 342.
110   'The German People have not started the war for the benefit of Europe.
      They had no intention of sacrificing themselves on the altar of a theoretical
      reconstruction of their continent,' Einzig, 'Hitler's "New Order"', p. 201.
111   'Der Südosten in der neue Wirtschaftsordnung', in *Völkischer Beobachter*,
      28th July 1940. *Berliner Börsenzeitung*, 26 October 1941.
112   As the banker Hermann Abs told an audience of business leaders on 17 July
      1941. Eichholtz, *Kriegswirtschaft*, Vol. 2, p. 397. Cf. Goebbels' diary entry
      of 15 October 1940, on acquiring complete control of Europe's film indus-
      try market, in F. Taylor (ed.), *The Goebbels Diaries 1939–1941*, (London,
      1982), p. 143. See also his entry for 1 October 1942: 'The most essential
      mineral wealth and territorial gains are in our hands. All that is needed now
      is a certain degree of patience and time to exploit them. Time is on our
      side', in Willi A. Boelcke (ed.) *The Secret Conferences of Dr Goebbels, October
      1939–March 1943*, (London, 1967), p. 282.
113   Eichholtz, *Kriegswirtschaft*, Vol. 1, p. 177.
114   Michalka, *Das Dritte Reich*, Doc. 67, p. 151.
115   Ibid., Doc. 68, p. 154.
115   Okey, 'Central Europe/Eastern Europe', p. 117.

Chapter 6

# 1848/49–1989
## *Two European Revolutions*

## *Dietmar Stübler*

Developments in the USSR and in European countries under Soviet influence entered their decisive phase in 1985 and 1988/89 respectively, leading to radical changes in political as well as social environments, that is, to revolutions.[1] What they achieved in the countries of 'really existing socialism' went far beyond changes in government. They brought about conditions in society which stood in irreconcilable contrast to existing ones. At the same time, the revolutions upset the existing balance in international relations. Soviet-dominated alliances collapsed, and the countries thus liberated formed new ones.

There is now widespread interest in a scientific reassessment of our approach to these developments. The factual knowledge of historians, political scientists and sociologists lags far behind the historical detail stored up in the memories of many first-hand witnesses who were members of now dissolved governments or of those engaged in civil rights movements. However, historians whose interest is focused on contemporary history are often faced with that kind of problem, and we are conscious of the fact that we can only offer *preliminary* answers to questions arising from continuous processes.

Let us choose as our point of reference for the 1989 European revolution another continental revolution, that of 1848/49. To start with, it is worth considering whether both were, in fact, *revolutions*.

For contemporaries of the 1848/49 revolution that was beyond doubt. On the extreme left wing, Karl Marx and Friedrich Engels involved themselves in the revolution in line with the doctrines of the manifesto of the Communist Party: communists everywhere support all revolutionary activity against existing social and political conditions.'[2] By contrast, Bismarck and his friends from the Association for King and Country stated as their political conviction 'that we shall not collude in any way with the revolution'.[3] King Frederic William IV, moreover, declined the imperial crown offered to him by the Frankfurt National Assembly of 1848 because he considered it 'sullied by the carrion stench of the revolution'.[4] Despite their different standpoints, those protagonists of 1848/49 unanimously referred to the events of the time as 'a revolution'.

In 1989, the picture is not as clear. Our confused judgement derives from the experience of the two great revolutions: the French Revolution of 1789 and the Russian Revolution of 1917. Both those revolutions had to do with violence and terror, with interventionist and civil wars. That is precisely why many civil-rights campaigners are reluctant to accept the term revolution for 1989. Adam Michnik, at one time a strong supporter of Lech Walesa and today his most pronounced critic, addressed that very point. For him, the term revolution does not apply to the events of 1989 because he despises all kinds of revolutionary force: 'Let those methods be their own', he told Timothy Garton Ash, the best contemporary reporter and commentator in central Europe from 1980 to 1990. The Hungarian author György Konrád too, known for his critical stance against the regime, rejected the methods bemoaned by Michnik on the grounds that they were rooted in the traditions of Jacobean-Leninist rulers.[5]

The chairman of the Hungarian Federation of Free Democrats, Zóltan Lovas, spoke of the 'quiet Hungarian revolution'. The main slogan of the GDR revolutionaries was: 'No violence!' The President of the Czech Republic, Václav Havel, called the revolution in the CSSR the 'gentle revolution'. In preparation for the general election on January 3, 1992, the fifteen parties represented in the Bulgarian parliament agreed on a 'Resolution for the Peaceful Transition to Democracy in Bulgaria'.[6]

It is, indeed, one of the most striking characteristics of the European revolution of 1989 that it triumphed without any form of military contest. That is what distinguishes it from 1848/49. We need only think of General Cavaignac in Paris, June 1848; of General Windischgraetz in Prague, June 1848, in Vienna, October 1848 and in Budapest, January 1849; or of William, Prince of Prussia in Baden and the Palatinate, July 1849. If need be, counter-revolutionary forces showed solidarity in their determination to crush the revolution, for example when Russian troups, following an agreement between Russia and Austria, launched an offensive against Hungarian volunteer battalions, the Honvéds (June 1848) who were forced to capitulate in August 1848.

In 1989, none of the Russian garrisons left their barracks (as they did in Hungary in 1956 or in the CSSR in 1968) in order to march against the revolutionaries and re-erect tumbling governments. Even party leaders and governments forced to abdicate did not use their armies against civil-rights campaigners. That – with one notable exception which we shall discuss shortly – is the fundamental difference between the situation in European socialist states and in the People's Republic of China. In Peking in June 1989 the army, acting without any directive from Moscow, created a ghastly bloodbath in the Square of Heavenly Peace in order to crush a mass demonstration. Nothing comparable occurred in Europe except in Romania which had relaxed its ties with Moscow to a greater degree than other socialist states. In December 1989, army and security forces fired without warning on mass demonstrations in Timisoara and Bucharest.

For the time being it is impossible to assess with fairness and impartiality to what extent the European revolution owes its peaceful nature to the strength of civil-rights movements and the strength of the crowds sympathising with them, and to what extent it merely reflects the weakness of burnt-out over-aged leadership in parties and governments.

If we acknowledge the events of 1989 as a revolution we still need to ask ourselves whether this was a *European* revolution. For the 1848/49 revolution, its continental characteristics are evident twice over. First, the wave of revolution covered the best part of the continent: 'France, the German and Italian states, the entire multinational state of Austria and the border areas of the Ottoman empire on the Balkans (the principalities of Moldavia and Walachia) were swept along. The pace of reforms also accelerated in Belgium, The Netherlands, Switzerland and the Scandinaviean countries without, however, turning into revolution. There were sporadic rebellious attempts in Ireland, Spain and Greece which were as unsuccessful as those in England. Only Russia remained unaffected by the European wave of revolution.'[7] Second, the pan-European aspect of the revolutionary movements was matched by the common purpose nearly all countries shared, that is, 'The setting up of nation states, democratisation of political systems, and the reorganisation of social welfare legislation.'[8]

The 1989 revolution was limited to Central Eastern Europe, South East Europe and Eastern Europe. So far, Western and Central Western Europe has seen neither reform movements nor, indeed, 'parliamentary revolutions'. In our view, that European quality of the 1989 revolution stems from Eastern Europe concurring on an overwhelming scale with Western European values. The dissident Hungarian writer György Konrád put it like this: 'We East Europeans are oriented to the West in our interests, in our migration. In the course of our history we have endeavoured to achieve integration with the other part of our Continent, and now we are again seeking rapprochement.'[9] The title of one of his books is *Mein Traum von Europa* (Europe My Dream).[10] Jens Reich, co-founder of New Forum, one of the civil-rights organizations which were most influential at the start of the GDR revolution, called his own report of the events of 1989/90, *Rückkehr nach Europa* (*Return to Europe*).[11] Bulgaria, too, according to a statement by its President Shelju Sheleff, has always understood itself as being part of the European cultural scene despite Ottoman and Russian bondage.[12] Asserting a European dimension of the 1989 revolution we are not ignoring the fact, however, that bilateral relations have been hampered by reticence, lack of understanding and mistrust between civil-rights movements in the east, and between opposition parties and extra-parliamentary movements in the west.

When he was awarded the Peace Price of the German Book Trade, Václav Havel said in his acceptance speech in October 1989: 'It is obvious that the new German *Ostpolitik* meant the first glimmer of hope for a Europe without the Cold War and without the Iron Curtain. At the same time, however, it also meant – more than once – giving up freedom and thus the fundamental prerequisite of peace in a real sense.'[13] In our view, the Conference for Security and Cooperation in Europe, culminating in the signing of the Helsinki Final Act in August 1975, encouraged opposition movements in the socialist countries of

Europe. *One* piece of evidence for this was Charter 77 in the CSSR, dating from 1 January 1977, in which Václav Havel played a leading role. Another can be found in Poland. The Worker Defence Committees (from 1977 onwards) and the Socialist Self-Defence Committees (from 1978 onwards) were direct forerunners of the Solidarnosz (founded 22 September 1980) to which Lech Walesa owed his political stature. Furthermore, it is no coincidence that 1976/77 saw the disputes within the GDR Writers' Federation which led to Wolf Bierman being stripped of his GDR citizenship and to several other writers being expelled from the Federation (including Stephan Heym and Christa Wolf). In contrast to the CSSR and the Peoples' Republic of China, the GDR was able to suppress new departures which had attracted widespread attention.

However, in the West where politicians are used to long-term planning, Eastern opposition leaders met with little understanding when they impatiently pleaded for a change in the really existing socialism. Václav Havel had intended to explain to the delegates of the Amsterdam Peace Congress (1985) that 'today peace in Europe is no longer threatened by the possibility of change; it is threatened by the unchanging *status quo*.'[14] However, he was unable to attend because Prague refused to give him an exit visa. But the West European architects of the Helsinki Final Act ran into similar difficulties trying to convince eastern civil-rights campaigners sitting like cats on hot bricks that the west was prepared to accept the *status quo* in order to be able to change it in the long term; that it was prepared to put up with impenetrable borders in order to wrest from eastern governments a commitment to respect human rights so that, in the long term, those impenetrable borders might be opened up.

Relations between the *extra-parliamentary* opposition in the West and dissidents in the East proved to be no less difficult. The so-called students' revolt of 1967/68, and the peace movement aimed against the NATO dual-track agreement at the end of the 1970s and the beginning of the eighties were directed against precisely *those* economic systems on which civil-rights campaigners in the East had pinned their hopes. That was bound to evoke contradictions.

In our view, they do not invalidate the European nature of the 1989 revolution which derives from the concord in focussing on the values of bourgeois democracy and a free market economy. Both of those were helped on their road to success in Europe by the industrial revolution in England and the French Revolution of 1789.

The aim of the European revolutions of 1848/49 and of 1989 was to wreck international peace agreements, that is, the Congress of Vienna 1814/15 and those of the Yalta and Potsdam Conferences. But the order of Vienna withstood the revolution. Right at the beginning, Lord Palmerston wrote to Tsar Nicholas: 'At the present time we are the only European powers that have remained unchallenged, and we should look upon each other with trust and confidence.'[15] By averting the threat of a French intervention in Italy, England prevented a French war against Austria, and by averting the threat of a Prussian intervention in Poland it prevented a Prussian war against Russia. Tsarist Russia assumed the role of guardian, watching over the balance of power in Eastern and Central Europe and retained that role even in 1850 when Prussia, against Austrian opposition, tried to force through the *kleindeutsch* concept under its own leadership, albeit unsuccessfully (Olmütz Punctuation, 29 November, 1850). It was only with the Crimean War (1853/54–1855/56) waged by England and France in support of Turkey against Russia, and with Italy's and Prussia's wars of independence and unification against Austria and France (1859/60–1870/71) that the political order of Vienna collapsed.

The year 1989 was different from 1848/49 in that it removed the existing international order. The collapse of the eastern bloc brought about the end of the Cold War which had followed on from the end of the Second World War. Russia is now turning its back on Central Europe – as it had done after its defeat in the Crimean War. The Slavonic multinational states, the Union of Socialist Soviet Republics, Yugoslavia and Czechoslovakia have disintegrated. By contrast, Central Europe saw a considerable expansion of the Federal Republic of Germany when it was joined by the German Democratic Republic. These enormous historic processes are unfolding now without triggering a European or world war, which confirms the point made earlier that there is no longer a link between revolution and military power.

In the European revolutions of 1848/49, national conflicts were of prime importance. In 1848/49, problems of a highly complex nature had to be faced by the Habsburg Monarchy with its mixed population of 7.5 million Germans, 18.7 million Slavs, 5.5 million Italians and 4.5 million Hungarians; by Italy, where Austria's foreign rule had put unbearable stress upon the country and its people; by a Poland divided into three; by Ireland and by the Danubian principalities of Moldavia and Walachia. The various nationalist movements were an important driving force in the 1848/49 European revolution, but their emergence was uncoordinated. Indeed, their mutual rivalries constituted one of the main causes for the demise of the revolution.[16] In each case the problem of creating uninational states remained unresolved, deferred to the 1860s and 1870s (Italy 1861; Germany 1871; Romania, Bulgaria, Serbia, Montenegro each in 1878) or to the Paris Peace Conference at the end of the First World War (the Serbian-Croatian-Slovenian monarchy, from 1929 onwards Yugoslavia; Czechoslovakia).

The redrawing of national boundaries, resettlement programmes and expulsion immediately before, during and just after the Second World War defused the conflicts of national identity in some respects – only a very small German-speaking minority was allowed to remain in Poland – while aggravating them in others: some 2 to 2.5 million Hungarians and just under 23 million Romanians reside in Romania. The dictatorships in the Eastern Bloc hushed up existing tensions or used force to contain them. The end of really existing socialism has meant that these tensions were discharged without there being generally accepted norms or institutions to regulate these processes.[17]

Poland was an exception. The loss of land in the eastern part of the country (approximately 175,000 square kilometers) as agreed at Yalta and Potsdam was more than compensated for by the gain of land in the West, smaller in area (just under 100,000 square kilometers) but of significantly higher value. For Poland, the political consequences were painful and lasting: 'even the most anti-Soviet Pole felt himself tied to Moscow by a chain of fear – fear of German revisionism.'[18] At the end of the 1960s and the beginning of the 1970s, the *Ostpolitik* of the socialist-liberal coalition (Brandt/Scheel) was a contributory factor in enabling Warsaw to relax the shackles and eventually discard them. At the present time, Poland is not experiencing any problems with the presence of a strong national minority within her boundaries, or from her commitment and obligation to look after the interests of Polish minorities in neighbouring countries.

Yugoslavia is, of course, a different matter altogether! Here the dissolution of the former state follows the route of civil war, predominantly fought by the numerically strongest populations, that is Serbs (40 per cent) and Croats (22 per cent). A number of factors other than the inherent potential of national conflict contribute to this disintegration: the economic north-south divide (from developed Slovenia down to underdeveloped Montenegro); the abuse for political purposes of religious contrasts between the Serbian orthodox Chistians, the Roman Catholic Croats and the Muslims in Bosnia and Kosovo; and, last but not least, people's differing perception of their culture and history in the Ottoman empire (Croatia, Slovenia).[19]

By contrast to events in Yugoslavia, the formal dissolution of Czechoslovakia is an historical fact, and the process has, so far, been peaceful. More than 30 million Czechs live predominantly in the Czech Republic, some 15 million Slovaks (and some 1.5 million Hungarians) predominantly in the Slovak Republic.

The question of national identity helped trigger the revolution in Hungary, Bulgaria and Romania. Let us recall just some of the more salient events. After the General Secretary of the Hungarian Socialist Workers' Party, János Kádár, had been overthrown (21 May 1988) by reformist Communist forces within the party, the Communists tried, albeit unsuccessfully, to steer the popular movement on to a nationalist course. (On 27 June 1988, a mass rally took place on the Budapest Heroes' Square against the policies of the Bulgarian Communist government towards Hungarians living in Transylvania.) Regarding the situation in Bulgaria, a direct link existed between the overthrow of Todor Zhivkov, General Secretary of the Bulgarian Communist Party (10 November 1989) and the mass exodus of the Turkish minority from Bulgaria and into Turkey (from May 1989 onwards) at the height of the Campaign for the Assimilation of Turks in Bulgaria. The Romanian revolution had begun in Timisoara (17 December 1989), a Transylvanian town with a majority population of Hungarians and Germans. When pastor Laszlo Tökes, known to be critical of the regime was arrested some 10,000 inhabitants of Timisoara staged a protest, and large numbers were massacred by security police and the army. On 22 December, 1989, the General Secretary of the Romanian Communist Party, Nicolae Ceausescu, was arrested and, following demonstrations in Bucharest, was executed three days later.

The question of Macedonia, which involves Bulgaria, Serbia, Greece, the unification of the 'Second Romanian State' Moldavia with Romania, and Albania's claims to Kosovo are just three issues which are moving further and further into the limelight without us being able to foresee, at the present moment, how they are going to be dealt with.

Referring back to the question of national identity in the context of the European revolution 1989, let us now consider the revolution in the GDR in some greater detail. There were two reasons why party leaders and political leaders in the GDR failed in their attempts to refute or suppress the historical fact that, at the end of the Second World War, the German question had been left unresolved: one was the way in which Germans experienced their common intellectual and cultural history; the other was personal contacts which existed across the political divide and which, at the same time, were continually renewed. During the 1980s, the economic gap between the East and the West widened to the detriment of the East where it reactivated bonds with the West.

The summer of 1989 saw a mass exodus from the GDR to the FRG, with signs of panic. Hundreds of thousands of refugees from the GDR occupied diplomatic missions of the Federal Republic of Germany in socialist countries. On 8 August 1989 the GDR mission of the Federal Republic of Germany closed, followed by the closure of the West German embassies in Budapest (14 August) and Prague (23 August). When Hungary opened its borders with Austria on 11 September 1989 some 15,000 GDR emigrants poured into the West within a few days. An equal number of GDR citizens arriving in the West had travelled by train from Prague via the GDR.

For those who had stayed behind, the mass exodus from the GDR was a sign of the instability of the state and gave them the courage to speak out openly. It was then that the demonstrations began in Berlin, Dresden, Leipzig and elsewhere. The Monday demonstrations in Leipzig proved the most significant in triggering the revolution. On 2 October 1989, 20,000 people took part in rallies, on 7 October there were some 70,000, and by the end of the following month some 300,000 people participated. Following the Leipzig example (up to mid-March 1990), similar mass rallies took place in the streets and on the squares of most large and medium-sized towns. They prompted the resignation of the government on 7 November 1989, the opening of the borders between the GDR and West Berlin as well as between the GDR and the Federal Republic on 9 November, 1989, and the resignation of the Socialist Unity Party of Germany (SED) leadership on 3 December, 1989.

When the demonstrations began in October, 1989, their slogan was: 'We are the *people!*' The men and women who carried the placards believed that socialism could be reformed and democratized. By the end of November and the beginning of December, the motto had changed to: 'We are *one* people!' In no time, that motto rendered all other issues irrelevant. 'The majority of people totally rejected ... the renewal ... of the GDR.' [20] They were calling for unification by the shortest possible route. Marked by the milestones of the monetary, economic and social union, which introduced the West German deutschmark into the GDR, on 1 July 1990 (State Treaty on Economic and Monetary and Social Union dated 21 June 1990), and the Treaty on the Final Settlement on Germany signed by the foreign ministers of the four wartime allies and of the two Germanies on 12 December 1990, that route led to the GDR formally joining the Federal Republic of Germany on 3 October 1990 (Unification Treaty dated 20/21 September 1990). With the signing of that treaty, the division of the German nation into two separate populations had ended. Now there is only *one* German state in the centre of Europe, a Federal Republic of Germany considerably larger than before. That factor will be of increasing importance for the course of European history, particularly if we compare it with the dissolution of the Soviet Union, Yugoslavia and Czechoslovakia during the European revolution of 1989.

Revolutions are always periods of intense constitutional politics. According to Ralf Dahrendorf, the latter is concerned with 'the framework of a social order, with the social contract, as it were, and its institutionalised manifestations. Normal everyday politics, on the other hand, is concerned with certain directions of action which are determined by individual interests and preferences.'[21]

While the European revolution of 1848/49 did not achieve its aim of establishing nation states, the prospect for constitutionalism was rather different. France's constitution of November 1848, replaced by the imperial constitution after Napoleon's coup *d'état* in December 1852, is a special case in continental Europe because political and social conditions were more advanced here than elsewhere in Europe. In Prussia, Frederic William IV dissolved the National Assembly and, from a position of unchallenged power, decreed a constitution on 5 December 1948. Subsequently revised by the monarch on 31 January 1850, it remained in force until 1918. In Austria, too, the Emperor sent his Imperial Diet packing and proclaimed a constitution (4 March 1849). However, its fortunes differed from the Prussian example. The constitution remained but a piece of paper, and even that was scrapped by Francis Joseph in 1851. In Italy, the situation was similar with one notable exception. The constitutions proclaimed in February and March 1848 were subsequently repealed by the princes (1848/49). Only the Albertinian Statute of the Kingdom of Sardinia-Piedmont (5 March 1948) remained in force until the end of the monarchy in 1946.

But unrelated to any one constitution, liberalism was also evident in practical politics in varying degrees. Nevertheless, the constitutions were an important factor when it came to taking full advantage of the enduring upturn in the economy which had begun in the 1830s and were thus increasing the pace of transition to a modern industrialized world.

The European revolution of 1989, too, offers a challenge to constitutional politics. The GDR is an exceptional case. From the day it merged with the Federal Republic (3 October 1990) the FRG's Basic Law, dating from 23 May 1949, has been in force in the five new *Länder*. Since 1989, however, new constitutions have been passed surprisingly quickly by the parliaments of

Romania (4 January 1991), Albania (15 April 1991) and Bulgaria (12 July 1991). In Poland, Hungary, Czechoslovakia and the Soviet Union the relevant institutions approved amendments to their constitutions. In Hungary they also approved a transitional constitution (18 October 1989) and in Poland a so-called 'small constitution' (1 November 1992).

As regards the 1989 revolution, constitutional politics had to deal with two entangled and complex issues: the monopoly of power, reflected in the generally accepted view of the party's leading role, and the concept of national property or property owned by the people which served as a decoy for the fact that both the state and the party did, in fact, hold the monopoly of property. 'It is charac- teristic of state-institutionalised socialist societies that both, political power and the power inherent in capital ownership are combined and controlled by one authority, that authority being incapable, in principle, of doing justice to the enormously increased political tasks it has to deal with.'[22] With that in mind, György Konrád demanded in his *Stimmungsbericht* written before the revolution the 'reduction of the state organism to operations that no one other than the state will be able to apprehend.'[23] Indeed, in all countries the first step in amend- ing the constitutions of the people's republic was to delete the article which referred to the leading role of the (Communist) party. Then, after a certain time had elapsed the article relating to the socialist-planned economy and to national property as its ideological basis disappeared from the constitutions. According to Adam Michnik, these changes signalled a 'farewell to communism':

> We are saying farewell to a system in which the state was owned by a political party and the individual was owned by that state. We are saying farewell to a system whose utopian ideal of planned economy and social justice turned out to be a temptation and whose idea of equality and har- mony in human relationships turned out to be deception. [24]

Plain words of farewell! But what about a welcome? Several academics who have commented on the 1989 revolution (including Ralf Dahrendorf and Hartmut Zwahr) point out that it produced no new ideas and, we would add, no Utopian ideas. [25] The 1989 revolution derives its strength from reinvoking ideals which ruling parties and governments had considered historically redun- dant if not extinct. This spiritual rediscovery of their own and of European history indicates that people are turning their backs on a socialist present which for civil-rights campaigners and the sympathizing crowds had become unbear- able. It also means that both, civil rights campaigners and the sympathizing crowds, are looking for a model which points the way into the future and which, they believe, has been realised in Western European countries to a greater or lesser degree. Timothy Garton Ash speaks of a renaissance of the term *Bürger* during the 1989 revolution, and also points to the corresponding pejora- tion of the term 'comrade'.[26]

Catchwords and labels prove him right. In socialist countries, the critics of the regime called themselves *Bürgerrechtler*, literally citizens' rights campaigners.

In Poland they were organized in *Bürgerkommitees* (citizens' committees), in the GDR in *Bürgerinitiativen* (citizens' initiative or action groups), in Czechoslovakia in the *Bürgerforum* (citizens' forum), in Romania in a *Bürgerallianz* (alliance of citizens). If we speak, with Timothy Gordon Ash, of the revival of the *Bürger* then we refer to the term *Bürger* in its ambivalent double meaning: the politically free *citoyen* enjoying equal rights, and the profit-oriented *bourgeois*.[27] The ambivalence reflects the two basic perspectives which we also find in the catalogue of demands put forward by the civil-rights movements during the 1989 revolution and which have become manifest in constitutional policy: citizen-oriented parliamentary democracy with its division of powers, and social market economy. Acceptance of the leading role of the Communist Party has been replaced by political pluralism. Parties and movements compete for the support of free voters. The basic rights of the individual do not derive from an act of grace on the part of the state but are founded on the general acceptance of basic human rights (equality, protection against bodily harm, freedom of speech and religion, protection against oppression), rights which are preconstitutional and supranational. The concept of socialist ownership of the means of production on which management and planning of the economy was based has been replaced by the concept of *private* ownership. Within a legal framework, the constitutions guarantee an individual's legally acquired claims and unrestricted access to property. That is the first and most important step in the transition from a planned economy to a market economy.

In a separate paragraph, let us consider constitutional policy in the GDR. Three options offered themselves.[28] The first option was to draw up a separate constitution for a second German state as 'an alternative to the Federal Republic, maintaining friendly relations, yet full of the envy of a smaller brother who wants to do a few things better than his bigger and generally superior elder brother.'[29] That concept was based on a confederal coexistence of the two German states with mutual support for one another.

The second option was to draw up a completely new all-German constitution. This was suggested by Lothar de Maizière (CDU), the last President of the GDR's Council of Ministers, in his inaugural speech. Jürgen Habermas suggested that this constitution should be put to the people in a referendum so that 'it would be perceived as a deliberate political act serving as a focal point for the republican consciousness of future generations'.[30] This route would have led to the end of the GDR and the Federal Republic of Germany as independent states and to the birth of a new German republic.

The third option was to adopt the Basic Law of the Federal Republic of Germany. That meant that the GDR would join the Federal Republic of Germany, and that would leave 'no room for an independant development'[31] of the revolution within the GDR.

The first option floundered in the GDR's *Volkskammer* right at the beginning. The People's Chamber refused even to discuss the draft of a constitution for the GDR which had been hammered out at the Round Table discussions by

12 March 1990. Quite apart from the motives that may have moved individual members to vote against a constitutional debate, the decison of the People's Chamber reflected the prevailing mood of the people in the GDR. We have already spoken of them voicing their concern in public rallies. With surprising candour, the parliamentary elections on 18 March 1990 confirmed the impression gained from the mass demonstrations. The Alliance for Germany – the name already suggests a political programme! – collected 48.8 per cent of the votes. It was the political group that had campaigned most forcefully against *any* form of experimentation with the former socialist order of the GDR and had pleaded unreservedly for the *immediate* setting up of a unified Germany. The SPD had warned of the social and economic consequences that 'an over-hasty reunification' would bring about and gained only 21.9 per cent of the votes. Alliance 90 gathered a mere 2.9 per cent of the votes, even though it comprised the New Forum which, during September and October 1989 was the most important revolutionary organization. 'GDR improvers' they are now called somewhat disparagingly.

The second route to unification was barred by the Federal Republic. So the third option became reality: the integration of the GDR into the Federal Republic of Germany, thereby extending the sphere of influence of the Basic Law, the constitution of Federal Republic of Germany, to the incorporated territory. That is what the GDR's People's Chamber voted in favour of on 23 August 1990. In doing so it sought and gained access to the constitutional reality of Western Europe.

This important outcome of constitutional policy during the revolution in the GDR confirms the revolutionary processes in the GDR as being part of a wider pan-European revolutionary process: and to demonstrate this was the main objective of this article.

NOTES

1  See Theodor Schieder, *Staat und Gesellschaft im Wandel unserer Zeit. Studien zur Geschichte des 19. und 20. Jahr-hunderts* (Munich, 1958), p. 12.
2  Karl Marx, Friedrich Engels, *Werke*, Bd. 4 (Berlin, 1983), p. 493.
3  Ernst Engelberg, *Bismarck, Urpreuße und Reichsgründer* (Berlin, 1985), p. 325.
4  Letter to Karl Josias Bunsen (13 December 1848), in Leopold Ranke (ed.); *Aus dem Briefwechsel Friedrich Wilhelm IV. mit Bunsen* (Leipzig, 1873), p. 234.
5  Timothy Garton Ash, *Ein Jahrhundert wird abgewählt. Aus den Zentren Mitteleuropas 1980–1990*. München, Wien 1990, p. 206 (A. Michnik); p. 199 f. (G. Konrád).
6  Winfried Maß (ed.), *Der Eiserne Vorhang bricht* (Hamburg, 1990)
7  Dieter Langewiesche (ed.), *Europa zwischen Restauration und Revolution 1815–1849* (Munich, 1989 2nd edn), p. 90.
8  Ibid., p. 71.
9  György Konrad, *Stimmungsbericht* (Frankfurt am Main, 1988), p. 86.
10  György Konrad, *Mein Traum von Europa* (Frankfurt am Main, 1985).
11  Jens Reich, *Rückkehr nach Europa. Zur neuen Lage der deutschen Nation* (Munich, 1991).

12  Speech before the Parliamentary Assembly of the Council of Europe in *Archiv der Gegenwart*, Vol. 61 (1991), Nr. 35320 B3.

13  Vaclav Havel, *Am Anfang war das Wort. Texte von 1969–1990* (Reinbek bei Hamburg, 1991), p. 219.

14  Havel, *Am Anfang war das Wort*, p. 148.

15  Quoted in Gordon A. Craig, *Geschichte Europas 1815–1980. Vom Wiener Kongreß bis zur Gegenwart* (Munich, 1989: 3rd edn), p. 124f.

16  Langewiesche, *Europa zwischen Restauration und Revolution*, p. 165.

17  See GertJoachim Glaeßner, *Der schwierige Weg zur Demokratie. Vom Ende der DDR zur deutschen Einheit* (Opladen, 1991), p. 13

18  Andrzej Szczypiorski, 'Die polnische Revolution 1980–1990', in: Maaß (ed.), *Der Eiserne Vorhang bricht*, p. 51.

19  See Walter Laquer, *Europa auf dem Weg zur Weltmacht 1945–1992* (Munich, 1992), p. 676f.

20  Hartmut Zwahr, 'Die Revolution in der DDR', in Manfred Hettling (ed.), *Revolution in Deutschland? 1789–1989. Sieben Beiträge* (Göttingen, 1991), p. 134.

21  Ralf Dahrendorf, *Betrachtungen über die Revolution in Europa* (Stuttgart, 1992), p. 46.

22  Konrad, György, *Stimmungsbericht*, p. 13 f.

23  Ibid., p. 14.

24  Adam Michnik, *Der lange Abschied vom Kommunismus* (Reinbek bei Hamburg, 1992), p. 15.

25  Dahrendorf, *Betrachtungen über die Revolution*, p. 38; Zwahr Hartmut, 'Die Revolution in der DDR', p. 134 f.

26  See Garton Ash, *Ein Jahrhundert wird abgewählt*, p. 467f. and 428

27  Ibid., p. 468.

28  See Zwahr, 'Die Revolution in der DDR', p. 123.

29  Jens Reich, *Rückkehr nach Europa. Bericht zur neuen Lage der Nation* (Munich, 1991), p. 261.

30  Jürgen Habermas, *Die nachholende Revolution* (Frankfurt am Main, 1990), p. 218.

31  Gert Glaeßner, *Der schwierige Weg zur Demokratie*, p. 22.

# Index

# List of Contributors

Dr Steven Beller is currently a member of the Institute for Advanced Study at Princeton. His publications include *Vienna and the Jews 1867–1938: A Cultural History* (1989) and *Herzl* (1991).

Alan Foster is Head of the Politics Division at the University of Greenwich. He has published widely on the press and foreign policy and has recently contributed to John Morison (ed.), *Eastern Europe and the West* (1992).

Dr Anthony McElligott is Lecturer in Modern History, University of St Andrews. His *Contested City: Municipal Politics and the Rise of Naziism in Altona 1917–1937* will shortly be published by the University of Michigan Press.

Dr Peter M. R. Stirk is Lecturer in Politics at the University of Durham. He has edited several books on aspects of European unity, including (with D. Willis) *Shaping Postwar Europe* (1991) and (with D. Weigall) *The Origins and Development of the European Community* (1992).

Professor Dietmar Stübler is a member of the Fachbereich Geschichte, Universität Leipzig. He has published several books on Italian and European history.

Walter Weitzmann is Emeritus Professor of History, State University of New York. He has written on the history of the Jewish community and is currently working on the ethnic cleansing in Spain between the conquest of Granada and the expulsion of the Moors.